The Master Plan

To Ralph J. Duff, Sr.
God bless & keep you.

Al Duncan

1999

THE MASTER PLAN

BY
AL DUNCAN

Ambassador House
P. O. Box 1153
Westminster, Colorado 80030

The Master Plan by Al Duncan

Copyright © 1999 Al Duncan. Published by Ambassador House, P. O. Box 1153, Westminster, Colorado 80030. (303) 469-4056

Cover design by: Mike Leon
Text layout by: Ambassador House

Library of Congress Catalog No. 99-72428

Manufactured in these United States of America

Categories: 1. Fiction   2. Bible Prophecy   3. Politics

ISBN: 0-9663533-3-1

ACKNOWLEDGMENTS

The hours turned into days and the days turned into months, stretching for almost two years. Utilizing her critical eye, my wife, Socorro, provided much needed assistance. She encouraged, sacrificed, and never complained. I thank God for the wife He gave me, and I thank my wife for her forbearance during those difficult times.

My heartfelt thanks also go to Dr. Stanley and Barbara Monteith who were both invaluable in their help in getting this book published. Dr. Stan's broad knowledge of the facts surrounding the New World Order establishes him as one of the most knowledgeable people on the subject today. Thus, I am honored beyond expression for him writing the Introduction. I also offer a very special thanks to his wife, Barbara, for her many tedious efforts editing the manuscript.

My thanks also goes forth to Publisher, Sandra Myers, for her encouraging words, helpful suggestions, and, her professionalism and expertise in the area of publishing. A special thanks to Michael Leon and Sharon Kisleing of MJL Design for their outstanding cover design.

I could not continue without extending my gratitude to Chuck Missler and John Loeffler, *The Missler Report*; Dr. Noah Hutchings, Southwest Radio Church; Ken Klein, *The Millennium Bug and the Year Two Thousand*; Texe Marrs, Power of Prophecy; and all of you who have extended your time, efforts, and finances to make known this insidious conspiracy to bring about a New World Order.

It was while reading one of Des Griffin's books that I was introduced to the hidden agenda behind the New World Order. It was also his writings that were instrumental in bringing me to the Lord eighteen years ago. Since then, Mr. Griffin and I communicate occasionally. I'm still amazed at his investigative research, as he continues to uncover facts that are beyond reproach. And, his writings derived from those findings are utterly priceless.

I also extend my deepest gratitude to Dr. Henry Lamb of ECO, *The Rise Of The Global Green Religion*; Dr. Dennis L. Cuddy, *The Road to Socialism and the New World Order*; Mr. Des Griffin, *Fourth Reich of the Rich*; Don McAlvany, *The McAlvany Intelligence Advisor*; Michael Coffman, *Saviors of the Earth*; Terry L. Cook, Second Coming Ministries; Tim Cohen, *The AntiChrist and a Cup of Tea*; and Dr. Stanley Monteith of *HIV-WATCH* for giving me permission to use portions of their invaluable, well-researched material as the foundational theme for *THE MASTER PLAN*.

PREFACE

This novel is a work of fiction. All characters are of the writer's imagination. Any similitude to people living or dead is entirely coincidental.

I wrote *The Master Plan* as a timely wakeup call to believers and an eye-opener to unbelievers searching for the reasons behind the intellectual, moral, and economic descent. This exciting End-times novel revolves around the unprecedented events occurring daily within our nation and the world. It is a controversial story that exposes the truths behind the present state of our economy, the political arena, the failing educational system, the expunging of our Constitutional liberties, the violent behavior of our youth, the Gay and Lesbian agenda, the vast emergence of deadly diseases, the Y2K, and much more. This story also depicts the ultimate results of the world's descent, while offering the only solution.

Unfortunately, these happen to be the hottest issues transpiring daily throughout the world. People want to know what's going on and what they can do about it. *The Master Plan* addresses these questions in the form of an intriguing, exciting, and heartwarming story.

INTRODUCTION

This may be one of the most important books that you may ever read. I don't ordinarily read novels, but once I started reading *The Master Plan* it was difficult to put it down. It's the story of a young engineer who uncovers a plot to seize control of the world. Using well-documented research material as his foundation, the author outlines a plan to utilize the United Nations to bring about a Federation of the World under the control of a wealthy elite. He weaves an intricate, fast-moving, End-Times adventure story that will hold you transfixed from the opening pages until the final shocking climax.

There are many other excellent End-Times novels, but *The Master Plan* is unique because of its theological interpretation, its Biblical implications, and the fact that it is politically *incorrect*. Al Duncan's book is well grounded in the Scriptures; it will challenge the beliefs of many Christians, and it will hopefully help prepare them for the difficult times that may lie ahead.

One of the great tragedies of today is that many well-meaning Christian leaders have become so intrigued with the approach of the Rapture that they have focused their attention almost exclusively on this event and convinced their followers that there is no reason to be concerned about other contemporary issues. As a result, many believers have become so heavenly minded they are no earthly good, while Lucifer and his supporters honor the fact that many Christians have abandoned their obligation to be good stewards of His bounty. Do you think that those who have allowed evil to prosper here on earth bear no responsibility for what is happening today? I personally believe that Jesus Christ is coming very soon, but can anyone guarantee that we will all be Raptured from the earth before persecution comes to the United States? Where is that recorded in the Scriptures? Time and again we are told that the Second Coming is imminent, and I believe that is true, but what will happen if deliverance comes 10 or 20 years after America has been destroyed, and its citizens martyred? In Matthew 13:18-23, we find the Parable of the Sower where our Lord warns that many will fall away from their faith in bad times because:

"...then cometh the evil one, and catcheth away that which was sown in his heart. This is he who received seed by the wayside."

Tragically many Christians have forgotten the dictum that men and women become accomplices to those evils they fail to oppose, and have become indifferent to the suffering of others. They are assured of a place in Heaven and falsely believe that their only further obligation is to tithe and study the Scriptures. I believe that studying the scriptures and tithing are both important, but participating in those activities does not relieve us from a responsibility to try to play some part in the unfolding of current world events. That is why the story line of *The Master Plan* is so important. It will help prepare you and your loved ones for the future. No place in the Bible are we promised that we have nothing to fear, or that God will always protect us from adversity. What we are promised is that God will always be with us, even unto the end of the age. A careful reading of The Revelation of Jesus Christ 6:8-11 reveals:

8. And I looked, and behold a pale horse: and his name that sat on him was Death, and Hell Followed with him. And power was given unto them over the fourth part of the earth, to kill with sword, and with hunger, and with Death, and with the beasts of the earth.

9. And when he had opened the fifth seal, I saw under the altar the souls of them that were slain for the word of God, and for the testimony which they held:

10. And they cried with a loud voice, saying, 'How long, O Lord, holy and true, dost thou not judge and avenge our Blood on them that dwell on the earth? (Emphasis added)

Thus in Revelation 6:8 we are told that one-fourth of the inhabitants of the earth will be murdered, and in Revelation 6:9 we learn that those who are to be killed are Christians because they will be slain for the Word of God, and for the testimony which they held. Obviously the events prophesied in Revelation 6:8 have not yet come about because they precede the misfortune prophesied in Revelation 8 when an additional one-third of the remaining creatures on earth will be destroyed.

The Master Plan is important because it portrays the spiritual struggle taking place in the world today and challenges the widely held belief that nothing bad will ever happen to Christians. I would like to believe that to be true, but I fear that Lucifer and his Legions are encouraging that deception to facilitate their conquest.

You will never forget the concluding pages of *The Master Plan*. Al Duncan is to be commended for taking a controversial subject, weaving a detailed story, and defying commonly held beliefs. I pray that the Lord will utilize his effort to bring readers closer to Him, and to cause many unsaved people to come to a knowledge of His redeeming Grace.

Dr. Stanley Monteith

I couldn't feel any pain as I slowly regained consciousness. Due to the total darkness and the moans and groans around me, I wondered whether I was all right. I felt like I was recovering from the effects of a powerful drug.

Gradually my senses came to life as the smell of stale human bodies roused me. Although I couldn't see, the sound of tires on the pavement and the bumping movements led me to believe that I was riding in some type of huge truck. The heat was almost unbearable, and the stench from vomit, urine, and feces was noxious. I had no idea how long I had been riding, from where I had come, nor where I was going. However, it wasn't long before the truck pulled to a bumpy stop.

Suddenly, a door at the rear opened. A flood of blinding sunlight filled the compartment causing gasps and cries from the men around me. Uniformed guards shouted commands instructing us to unload, as they set a ramp for us to exit. Everyone struggled to their feet and stumbled toward the rear of the truck. The sight and smell were so unbearable that the guards wore masks. Judging by our present condition, it appeared we had been riding for a couple of days.

While descending the ramp I filled my lungs with deep breaths of fresh air. The guards marched the group of us across a highway. Other trucks were also arriving. They formed a long row, with each truck being unloaded in a similar fashion. Beyond the trucks, empty land stretched to distant hills and mountains. Across the highway stood a high, chain-link fence topped with barbed wire that surrounded a yard. In the near corner was a large gate. Beyond the fence was more barren land which stretched to a tree-line almost a half mile away.

The penetrating sun sapped moisture and much needed strength from my weakened body. There wasn't any shade in the yard to protect us from the sun's direct rays, and the heat was scathing.

As cattle being herded into a stockyard, the guards herded the group of us through the gate and into the yard already packed with men. We pressed closer together as the guards ordered us to join the others.

Muscular, scruffy-looking men in T-shirts, coveralls, and tennis shoes pushed their way through the crowd demanding that we, "Shut up, and keep moving!" I noticed that the uniformed guards called these men *goons*. I also noticed that the men filling the yard were of all nationalities and ages.

To avoid bumping the men in front of me, I slowed my pace before entering the gate. Suddenly I felt a sharp blow to my back. It was a powerful blow delivered by one of the goons. I turned instinctively, ready to defend myself. As I was about to retaliate, one of the uniformed guards warned me: "These goons would just as soon kill you as look at you; so you'd best keep movin'!" There was a strange, distant look of viciousness in the eyes of the goon who struck me. Deciding the guard was right, I complied by picking up my pace in step with the rest of the men that were being unloaded from the truck I was riding in.

We headed toward the opening of a gray, two-story wooden building. On the top of the building was a billboard that displayed in bold letters: LABOR CAMP – 1100, the time: 1:30 p.m., the date: August 13, 2002, and the temperature: 103 degrees.

The inside of the building resembled a large ward with hard linoleum floors, gray walls, and the smell of disinfectant mingled with body odor. Although the building provided shelter from the direct sun, without an air conditioning system it afforded only minimal relief from its heat.

Farther along the wall, to our right, was an open shower area that extended the 150-foot length of the building. In compliance with the guards' orders, about 100 of us removed our clothes and tossed them into one of the laundry carts that formed a row in front of the showers. One of the guards asked for the water to be turned on and it instantly spurted out of the showerheads positioned along the wall. No sooner had we lathered our bodies with soap when orders to "Hurry up and get out for the next group of men! Showers go off in two minutes," echoed throughout the large, tiled area. We all tried frantically to rinse the soap from our bodies before the water was turned off.

After drying, I wrapped the towel around my waist the same as everyone else. The guards ordered us to follow the group of men before us that were also wearing towels around their waists. We slowly made our way to a long row of tables covered with white sheets and filled with syringes, cotton swabs, and small bottles of clear vaccine. A number of men dressed in white smocks stood in front of the tables making sure each man had a vaccination before he passed.

When everyone in our group was vaccinated, the guards ordered us to continue following the men in front of us. Sweating from the heat, and the bodies around me, I gradually worked my way to the second floor with the rest of the men in our group.

At the top of the stairs a crew of men were issuing clothing from an open doorway. These men asked our clothing and shoe sizes, then wrote them down on pads. After locating our sizes, they returned and handed each of us a clean but well-used khaki-colored shirt and trousers, and a pair of well-worn work boots.

While dressing, we inched our way down a hallway lined with open windows on one side and guards on the other. Billowing curtains spewed gusts of fresh, but warm air. The hallway intersected with another hallway at the end. Directly ahead at the other end of the hall was an open door with two lines of men entering a room from both sides. A guard stood on the opposite wall, directing each man through the doorway and into a room; first a man from the group I was in, and then a man from another group.

I didn't recognize any of the men from the other group, nor did I recall seeing them as we entered the yard. They appeared healthy, with toned bodies and tans. They also seemed familiar with these procedures and were confident about what they were doing. We all wore the same khaki outfits, but theirs were grimy, as though they had been working in the fields.

The doorway we were entering was at the corner of a room filled with long rows of hard, flat wooden benches. The first bench started directly inside the door at the left. Men of various ages, sizes, and nationalities sat side by side talking freely back and forth across the room. Posted on the walls were signs that read: "TALKING ALLOWED".

At the far end of the room were desks with a chair beside them. When someone moved into a vacant chair beside one of the desks, we all slid over to make room for the next man in the hallway.

Seated behind the desks were the first women I had seen since my arrival. They were shapeless, unkempt women, who apparently didn't care about their appearance. These women were either talking with one of the men seated at their desk or writing down information that was being given to them.

With permission to talk, everyone seemed eager to exercise his ability to speak. Being in a strange place with a room full of strangers, I thought that it was best to keep quiet.

A young man sitting in front of me turned around and asked, "You just got here, huh, mister?"

"I just arrived today," I answered.

He paused momentarily before continuing his conversation. "I've been here over a year now. On the last Monday of every month they bring a bunch of us over from the barracks. This is where we pick our women. We can choose as many as four. Some guys only pick one woman to be with them for the whole month, but after a week I get tired of the same woman. So I pick a different woman for each week. I've had a different pretty face every week since I been here.

"See those hags up front?" he continued. "They check your file to see what kind of females you're best suited for. They got catalogs with hundreds to pick from. If you really like one, they'll let you keep her for as long as you want.

"The work's hard, but the food's good. They give you a nice place to live in, and with a pretty woman to take care of you every day, it ain't all that bad. Can you remember anythin' yet?"

"My mind's still somewhat foggy," I answered. "I don't recall much of anything before regaining consciousness in the truck on my way here."

"That happens to everybody. You can remember basic stuff, you just can't remember things like what you did before you got here, people's names, and stuff like that. But don't worry, it'll all come back to you in a day or two."

A steady hum of voices filled the room. As I looked around at all the faces I couldn't help thinking about what this young man just told me. I appreciated his concern, but I was interested in when I would be permitted to leave. To avoid appearing preoccupied with my own affairs, I asked him, "How much longer will you be here before you're able to leave?"

"Leave... I ain't never getting' out of this place....Or you either!" he added as if he suddenly realized my intention for asking the question. "We're here for life. I've seen a lotta people try to escape. None of 'em ever got too far, though. They were all caught, tortured, and killed. Those goons'll kill you in a heartbeat!" he said with a snap of his finger and a distorted expression on his face. "They say there's a thing in their head that drives 'em mad when a guard blows his whistle."

I was sure he was mistaken about never being released. He had to be here under different circumstances than I was, and I couldn't imagine doing anything that would cause me to be here for the rest of my life.

"What is this place?" I asked.

"This here's a old military base that's been turned into a labor camp. They send all the troublemakers here who won't conform to society.

I ain't seen my folks since I been here, and I probably won't ever see 'em again. Nobody knows where I am, 'cause there ain't no way to get in touch with nobody.

"Something else you probably ought to know, nobody in the labor camps lives past fifty. So don't be surprised when one of the old folks disappear."

He let out a soft chuckle, as though this was the first time he seriously considered the matter. "They call it euthanasia," he continued, removing the smile from his face. "They say anybody fifty years old ain't able to keep up the pace with the rest of the laborers. But that ain't so. They have enough people to do all the work they need done anyway. Controllin' the number of people in this camp is what they're doin'. They don't care *nothin'* about a man's life!"

Suddenly there was a loud commotion outside. Some of the men leaped up from their seats and ran to the windows positioned around the room. The young man I was talking with ran toward a window in the corner. He took one glance before he started waving and shouting. "Come here and look. This is what I was to tellin' you about. Now you can see these goons in action for yourself."

He was pointing down in the yard where we entered the gates after being unloaded from the trucks. Within the crowd of men in the yard below was a young man in his early twenties. He was calling to someone he apparently recognized, who was about 25 feet away. One of the goons saw him and started pushing through the crowd and telling the men around him to shut up and keep moving. When the goon was within reach the young man hit him with all his might. The goon didn't fall because the crowd supported him. When the surrounding men realized the possibility of being mistaken for one of the instigators, they backed away from the young man as far as the crowd would allow.

One of the guards blew a whistle with a sharp, piercing sound that was so painful everyone in the yard immediately covered their ears. Seemingly from nowhere, four more goons appeared; two of them grabbed the young man's arms on both sides, and two more grabbed his legs.

His friend was frantically trying to make his way through the crowd. "Stop fighting them!" he yelled. Suddenly there was another sharp blast from a whistle and four more goons rushed to subdue this young man in the same manner as his friend.

I looked through the crowd for the first young man, only to see the goons carrying him kicking and screaming through the parting crowd and across the yard. They held the young man between them like a battering ram. At first the goons were walking, and then they gained their momentum until they were running at top speed. With the young man secure in their grasp, they headed straight for a concrete pillar.

The first thing to hit was his head. It splattered like a pumpkin. Then there wasn't any head, and then there wasn't any neck. They continued until there wasn't anything left but pieces of the young man's body. They did the same thing to his friend.

Afterward, one of the goons went over to a shed and picked up a garden hose. He and his comrades rinsed each other off, and then washed the remains into a gutter that ran under the fence line into an open field.

Men kept filling the yard while the goons ducked in and out of the crowd pushing and shouting, "Shut up and keep moving!"

Fear struck me. If I hadn't taken heed when that guard warned me, like the two young men, my remains would have been washed into the gutter.

After returning to my place on the bench I noticed that the man in front of me had proceeded to a desk, and I was next. Although there was little continuity to my thoughts, I knew my situation was more serious than I had first imagined. The youngster was right, these people didn't care about human life. If I wanted to maintain my sanity and keep my life, I needed to come up with an escape plan.

I was stunned by the cheerful manner in which the woman behind the desk asked my name. She was completely oblivious to what had just taken place. "I know my name is Lance Roberts, but I'm not sure of anything else," I answered in response to her question.

She thumbed through a group of files in a cabinet behind her desk and pulled out my folder. After briefly studying its contents, she raised her head and looked at me intently. Suddenly a smile filled her face. "I have quite the catalog of beauties for you, Mr. Roberts. I'm sure you'll find one to suit your fancy."

She reached into the desk drawer and placed before me a color catalog of glossy photographs with females in various poses and suggestive captions written beneath them. "According to this partial file I have here, you are not gay. However, I am required to show you this catalog of males," she said, handing me another catalog similar to the one she had handed me previously. When she detected my disapproval and saw the look on my face, she quickly removed the catalog and placed it back into one of the drawers.

Near the end of the catalog, a beautiful young woman caught my eye. I pointed her out to the woman at the desk, gave her the page number as she requested, and told her, "She will be fine."

The woman at the desk nodded, "You have very good taste. She's a beauty. But I think I should warn you. This girl's personality is one of the worst in our lot!"

She searched through a long list of names attached to a clipboard on her desk and when she found my name she highlighted it in yellow.

"Your number is 3900, this camp is 1100, and your cabin is number 4."

After pausing for a moment, she added, "Here is a word of advice, Mr. Roberts, and I hope you take heed for your own sake. Ignorance, even stupidity—though they must be punished—are both common behaviors around here. But cunning intelligence is a threat to everyone; those who demonstrate it are quickly eliminated."

"I accept your advice," I said appreciatively. After witnessing their example of elimination in the yard below, I didn't want any part of it. If I planned to go on living long enough to escape, I had to be discreet.

After her warning, she lowered her head, examining the papers on her desk. "Next!" she hollered. With an outstretched arm, and a pointed finger, she directed me to a line of men exiting through another doorway at the opposite end of the room.

My next stop was the clothing room. A week's supply of clothing had been thrown into a large sack and was handed to me as I passed. I swung the sack over my shoulder, imitating the man in front of me.

Uniformed guards and goons marched a hundred of us to our cabins about two miles away. The dusty road we traveled ran beside a twelve-foot high, chain-link fence topped with rows of razor wire. Far in the distance the sun was slowly descending behind a grove of trees. The heat was sweltering, and the load I was carrying only made the situation worse.

All I could think about was getting out of here. The question was how. If someone was able to scale the fence unnoticed, there was a constant patrol of guards, and miles of flat land to cover before reaching the seclusion of the trees. Although I was determined to find a way to escape, for now I had to bide my time. My biggest problem would be staying alive until then.

By the time we reached the barracks my body was covered with perspiration. Each man had a cabin, and when we reached number 4, I obediently climbed the steps and went inside.

The living room contained a well-used couch. Standing before it was a battered coffee table. Two end tables with lamps stood on both sides. The kitchen was barely large enough to contain the two-burner stove and oven, the doll-sized refrigerator, a washer and dryer, and the table and chairs.

I opened the bedroom door, set the sack of clothes on the floor, squeezed past the double bed and entered the bathroom. There was a toilet, a small mirror over the sink, and a bathtub and shower combination.

When I saw the shower, I took off my clothes, threw them on the bed and stepped into the tub. I turned on the water, adjusted the shower and moved underneath it. It was the most relaxing and refreshing feeling

I had experienced since, when...? I tried to remember what my life was like before regaining consciousness in the truck. I knew there was a different kind of world beyond the perimeter of this fence, but it was too distant for my mind to recall.

As I finished rinsing myself, I heard a door shut. I remembered dropping my sack of clothes in the bedroom, and I didn't have a towel with me. Suddenly I found myself staring into the face of the girl I had picked out of the catalog. She was wearing a khaki dress that gathered around her small waist and stopped just above her knees. The pictures in the catalog did her little justice; she was infinitely more beautiful in the flesh. Her eyes seemed as large as silver dollars, and her full mouth glistened with moisture. She stood there, staring at me with a look of indifference.

Attempting to cover myself was useless; I would only look more foolish. So I politely asked, "Would you please hand me a towel out of my sack in the bedroom?"

Before I could think of anything better to do, she was back, handing me a towel. She folded her arms and leaned against the doorframe. Without a word she continued watching me with that look of indifference.

I thanked her for bringing me the towel, but I felt ridiculous standing in front of this stranger, as naked as the day I came into the world. When I couldn't take it any longer, I wrapped the towel around me and walked toward the door leading into the bedroom. "Excuse me," I said as I passed her. "If you don't mind, I'd appreciate a little privacy while I get dressed."

She followed me into the bedroom, causing me as much discomfort as before. I searched through the sack until I found something to wear. To distract her attention from what I was doing, I asked, "What is your name?"

"Why?" she retorted antagonistically?

"Since you seem intent on watching me dress, I'd at least like to know who it is I'm entertaining."

"My name's Monique Duval, and this is a prison labor camp, not the Boy Scouts. If you're that sensitive, you'll never survive here!"

It had been a long, hectic day and I didn't care to put on a show for a sarcastic female spectator. I walked past her again, shut the door behind me and finished dressing in the front room.

While examining the contents of the refrigerator for something to eat, I heard the door open. Monique came out of the bedroom and walked over to the table. "Have a seat," she said, pointing to one of the two chairs. "I will fix you something to eat."

When Monique finished cooking she placed the plate of food in front of me, folded her arms and leaned against the sink, and without a word she watched me eat. As soon as I finished I thanked her for the meal, set my dirty dishes in the sink and went into the bedroom. I set the sack of clothes in the corner out of the way and lay across the bed. I could hear Monique in the kitchen washing the dishes, while the room grew dimmer and dimmer with every passing moment.

Suddenly, I heard loud noises coming from outside the window. I reached over and pulled the curtains back in time to see a guard and two goons dragging a man and woman shouting obscenities from the cabin across from mine.

Monique came up beside me and whispered, "Don't let them see you. If the guards know you are watching, they will take us with them. To stop news from spreading that there are conflicts, the authorities always take eyewitnesses to any altercation."

I cautiously released the curtain, and returned to the bed.

"Before I forget, let me show you where the security buttons are in each room."

After she pointed them out we returned to the bedroom.

"What's *your* name?" she asked, having an apparent change of heart.

"Lance Roberts," I answered.

"Has your memory returned yet, Lance?"

"No, not completely" I replied. "However, a young man I met while I was being processed in assured me that it would return within a couple of days."

With an air of authority, she began: "What you're experiencing now is partial amnesia. Two months ago you were given a drug called a *Memory-Enhancer*. Since our thoughts and experiences are retained in the memory banks in our minds, this drug breaks down the memory inhibitors and stimulates recollection. To put it simply, the drug enables you to recall your past as though it was current. Once the gates to your memory banks are opened, your past can be duplicated, translated, and digitized for reading by a computer. The actual process is Thought-Image-Duplication, which is done by what is called a Memory-Scan. Any thoughts you've had since you were born have been written onto a Compact Disk."

"Are you saying that these people know everything I've done since I was born?" I asked.

"That's right," she answered confidently. "Every thought and impression you've ever had has been digitized and written on a disk. Teams of experts comb this data to interpret the information, and then they categorize the information to determine your psychological profile. They do have one defect in their system, though. Things that we dream, imagine, or fantasize are so obscure they are usually not interpretable.

When viewed through a computer they just appear as imperceptible bits of data that can't be confirmed.

"During your ride here the drug started wearing off. Within a day or two you'll be able to remember everything. Then you'll know what crime they *claim* you've committed against the State. I use the word claim, because you may or may not have committed a crime at all."

I couldn't imagine doing anything that would cause me to be imprisoned for the rest of my life. And yet, I was here. Apparently she knew what she was talking about, but I wanted to believe that each case was different, particularly mine.

"During the week," she continued, "at 5:30 a.m., a buzzer goes off. Thirty minutes later it goes off again and you have to be standing on the steps ready for work. I don't know what they'll have you doing, but I am sure it'll be hard work. All laborers are due back by 5:00 p.m., unless there's some unforeseen problem.

"Where are you getting all of this information, Monique?" I asked, skeptically.

"I've had to stay with some high ranking officials, and I try to get as much information as I can from everyone I come in contact with," she answered before she continued, undisturbed by my skepticism.

"We don't have to work on Saturdays. However, all laborers and their roommates have to attend the weekly assembly in the Main Square. On Sundays we go to a religious service to give homage to Gaia, the prophet, and the prince. Later that day you'll meet with your counselor. The rest of the time we're locked in this cabin unless you're told otherwise."

My thoughts were racing. The more I heard, the more I wanted to get out of this place.

"Who's Gaia, the prophet, and this prince?" I asked.

"Gaia is mother earth. She's the source of all life. Humans are Gaia's mind, her intellect and soul, and we constitute the Universal Church. The great prophet is sometimes referred to as the Most Holy, and the prince, why, he's the savior. I've never seen anyone perform miracles like the prophet. And some say the savior is the Son of God; some say he *is* God.

"Have you experienced the goons yet?"

"I have," I answered, remembering the incident in the yard and the painful blow given me by one of the goons when I first arrived. "I was hit in the back by one of them when I first came. I also watched them unmercifully kill two young men."

"They're inhuman!" she spat with vehemence. "Each goon has a computer chip surgically inserted behind his ear. This chip is a receiver that transmits signals to the brain. When a guard blows his whistle it triggers a violent reaction inside their heads. With the type of neural surgery they've had, and all the drugs they're given, they're not human. The only emotion they're capable of exhibiting is brutality.

"You need to always be prepared to cover your ears when you see a guard start to blow his whistle. The shrillness of those whistles can damage your eardrum if you're subjected to the sound for a long period of time. Some people wear earplugs whenever they leave their cabins. But even at that you have to be careful, because if you don't respond to an order, that's a reason to kill you."

"How long have you been here?" I asked.

"It'll be two years next month," she said with disdain. "I don't know how many different men I've stayed with. Since I've never willingly submitted to any of their sexual pleasures, I was always taken by force. There've only been three men that haven't raped me, and that, I believe, is because they preferred men. Excluding those three, you're the first who hasn't tried to seduce or rape me within the first five minutes of being with me.

"Have you told the authorities about this?" I asked with concern.

"Apparently you don't understand! Just today my Counselor warned me about my indifference toward the men, and then I was threatened with punishment if the complaints continued. Sometimes I think it'd be best if I were dead."

"Committing suicide isn't going to help. And your death certainly isn't going to hurt them. Just because things aren't going your way at the moment is no reason to give up hope."

"Look, Lance, the only reason for my existence is so I can be used by the State!"

"Monique, the human mind is the most complex mechanism there is. We can dream and imagine; we can even fantasize. If we weren't able to look forward to a brighter tomorrow, *then* life would be hopeless. But as long as we have a mind that functions properly, we *can't* allow ourselves to lose hope!"

Darkness filled the room. The moon shone brightly through the window behind Monique, causing a silhouette around her shadowed image. There was a period of silence before she asked in a low, distraught voice, "What is there to look forward to *here*, in this Godforsaken place?"

I thought for a moment before answering. If she were an informant or one of the authorities, I would be exposing my intentions. After a quick assessment, I answered her honestly, "Your freedom, Monique. What else?"

She quickly moved closer to me and whispered, "If they hear you talking about an escape, or a plan to overthrow the State in any way, the punishment is solitary confinement, indefinitely. If they catch you attempting to escape, the punishment is death!"

A splinter of fear shot through me. Solitary confinement would close the door to any plans of escaping. My only consolation from her last statement was learning that she wasn't one of them.

"Tomorrow I'm scheduled to attend a preparation class before I start a special training session, and you have a big day ahead of you, too, Lance. I think we'd better get some sleep."

The loud buzzer echoing throughout the tiny cabin woke me. I could smell food cooking in the kitchen. I jumped out of bed and went into the bathroom to shower and dress. As I finished, Monique announced, "You had better hurry, Lance. You have twelve minutes before the final buzzer sounds. And I hope you like eggs?" she asked. "I've fried you three, along with potatoes and bacon, toast and coffee."

"I love eggs, any way you cook them. And how are you this morning?" I asked as pleasantly as possible.

"Well, so far, it's one of the best days I've had since I've been here."

Arranged neatly on the couch was everything I needed for the day ahead. There was a handkerchief, a watchman's cap, and a jacket to ward off the morning chill. Monique also warned me that the latch to the lunch box was faulty and may come open at any time. Inside the lunch box were three sandwiches, an apple, and a thermos bottle filled with lemonade.

I hurried to finish my breakfast and collected the items she had laid out for me. When the second buzzer sounded I was standing on the front steps anticipating the day ahead. A large mass of men filed past. One of the guards bringing up the rear ordered me to fall in line behind the last man. The guard repeated his command as we passed each cabin in the barracks.

We marched to a large square a fourth of a mile away. In the middle of the square was a platform. Upon the platform sat a recorder connected to loudspeakers. From the loudspeakers we were given orders to form a tight circle as close to the platform as possible. In compliance, the last of the men crammed into a semi-circle around the platform.

We were then instructed to divide into sections according to our last two numbers. Everyone with identification numbers ending in the same ten digits, such as 0-9, 10-19, and so on, assembled together with the section of men whose numbers corresponded with theirs. According to my last two numbers, the section I worked with was responsible for irrigating the fields.

A group of guards and goons marched our section to a field about a mile from the main square. The warmth of the sun was gradually breaking the chill of morning. Tiny beads of dew resting upon blades of grass glistened from the sun's reflection. It was a beautiful morning to be anywhere, anywhere except where I was.

It was 7:30 a.m. when we reached the fields. They divided us into two groups and explained the procedures. One man from each group was in charge of the "on" and "off" valves. These men were also responsible for locating the leaks caused by a faulty or broken coupling. The other men positioned themselves at various coupling points along the 300-foot length of aluminum pipe. This aluminum pipe supplied the water to operate the sprinklers mounted on top. Each man grabbed the neck of the sprinkler with one hand, the base of the pipe with the other, and together they ran the entire length of pipe over fifty feet. Once the 300 feet of pipe was properly connected, the group in charge of the "on" and "off" valves turned on the water.

Sometimes there were leaks or bad connections that needed repairing. Finding the source of the leak took time; it often took as long as thirty minutes before we would locate the source of the problem. But our day was usually spent repeating the same mundane process of disconnecting the pipe, lifting it, and then running to the next connection point. When properly assembled, sufficient water was available for a new plot of parched earth and thirsty growth.

During our noon lunch break everyone gathered into small groups. They discussed a variety of subjects, such as encounters with their favorite females, the killing of three men who recently tried to escape, and the dull, common happenings of the days before.

As I studied the grave faces of the men around me, I noticed a short, thin, bearded man with a bald head that gleamed brightly from the sun's reflection. He sat in a yoga-type position as though in deep meditation. Finally I approached him. " May I interrupt you for a minute?"

There was a brief instant before his eyes focused, as if coming out of a trance. The first real smile I had seen since I got here beamed up at me. "Sadly, I can only offer you a seat on the grass. But please, be seated," he offered in excellent English with an Asian accent. "It is obvious you are a new arrival to this domain of devils."

Interested in why he was here, I asked, "Where are you from?"

"I was born in India," he answered. "At a young age my parents sent me to a Tibetan monastery for training in the priesthood. My temple is hidden high within the Himalayan Mountain range."

"Are you going back there, when you finish serving your sentence?" I asked, hoping he would relieve my fear that all offenses are punishable by life imprisonment or death.

"I know of no one being released from here," he replied. "At any case, my fiftieth year will commence at the end of this month. As I am sure you have been informed, my death is imminent."

Before I was able to question him further, the bell rang, ending our lunch break. One of the guards ordered us to return to work. The remainder of the day continued in the same dullness as the morning.

At 4:30 p.m., the guards lined us up into columns of ten and marched us back to our cabins. The sun slowly made its way across the heavens, sliding toward the edge of the earth. The relentless heat seemed unaffected by the sun's disappearing act, its oppressive shroud dogging our every step.

The trek from the fields seemed much longer than the trek to the fields. My back ached, my muscles were tight, and my feet were contorting with pain from standing on them the majority of the day. As we arrived at cabin number 4, I almost felt regard for this modest dwelling that was now my home. It was strange how a woman I barely knew and a bald man whose name I still didn't know were the only people of importance in my world.

As I opened the door the smell of food stimulated my hunger. I stood watching Monique's graceful movements as she prepared the meal. Minutes passed before she sensed my presence and instinctively turned around to face me. Her large, hazel eyes seemed to look right through me.

"Hello, Monique," I greeted her as pleasantly as possible under the circumstances.

"Hello, Lance," she replied, with an air of skepticism. For a brief moment she studied my face as if searching for a clue that might reveal my thoughts. I, in turn, studied her facial expressions closely. Gradually the look of uncertainty subsided as she relaxed, realizing nothing had changed between us.

I went directly to the bathroom, hoping that a shower would wash away the tension and dispel the tedious memories of the day. While I was dressing, Monique knocked on the door. "You can eat whenever you are ready, supper is on the table."

Coming into the kitchen I asked, "How was your day, Monique?"

"This was my first preparation class for the Special Training

Session. That alone makes it a lot different than my normal day would have been; sitting in this cabin all day," she answered without showing much concern.

I remembered the priest and described the particulars of our meeting.

"Why are you interested in a person like him? What is the purpose of starting a relationship with someone who is in prison the same as you, especially someone who is about to be eliminated! It doesn't make sense to me."

"I don't have a profound answer, Monique. One thing for certain, he's the only person I've met around here who's shown any kindness. While I'm working with him, I hope to get to know him better.

"I worked pretty hard today and I'm very tired." I got up and went into the bedroom, lay across the bed and fell into a sound sleep. I dreamed a viciously frightful dream, with constant threats on my life. It was an obscure scene, like looking through smoked glass. And yet, the attacks on my life seemed as real as life itself.

The dream took place in Hong Kong, China. I entered the dojo where I had been studying under a Master of the martial arts. Positioned at one end of the dojo was a lantern. Shadows danced around the room as its flickering light grew dim and then brightened.

The Master sat in the center of the room on a thin mat. He wore a black silk kimono and sat in a yoga position. Smoke from herbs and incense lingered heavily in the air, causing me to feel light-headed.

I sat down facing the Master. We were both being drawn into a trance. He rose and began his kata. With the fluid, graceful movements of a cat, he fought with his imaginary opponent. I became transfixed, watching his exceptionally rapid moves. He flowed as smooth and graceful as a ballerina, while every powerful move was as deadly as the tiger he portrayed.

He beckoned me to join him. My kata was the dance of the King Cobra. I drove all other thoughts from my mind and began emulating the sleeking, slithering, floating movements of the cobra snake.

Suddenly, I was being attacked by my archenemy, the mongoose. He teased and taunted me with lightning-quick moves. I swiveled and swayed, luring him closer with undetectable deception, while cleverly avoiding his vicious attacks. With slight twists and turns, I eluded his attempts to bite me. I was very careful, knowing his bite was powerful and his vice-like grip was impossible to break. I also knew that a miss by a fraction of an inch was no closer than one by a mile. By exerting less energy, I reserved my strength.

I was at my best, and he was beginning to tire, growing slow and careless. To reserve my energy, I struck less frequently. All of my senses were alert. I waited patiently for him to make a mistake.

Then it happened. He lunged toward me in a menacing attack. It was a telegraphed move that my instincts perceived the instant he began. As if in slow motion he thundered toward me with his razor-sharp teeth positioned to bite. I swerved to avoid his reach by a fraction of an inch.

It was during his backward retreat that I struck him first. I watched his eyes focus upon me with shocked dismay. He seemed to reflect a slight pain from the bite I had delivered to the back of his neck. There was no hope for him now. He studied me for an instant, and I could see the fearful awareness on his face. He watched as the poisonous venom dripped from my long, sharp fangs. He knew that he was doomed.

Before he could run, I struck him again. His once-vicious onslaught had now turned to meek despair. *"Too late, my persistent enemy. It's much too late to cry for help. In an instant you will be paralyzed; in another, you will be dead!"*

I heard Monique calling my name. She was sitting in the chair, watching me intently. "You were having a nightmare," she said, with a puzzled inflection in her voice. "I started to wake you earlier."

"You should have," I told her. "I was fighting for my life, and then I heard you calling me from a distance."

The moon beamed through the window amidst the ebony sky. I silently studied its face-like image, transfixed by its radiance.

"What are you thinking about?" Monique asked, breaking the silence.

"You, and your present situation," I replied as pleasantly as possible. "Considering what you said—about being forced by most of the men you've had to stay with—would you like to learn a form of self protection so that you can defend yourself against an attacker?"

"Sure," she replied with a definite interest in her voice. "How long will it take me to learn?"

"In a few hours I can show you enough for you to defend yourself. It's up to you how quickly you learn how to execute the moves by the amount of time you practice. When you've developed the skills as second nature, you won't have to worry about the same person bothering you twice.

"It's been a long, hard day, Monique. I'll see you in the morning."

The sun brought the new day. We marched to the fields and irrigated them. Today was hotter than yesterday.

During our lunch break I learned that the small bald-headed man's name was Haile. He told me about his homeland and the functions that he performed as a priest. He knew his days on earth were limited, and he planned to make the remainder of his life count, in a different way than ever before. I listened attentively until the bell sounded and the guards commanded us to return to our work assignments.

For some unknown reason a large man with a thick neck the color of a partially ripe strawberry, and unruly hair that stuck to the sides of his face and forehead, sat upon a log whimpering like a child. In a high-pitched voice he whined and boldly protested about going back to work. One of the guards commanded a goon to convince him that working was not so bad. With two sharp blows, the goon persuaded him to return to his work assignment. The rest of the day inched by slowly. Finally, it was time to return to our cabins. They counted us, and then marched us back to the barracks.

Monique looked exceptionally attractive this evening. She wore a colorful scarf that had been cleverly tied in the back with the pretty flowered material resting on her shoulder. I fought off the inclination to walk up behind her and hug her gently around the waist.

While eating, I playfully remarked, "You look especially lovely this evening. Is there a special occasion?"

Her sincere reply extinguished my flirtatious thoughts. "No, there wasn't any *special* occasion. I thought about your offer to show me how to protect myself. So I wore the scarf to cover my hair and keep it out of the way."

"So you did think about me while I was gone, even if it was as a self-defense instructor," I said in jest."

With a slight smile and resignation in her voice, she responded, "Okay, Lance. Let's be friends. If nothing else, you've convinced me that you're not out to harm me."

"You catch on fast," I said with sarcasm, before moving on to a more serious note. "Tell me, Monique, don't you have any family or friends that can help you?"

Ignoring my sarcasm, she replied. "My mother was an Afrikaner and my father was a Frenchman. My father became wealthy through the gold and ivory trade—the right timing, I guess. Whichever, he discovered one of the richest gold mines in Africa. The ivory trade was more a hobby than a financial venture, and when he learned of the vast slaughter of animals for profit—long before it became illegal—he severed all ties with the trade.

"At an early age I was sent to school in Europe. I returned home to spend the summers with my family. Mother always planned my summer vacations around the three of us. They were some of the best times of my life; I can recall them as if they were yesterday.

"One semester, before the summer break, mother came to visit me at school. She told me she would stay with me during the summer, since I wouldn't be going home that year due to intense tribal fighting in the surrounding villages.

"The following year she brought me the same report, which meant I had to stay in Europe for another full year instead of being able to return home for the summer.

"And then it happened. One day shortly before Christmas I was summoned from class and told to report to the Dean's office. Two men employed by my father were there to take me home. A private jet was waiting for us at the airport, and we left for Africa immediately.

"It had been two years since the last time I was home. When I arrived, I sensed a dreadful foreboding over the entire continent. War, disease, and famine had spread over the country like locusts; entire villages were destroyed. The devastation and destruction were insufferable.

"Prior to my return, thousands of people were butchered only a mile from our family's estate. Defenseless men, women, and children were systematically hacked to death in their homes, schools, churches, workplaces, and hospitals. The media propagandized these murderous actions as tribal disputes and strongly discouraged other countries from interfering. These false reports, along with policies that blocked intervention by other countries, only intensified the bloodshed.

"My father, however, told an entirely different story from the reports given by the media. The people that were slaughtered hadn't done anything to deserve death. They were martyred because of their religious beliefs.

"My goodness, who would slaughter innocent women and children for their religious beliefs?" I asked.

"According to the information my father had discovered, these people were peaceful Christians. In every case, shortly before a town was attacked, a government decree was issued ordering the confiscation of arms and ammunition. The helpless villagers were sitting ducks for the heavily armed military forces.

"My father and some of his trusted colleagues made an independent investigation of these atrocities. Their findings staggered my imagination. At first I thought they might have been a bit paranoid, but as I studied the facts, I noticed a subtle, methodical agenda weaving its way throughout the whole affair. After thoroughly examining the documented facts, I couldn't have agreed more with their conclusions.

"Father's reports contained photocopies of documents and maps that came out of a number of United Nations conferences such as the Convention on Biological Diversity and Agenda 21. Through international agreements and treaties, harsh policies restricting people's rights and liberties were subsequently ratified.

"What was happening in Africa was only a part of what was taking place all over the world. After connecting all the dots, there was an obvious plan to reduce the world's population, seize control of large landmasses, and confine humans to designated island areas.

"We also noticed government-instituted, family planning centers being set up in every town. These family planners held town meetings that included videos that strongly advocated the use of contraceptives, sterilization, abortion, and alternative lifestyles.

"This was a definite contrast to African culture, which favors large families, strong family ties, and heterosexuality. Under normal circumstances these people would never have agreed to anything like sterilization or abortion. But due to the compulsion for aid, badly needed food, medical supplies, and protection from rebels, they were forced to submit to these acts of aversion.

Wasn't there anything your father and his friends could have done to prevent these atrocities?" I questioned.

"Actually, they were doing all they could," she answered. "You see, the architects of this conspiracy weren't under any pretext that birth control and alternative lifestyles were the only methods to control the population. The documents father had discovered contained detailed accounts of how advisors to heads of governments successfully orchestrated every war in the past century.

"And yet, war hadn't significantly decreased the population the way they desired. By spreading diseases throughout the world, survivors could procreate freely without making the world too full.

"Father's findings revealed documented proof that AIDS and a number of other fatal viruses had been artificially engineered. Under the cloak of germ warfare, the World Health Organization employed a major laboratory to produce a virus capable of deteriorating the human immune system. During the developmental stages, they grafted an assortment of animal viruses that had been mutated in monkeys and chimpanzees. These viruses were eventually cultured with human cells and ultimately injected into human genes. The final result was a number of very powerful, independent viruses commingled into one. What makes the AIDS virus virtually impossible to eradicate is the number of individual viruses constituting different strains.

"Once the virus was engineered, the true intent was revealed. The first human experiments involved a hundred retarded children from an institution in New York. Naturally, each child inoculated ultimately died. After verifying the deadly effects this virus has upon the immune system, they were ready to disperse the virus throughout the world.

"The homosexual lifestyle was ideal for transferring HIV. Advertisements were placed in gay newspapers asking for volunteers; of course they weren't told that the results would be fatal. This is actually how they infected the gay communities. The remaining doses of this virus were taken to Africa and injected into thousands of Africans.

"By the time I returned home, hundreds of thousands of Africans had died of the AIDS virus. An equal number were currently infected, and hundreds were dying daily. The strain of AIDS virus injected into the African people is far more infectious than the normal strain in other countries. In some areas of the continent, seventy-five percent of the armed forces had tested HIV positive, and in other areas the toll was a hundred percent.

"There were a number of other reprehensible acts entitled *cleansing society*. The goal is the elimination of genetically inferior races—particularly races of color, but also morons, misfits, the maladjusted, and the aged.

"The major medium used to promulgate this plan was to protect the environment from the destructive forces of modern man. Man, as you probably know, is the most dangerous, destructive, selfish and unethical animal on mother earth. Threats of global warming, water shortages, famine, and the like, are all caused by human intervention. The real enemy is humanity itself. The damage people cause the planet is a function of demographics equal to the degree of development. The ecological crisis was really the population crisis. Cut the population by ninety percent and there wouldn't be enough people left to do a great deal of ecological damage."

"No," I interrupted. "I didn't know that. In fact, that philosophy seems to take it to a fearful extreme, don't you think?"

"Well," she continued in response, "they claim that the earth has the capacity to regulate or heal herself under natural conditions. But the human species has developed the technology to overwhelm the earth's capacity to heal herself, and she's therefore doomed to destruction unless the humans stop their technological assault. Global warming is the result of human assault on the earth. She is unable to relax because we have been busy removing her skin and using it as farmland, especially the trees and forests of the humid tropics. And we are also adding a vast blanket of greenhouse gases to the already feverish patient.

"They also claimed that the present population of the world is increasing at too fast a rate, and in order to stabilize the world population, they needed to eliminate 350,000 people per day. Although I agree that the world is over populated, killing 350,000 people a day would not be my solution to the problem."

"Even if their theory was correct," I interjected, "I wouldn't agree to killing anyone!"

"Most of their efforts," she continued without comment, "were directed toward the United States. They attributed much of the earth's devastation to the Americans' overall standard of living, such as industrialization and their usage of air and earth contaminating products. With all of their so-called scientific studies, they said that one American burdens the earth more than twenty people from an undeveloped country.

"Their estimate for the population of the United States was no more than a hundred and fifty million, for the industrialized world society at the present North American material standard of living was one billion people. At the more frugal European standard of living, two billion would be possible. The total world population should be no more than three billion rather than the current six billion.

"By the use of land management policies under a Biosphere Program they confiscated the best areas of the country, implementing Biosphere Reserves and World Heritage Sites. All major ecosystems in a region were reserved. To protect these ecosystems, buffer zones were established around them. They defined a buffer zone as an area surrounding any property with restrictions on its use.

"They charted the continent of Africa and divided it into major ecosystems for reserve. These conterminous states were encompassed in core reserves with inner corridor zones, which created a wilderness network that dominated a region with human habitations being small islands. They designated a half of the continent as wilderness areas with another fourth as buffer zones. These limits were necessary to restrict human activity and to protect Gaia against the destructive actions of mankind.

"Father decided it was safer to send mother and me out of the country. He intended to join us after he settled his affairs in Africa.

"Shortly thereafter we left for one of our estates in America. I had never been to the United States and was excited about going. At twenty, I was incapable of fully grasping the gravity of what was happening throughout the world.

"Six months later, Father was killed in a plane crash. He was an expert pilot who flew with the French Air Force before he retired. He was also an excellent mechanic and kept all of his aircraft well maintained in case of an emergency. And yet, his death was attributed to a minor mechanical failure. Mother and I were certain his death was a direct result of his discoveries and the attempts he made to stop these awful atrocities."

"I'm in total agreement with that," I stated. "There's no question in my mind that your father was murdered!"

"Everything was left to mother and me," she continued. "That's when I realized what a remarkable woman my mother was. Father's death forced her to take charge of everything. She spent hours, day and night, until she was certain the legal ramifications concerning my inheritance were proper in case something happened to her. With help from friends, it only took her a few months to settle the affairs.

"When time permitted, she continued to expose whatever facts she found concerning The Genocide Project. By now, everyone initially working with my father on the project had died, mysteriously disappeared, or simply refused to admit they knew anything about what was going on."

"I guess that pretty much substantiates the fact that your father was murdered," I added.

"Yes," she agreed, before going on. "I returned to school and completed a double major in Computer Science and Mathematics. I tried desperately to persuade mother to allow me to join her during the business meetings. She always refused; saying it was best that I devote all of my efforts to achieve an education.

"A year later, mother died. With me being the sole heir, she had transferred our entire estate into a Revocable Trust, with me as the sole beneficiary. She appointed our family attorney as Successor Trustee over the estate. On my twenty-fifth birthday, I'd be able to manage my own affairs, with the attorney as my financial advisor. However, the attorney was unable to execute his powers as Trustee. The estate was being examined by a special Probate Court and we were to be notified as to the date for the hearing. Being a Revocable Trust, this was not the usual legal procedure.

"A year and a half passed without a word from the courts. Then one day we received a notice informing us that the State had frozen all of my assets until after a complete review. Since the estate involved land out of the country, the attorney filed papers in Federal Court for a hearing. Shortly afterward we received a court date. To my dismay, my attorney had mysteriously disappeared. I had copies of the papers he had filed, but I had no idea what to do with them. I contacted a lawyer I met while going to school in Europe. I sent him photocopies of everything. Although he was young, he was an excellent estate attorney and graduated at the top of his class. He came from a family of lawyers who had been established in London for years. Before I received his reply I was arrested and sentenced to life in prison for fraud.

"That is my story, Lance. With the exception of the Authorities, you know more about me than anyone in this camp."

"That's quite a story, Monique," I replied. Now I understood why she detested these surroundings and why she displayed such contempt. "If anybody else told me that story, I would probably dismiss them as either insane, or a brilliant storyteller. But under the present circumstances, you've convinced me beyond a doubt.

"Why a mathematician, Monique?" I asked out of curiosity.

"I've been asked that question a hundred times before. I've heard all the reasons against it; that the study of numbers is not feminine; it's too taxing for a woman's mind; I should be thinking about finding a husband and raising a family. I've heard them all," she retorted.

I didn't say anything, but I detected an inner conflict. It was as if she was rebelling against the fact that she was female and the implications of being a woman. Her apparent disdain for family traditions also seemed to intensify her agitation.

When she realized her outburst was unjustified, she regained her composure and calmly addressed my question.

"When I became aware that I had two eyes, two arms, and two legs, I was fascinated by numbers. I believed, to thoroughly understand life, I needed a complete understanding of numbers.

"Everything is composed of, or calculated by, numbers. The galaxy consists of a number of planets that rotate at a certain speed, and numbers are used to measure that speed. Light travels at approximately 186,281 miles per second—without a means to calculate the distance of a mile, there's no way of determining the speed of light. The sun transmits a certain amount of energy, which stimulates life. After a given number of days, an accumulated amount of time, death takes its toll. Without a system of calculation, we could not derive a conclusion. The entire process of existence is calculated and concluded by numbers. But these are only a few reasons I chose to become a mathematician."

This was far more interesting than I had imagined, and so was she. I was at a loss for words, "Ummm, I see."

She smiled at my response, and asked if I would show her how to defend herself if she was attacked.

We went through some stretching exercises. When our muscles were limber, I demonstrated the basic positions, proper stances, the correct way to deliver blows and blocks, how to break holds, and the location of some vital points. I stressed the need to practice during her spare time. "Remember, Monique, the objective is to practice until your reflexes respond naturally."

I went to bed early. Monique came later. Fully clothed, she laid on top of the bed beside me.

Again, I didn't sleep soundly and woke up shortly before midnight. Not feeling Monique at my side, my eyes searched the dark room to identify an object. I finally focused on Monique's silhouette. She was sitting in the chair, staring out of the window at the star-filled sky.

"Monique!" I shouted, without restraint. "My memory's returned. I remember everything as clear as if it were happening now!"

Turning to face me, with a hint of surprise in her voice she replied, "It has?"

"Yes! Would you like to know why I'm here?"

"I would like that very much, Lance."

"Well, I achieved my degree in Architectural Engineering from the University of Specialization. I graduated with honors and accepted a position with World Construction, one of the most prestigious architectural firms in the country.

"During the ten years I was there, the firm grew to become the largest of its kind in the Western Continent. I had recently been promoted to chief architect with a staff of 32 and subject only to the firm's president, Isaac Burgess.

"As one of the fringe benefits accompanying my position I was allowed to reside on one of the firm's estates. It was a quaint manor rising magnificently above trimmed lawns and rolling terraces, and surrounded by four acres of landscaped pine, spruce, and walnut trees. The designer and builder was the founder of the firm. After his death it was arranged that the head architect utilize the estate until he no longer held that position. I declined the firm's offer for a limousine and driver, and purchased my own Cornice convertible.

"My parents were proud of me, their only child, and they spent a good portion of their summer vacations with me. For a thirty-five-year-old bachelor that worked his way up from a middle class family, I was doing fairly well.

"I was engaged to Greta, a twenty-five-year-old fashion model who worked out of an agency in Europe. She was tall, with long brown hair that bounced whenever she walked in those long strides so typical of models. We enjoyed tennis, racquetball, and swimming together, mostly on the estate. But my true pleasure was hang gliding. Whenever Greta was out of the country, I spent most of my free time hang-gliding or searching for unique cliffs to enjoy my hobby.

"One evening I was working late on a special project we were starting the next day. Because it was marked *Top Priority,* I wanted to study the set of specifications thoroughly before briefing my draftsmen in the morning. After a complete search of the office, I was unable to find the set of specs for the job. Isaac and I had discussed the details of the project earlier that day, so I wondered if he had mistakenly kept the files or merely failed to have them delivered to my office before leaving. While searching through his out-basket I found them attached to another set of specs for the same project. Puzzled, I studied them side-by-side. They bore the same *Special Project* heading, but the physical location of the site was different. One set of specs was apparently used to conceal electronic surveillance devices, secret codes, and a different location of the construction site. To complicate matters, Isaac's set of specs made repeated references to a mysterious *Manual IV.* I wasn't familiar with this manual but assumed it had to be important since the references were necessary to interpret the specs.

"Stimulated by curiosity, I started hunting for this mysterious *Manual IV.* After searching Isaac's office without a clue, I decided to wait until the following morning and ask Isaac about it. Then it occurred to me that I hadn't examined the walk-in safe that contained the firm's financial estimates and accounting records. Knowing the safe was only accessible to myself, Isaac, and the firm's accountant, I thought it might be a likely place to keep the manual.

"I dialed the combination and entered the safe. After examining the shelves and searching through the filing cabinet, I was still unable to find the manual. I didn't thoroughly check the last three drawers of the file cabinet because they appeared to be empty when I opened them. Having drawn a blank everywhere else, I decided to check them once more before leaving the safe.

"Examining the drawers again only confirmed my first conclusion, but when I slammed the last drawer shut, I heard a thump. 'Yesss!' I whispered, while opening the drawer again. Lying in plain view were two books. They had obviously fallen from their hiding place when I closed the drawer.

"I seized them and walked over to the leather chair positioned behind Isaac's desk. The smaller of the books was the mysterious *Manual IV*, which contained the information I needed to complete the project. The other book was much larger, it was bound in black leather and resembled a well-used Bible. Posted throughout the book were warnings against it falling into the hands of unauthorized personnel. It was simply titled: *The Master Plan*, revised edition 1999. The New Age One World Order, an exposé of Global Governance, designed by the Elite for world dominance.

"Although the information I needed to brief my staff would be lacking, I knew that Isaac had access to the information contained in the *Manual IV*, and he could brief them in the morning. My curiosity to investigate this master plan intrigued me beyond restraint.

"I opened its cover and began to read. Astounded by what I was discovering, I lost all concept of time. Realizing that I would never finish in time, I rushed to the copy machine to make photocopies. I had copied 196 pages of the 750-page document before noticing that the dark skies had turned the gray of dawn. Hoping that no one would come to work early, I rushed back to the safe and replaced the books. My watch showed 5:30 a.m., and I was due back at work in two hours. I had to rush home if I wanted to return on time.

"As I pressed the elevator button I pulled my handkerchief from my pocket to wipe the perspiration from my brow. During the ride down to the garage-level, a number of thoughts flooded my mind. I was positive Isaac was one of them, his copy of *The Master Plan* proved that. I didn't know how high he ranked within their structure, but his position as President of World Construction gave him a privileged monopoly over all major construction projects within the Western continent. I thought about the special meetings Isaac attended out of the country. When he returned he would have Special Projects like the one we were about to start.

"When I reached my car I placed the briefcase containing the partially copied document on the seat beside me. With jangled nerves I started the motor. Suddenly, as if on their own volition, my hands dropped into my lap. Overwhelmed by my discovery, I sat for an undetermined amount of time staring into space with a deluge of unanswered questions surging through my mind.

"Judging by the severe warnings against the manual falling into the hands of unauthorized persons, I was certain that knowledge of its contents constituted a threat to their organization. If I attempted to make any overt efforts to reveal their plans—such as in your father's case, Monique—I was certain my life would be in danger. Suppressing my fears, I regained my composure and drove out of the multi-level parking lot. Nobody knew about my discovery, and I wasn't about to breathe a word to anyone."

"Lance," Monique interrupted, "do you think this is the same group of people that had my father murdered?"

"I'm sure they are," I answered.

"My gosh," Monique exclaimed, looking at the clock on the wall, "it's almost four o'clock. They'll be calling you to work in a couple of hours."

"I had no idea it was that late. We'd better get some sleep. I'll tell you the rest tomorrow, when I come in from work. Good night, Monique."

"Good night, Lance."

The sky looked strange this morning. A haze seemed to cover its surface, impeding the clarity of the sun. The haze helped provide relief from the direct sun, but it increased the humidity.

While marching along the road, a young man in our group darted into a field for no apparent reason. I watched the reactions of the men around me, and they all acted like this was a routine occurrence. After questioning them, I learned that this was a common form of release from the continuous, mounting pressures from being imprisoned.

While he was running he tore off his shirt and cast it aside. By avoiding the potholes and chunks of dirt in his path he maintained his stride. Perspiration covered his back and shoulders. The reflection from the sun glistened off the muscular crevices of the young Afro-American's skin. I watched in awe as this athlete danced across the field with leaps and sudden turns that never impeded his stride.

Even with the head start he had, we all knew that he would eventually be caught. One of the guards raised a whistle to his lips. Instinctively my hands covered my ears, as did everyone else except the goons. I pressed my ears tightly with all my might. I still felt the painful pressure from the whistle's piercing sound.

Instantly four goons struck out in four different directions. Within minutes they were closing in on the young man. One of them dove for a tackle but missed. Another faked a move, and then he dove but missed. The young man had masterfully eluded them both. By the time he had reestablished his pattern, the two remaining goons had boxed him in. One of the goons hit the young man with a flying tackle and wrestled him to the ground. Instantly the other goon dove on top of him. They held him securely until the others joined them.

There were two more blows from a whistle with a slightly different tone and less painful to my ears than the first whistle. All four goons jogged back carrying their captive by the arms and legs. The young man was struggling desperately to free himself.

The goons approached us from the far side of the road when one of the guards raised his hand, stopping them in their tracks. He quickly walked over to them and shouted, "Make an example of this one!"

They threw the young man to the ground upon his face. Two of the goons pinned him down with their knees in his back to prevent his escape. The other two each grabbed an arm and began twisting and pulling his arms behind him and over his head. The young man couldn't contain his cries of pain. We all stood in silence, watching the torturous ordeal and listening to the sound of his bones breaking.

The goons dropped his arms; they hit the ground with a dull thump. They repeated the procedure with his legs. The young man had now lost all consciousness. He never felt the goon who grabbed his chin and the back of his head and continued to twist until his neck was broken.

At the start of our lunch break Haile beckoned me over to sit with him. "What do they call you, my friend?"

"My name is Lance, Lance Roberts," I replied.

"I will not be with you much longer, Lance; what we witnessed today makes this clear to me. It is equally apparent that this life is not for you. Have you made your plans for escape yet?"

For fear of possibly being overheard I felt apprehensive about revealing my intention to escape. After a slight pause, I answered. "No, I haven't."

"If you desire to escape, it can be accomplished."

"What is your opinion about taking another person?" I asked, considering Monique.

"An accomplice may hinder your escape and cause more trouble than help. I assume you are referring to a woman?"

"Yes," I replied reluctantly.

"If you must, be confident she can be trusted. Test her faithfulness to be certain."

"I haven't formulated a plan yet. All I know is that I'm not going to stay here. I'd rather die trying to escape than continue living as a slave!"

"The mind controls the body, Lance. The body will respond to what the mind tells it. Even pain can be disregarded by the strength of your will. Build an impenetrable mental shield against negative thoughts. Be mindful of your instincts when they warn you of danger, but do not allow fear to control you.

"Once you have learned what is realistically within your power, consider it carefully, and do not extend those boundaries. Direct all thoughts toward an escape plan and allow nothing to deter you from your goal.

"Above all, do not allow hatred to make its home within you. Hate is a debilitating sickness that does nothing but destroy the principles upon which life exists.

"You are still young; life is still plenteous for you. My life is over. I tell you this now, hoping you will do as I say and not as I do."

"Do you know a way that I can escape from here, Haile?" I asked enthusiastically.

"I do not. You must search within yourself until you discover the way that is perfect for you. When the time is right, and you will know that time, execute your plan with precision."

The bell sounded the end of our lunch break. Haile's words echoed through my mind, making the rest of the day's duties an aimless task.

When I returned to the cabin Monique was not there. All of her belongings were still there, but she was gone.

I made a sandwich, ate it, and lay down to rest. All I could think about was my helpless position. Every aspect of my life was controlled. The implements of war were food, shelter, clothing, and a beautiful woman. For those not as fortunate, such as the young man I met when I first arrived, this could be a utopia, a convenient way to avoid the challenges of life.

I recalled a pompous boast I had read from *The Master Plan*: *"We are not content with negative obedience, nor even with the most abject submission. When finally you surrender to us, it must be of your own free will. We do not destroy the heretic because he resists us. We convert him, we capture his inner mind, and we reshape him."*

I had enough to pacify me but not enough to satisfy me. I was looking forward to a meal I didn't earn, living in a house that wasn't mine, and functioning under conditions I wouldn't normally accept. And if that wasn't enough, I was trying to win the favor of a woman who was being forced to live with me.

The sound of Monique entering the house shattered my thoughts. The darkness had filled the little cabin. When Monique reached the doorway of the bedroom she called out, "Are you asleep, Lance?"

"No. I'm laying here trying to digest a dry sandwich I ate a little while ago. I'm sure glad to see you."

She removed the sweater from her shoulders and said, "I'm sorry I'm late. The new super-computerized information system finally arrived this morning, and I had to stay over for a full briefing."

I raised up and propped the pillow behind my head, "That's

interesting. What does a place like this need with a new computer?"

"Oh Lance, everything is done by computers," she said as though I had just stepped out of the dark ages. "Altogether there are 50 labor camps around the world. That constitutes a lot of tabulations taking place on a daily basis. This is the Capitol of the World-State, with the largest city and labor camp in the world. That's why we've been selected to house the most massive computerized system invented by man.

"From this location we'll maintain an active tabulation of all the arrivals, transfers, births and deaths taking place within the camps worldwide and maintain the exact whereabouts of every person in the world.

"When we complete the programming aspect, the system will contain everyone's medical statistics, work history, and financial reports. This will help determine whether a patient should be kept alive based upon health, usefulness, and other determining factors. And, naturally, the system will inform us when those in the labor camps turn 50 years old, which is why they call this system 'god'."

"Are you the one who programs that information into the computer?" I asked.

"Yes, I am. Look, Lance, I'm aware that this job has requirements I don't particularly like, but someone's got to do it, and it might as well be me. Anyway, once the data has been entered into the computer, it automatically prints out a daily schedule according to the information received.

"What else is this machine capable of doing?"

"Well, there's another procedure termed Embedded Electronics or Biochip Implants that include a Radio Frequency Identification Device. The RFID uses radio signals to read identification codes and other data stored in an RFID transponder. It contains a LifeChip, with a life span of up to 250 years. It's a reliable way to electronically detect, control, and track a variety of items like products, information, animals, and people.

"Everything on this planet, including people, will be marked, then tracked or monitored. If it moves, it'll have a transponder; if it doesn't move, it'll have a bar code of some variety. But everything made will have some form of tracking device using binary numbers or computer language, whether they be 3-D symbols or an RFID for distribution and warehousing.

"This transponder is a microscopic glass tube, made of soda lime glass for bio-compatibility. During manufacture, the tube is hermetically sealed to make it is impossible for body fluids to reach the internal electronics. Inside are three components. One is a computer microchip with a custom integrated circuit containing a unique ID number encrypted permanently into the surface. The second is a coil of copper wire wound around an iron core, which functions as a radio antenna to receive and send an encoded ID number from the external scanner. The third is a capacitor that tunes the signal to and from the microchip. When the scanner is activated, it digitally displays the encoded ID number on a liquid crystal screen. The number of possible code combinations is close to one trillion."

"Yes, I read about that right before my arrest. Would you explain it to me?"

"Each microscopic Biochip contains the person's DNA code, a digitized photo, social security number, car ownership and DMV driving records, arrest and warrant records, bank transactions, various consumer profiles, credit history and profile, tax returns, employment records, home ownership and personal property records, marital status, children, divorce records, medical and prescription records, and religious affiliation for each person in the world. Special injectors are used with an anti-migration tip. To prevent the Biochip from moving around, one end is sheathed in a polypropylene shell. This coating offers a surface with which fibrous connective tissue begins to bond within 24 hours after injection; it becomes a part of the body. Once implanted, the RFID is virtually impossible to retrieve. The right hand and the forehead are the two places on the body that are the easiest to scan by a computer scanner."

"That would make all of your personal information instantly accessible to the public. Why would a person want a computer chip injected into their forehead or hand containing their entire history?"

"There are a lot of advantages for people having this information at their immediate disposal, Lance. People who have chronic medical problems, or in case there's an emergency, they'll have all of their medical records available instantly. And they can't get lost. Nor does anyone have to worry about money, credit cards, or checks. It eliminates error, fraud, theft, and illegal drug purchases, it'll also cut down the overall cost of goods and services."

"Where you see convenience, I see a loss of privacy. I also see your finances, which should be confidential, now available for scrutiny from a number of government agencies. At the discretion of any personnel in any of these agencies, they can examine your medical history or financial records. And you don't have any control or voice in your own affairs if they decide to freeze your assets. No, we see it a lot differently, Monique.

"What else is this super-computerized system capable of doing?"

"They intend to start fusing computer technology into the brain. The proper term is chip grafting. This involves an implanted chip that can translate and digitize current thoughts, and then write them onto a disk that allows them to be read by a computer. I'm not talking about past thoughts, which can only be induced by a memory enhancer and processed by a memory scan. With this new process they're able to capture *current* thoughts, while they're actually being generated in the mind. Through electromagnetic emissions from the brain, using remote neural identification and screening techniques, they can alter individuals' brain waves, which ultimately alters their behavior. I'll also be in charge of maintaining this data on a continuous basis.

"The other procedure, included with the chip grafting, is a neural chip implant. A microscopic video camera is implanted behind the eye. This transmits a visual picture to a screen the same way the human eye transmits what we see to our brains. This will provide the authorities with a visual and audio record of every event in which a person is involved. The chip grafting reveals the thoughts and sensations and the neural chip implant provides the sights and sounds. That way, whatever a person thinks, feels, sees, and hears is recorded.

"Combine these new devices with biochemical and chemical mind-control drugs, it's easy to manipulate emotions and control reason. They ultimately intend to use this technology to prevent any disloyal ideas from taking shape in people's minds. With a record of each person's psychological characteristics, an approach can be devised to quickly persuade anyone to conform to the guidance of his or her advisors. If that won't work, they can completely wipe out a person's ability to think for himself. They can also preprogram someone to do various tasks and, by a remote control device, direct his or her actions.

"The original experiments were tried on the goons. Now that they've been perfected, the guards won't need whistles; they can do everything by remote control. Eventually everyone will have chip grafting and neural chip implants. In fact, this procedure is under consideration to be performed on children at birth."

"The capabilities of this new computer, along with the demented thinking of those in charge, are frightening! I'm afraid to ask what else it can do."

"Well, the authorities are pretty excited about this new computer, particularly my instructor. 'Now,' she told us, 'with the help of our new super-computerized systems, valuable time and labor will be cut considerably. We've been absolutely staggered, realizing that the computer has the capability to act as if it were ten of the top psychologists working with one person.'

"Close to a hundred people are attending these classes daily, mainly educators, psychologists, sociologists, and counselors. Only the instructor and myself have the technical experience to operate the new computer.

Until they recruit more experienced help, my instructor and I will have the obligation of running it."

"Do you realize the position you'll be in?" I asked inquiringly.

"Yes. I do, Lance. So what is my alternative; continue being a sex object and maid for the next 20 years?

"Look, I understand your situation, and maybe I'm being too judgmental. But there are issues you need to consider."

Disregarding my warning completely, she continued to share her thoughts. "I learned something today that's obviously been going on for some time. One of the educators related a story that may have been an actual account, or just a hypothetical case scenario. I don't know. In either case, this is what she said, *'Fred Moore is seven years old and a student in Public Education Concenter 419. Fred's classes consist of him alone. Pupils frequently gather in groups, for seminar-like discussions. But most of Fred's time is spent at the learning console, which consists of a computer.'*

Monique interrupted herself, "Until now, this is an exact description of my former education. It's the concluding portion that I wasn't aware of," she stated with difficulty. *"'Fred's computer—like all the other Concenter computers around the world—are connected to the main terminal in the Educational Resources Center. There, a team of psychologists, programmers, expert teachers of everything from arithmetic to zoology, remedial specialists, and guidance counselors comb Fred's record, and his progress is tabulated by the computers. No one knows Fred's grade level and it doesn't matter. He works at his own pace. No one can come between Fred and the curriculum we have laid out for him.*

"'The old, antiquated form of education was too concerned with a child's individualism, loyalty to family tradition, national patriotism, facts, and religious dogmas, and too little concerned with values. The children were fed all kinds of poisonous certainties by their parents, Sunday and school teachers, politicians, and priests. Their concept of right and wrong, which has been the basis of child training, the substitution of rational thinking for faith in the beliefs of old people, these are the outdated methods they used to chart the changes in human behavior. We are more concerned with values, attitudes, interests, ideals, and habits.

"'The global educative process is clear and easily understood. Education is tied directly to jobs—the job is our critical point in the State. We intend to start our educational process at birth, linking instruction with productive labor. Our teaching is a continuous, lifelong education. That is why we are raising children in communal nurseries; that way, any form of theology and history is suppressed.

"Our educative process gives incentives not to the one who wins more credit for himself but to the one who cooperates most effectively with others. Our educative process molds Fred's cognitive structure, including all his facts, concepts, beliefs, and expectations. We modify his valences and values. We prepare him for the realization of his best self in the higher loyalty of serving the State. World citizenship, a global principle, is the standard education of every child!'"

While studying *The Master Plan* this type of revolting information constantly confronted me. I had grown immune to their socialistic rhetoric and it no longer affected me the way it did initially. Monique was beginning to understand that she was a product of the system, and it wasn't just her. Most people around the world, including myself, had been brainwashed by this education process that was skillfully designed to enslave us mentally, physically and spiritually.

Aware of this, I thought I'd change the subject to something else. "Did you say that there are forty-nine camps besides this one?"

"Yes," she replied, enthusiastically, forgetting what she'd just told me. "I have a lot of work ahead of me. Every afternoon I'll be going over to the Main Complex to familiarize myself with the new computer. The following week I'll actually start programming the data for all of the camps. Lance, you should see this new super-computerized system, it's absolutely amazing!"

I understood Monique's excitement about the new computer and her new assignment, but I couldn't understand why it had suddenly become "*our* camp" and "*we* have, and *I* will."

"Oh, wow!" she exclaimed. "I almost forgot to tell you. Some of the staff members were talking about the building of a new Complex. They mentioned an architect with the experience for the position, and they said that he was temporarily assigned to the labor camp. I'm not positive, because I didn't hear the person's name, but according to what I did hear, it sounded like they were describing you."

I shook my head in denial. "I don't think they would take a chance placing me in a position that would allow me access to the plans of a campsite or its facilities; not with the information they know about me."

"Well," she replied, "we'll find out next week. If it is you, we'll be transferred to the Complex, together."

"This is the second time you've mentioned this Complex. What is it, and where is it?"

"The Main Complex is the capital of the World-State. It's literally the heartbeat of the world. It's a super, ultramodern, partially underground city about 20 miles from here. It has shopping malls, theaters, office buildings, and living quarters for the staff and the prisoners that work there. It's just like any other major city anywhere else in the world, only it's far more modern."

"It sounds impressive. Any improvement over my present condition is welcomed," I responded. "But I'm not going to start packing my bags based on such a slim possibility."

While we were eating, I described the incident that had taken place earlier that day. She listened, but she really wasn't concerned.

Later, Monique told me she wanted to practice martial arts, so we warmed up with a few basic exercises and stretches. When I felt she was limber, I taught her three basic but essential moves. We practiced until I felt she had mastered the mechanics effectively.

Without any forewarning, I decided to test her reflexes to see how she'd react if attacked. I came up behind her and pinned her arms to her side. To my surprise, she reacted naturally. By causing her body to go limp, she bent forward, simultaneously thrusting her rear into my pelvis. This broke my hold, causing me to fly over her head. I did a complete frontward flip and landed on my back about five feet away.

Although I hadn't expected her to throw me, I instinctively reacted by breaking the fall with the backs of my forearms, buttocks and the palms of my hands. Monique, thinking I was hurt, rushed over to see if I was okay.

"Oh, Lance, I'm sorry. I didn't mean to hurt you, I was just reacting the way you taught me. I didn't even realize what I was doing."

I'm all right, Monique," I told her while climbing to my feet and taking a seat on the couch. She sat down next to me and asked, "Would you finish telling me about these people who run the world."

"All right. I'll continue where I left off last night," I responded enthusiastically.

"Well, during the next few weeks I worked overtime until I had photocopied *The Master Plan* in its entirety. All my spare time was devoted to studying this plan. I wanted to learn how they intended to pull off this grandiose scheme of theirs. It's not every day somebody can come up with a feasible plan to direct each detailed event and control the world."

"No it's not!" Monique agreed. "I'd like to know how they were able to do that myself."

"I learned that the executive body of this tightly knit organization was referred to by a number of titles, the Society of the Elect, being one. This group of men, initially comprised of one family, were British elitist socialists and some of the wealthiest and influential men in the world at that time. They had united with one aim in mind, to create a New World Order.

"Knowing it would take generations before achieving their ultimate aim, they devised *The Master Plan*. The ideal was universal peace, the creation of one language founded on the unity of mankind, with all States crushed, disciplined, and subject to one law under global governance. Nationalism had to be overcome, the architecture of the present world dismantled, and a common creed or ethical-religion established. Depopulation was a necessity, with a subsequent zero-growth society. Mankind's desire for peace could only be realized by the creation of an authoritative New World Order so great and powerful that wars would be rendered impossible."

"It's beginning to sound like totalitarianism to me," Monique stated.

"You're absolutely correct," I responded. "Once drafted," I continued, "*The Master Plan* was continuously revised and covertly passed among the members. Only the Elite's inner Circle of Initiates and the Association of Helpers knew the detailed account of their aim. Through semi-secret discussion and lobbying groups, later known as the Round Table Groups, they initiated their plan.

"A strong emphasis was placed on maintaining utmost secrecy. The success of *The Master Plan* would be established by two determinate facts—loyalty of its members to each other and punishment of its enemies. Only select, proven, and trusted men knew the true identities of the Elite's inner circle. It was the outer circle, the Round Table Groups, which initially engaged others to do the Elite's bidding.

"Achieving world dominance required expertise in every sector of life. Trusted subordinates were instructed to cull specialists from among their administrative brains—specialists reared on investigation, observation, and the delicacies of fine calculation. These specialists closely studied the events of history—observing every moment as it passed—and then drafted their plans accordingly. They didn't want to merely analyze and interpret international policy, but make it.

"After succeeding in Europe, they turned their gaze upon the United States. For some time this organization coveted America's return to subjugation under British rule. America, however, was a young, independent country founded upon a bureaucratic system that created immense adversity to the fulfillment of global governance. The North American Republic furnished its own money without cost. And its Constitution was written to limit the power of government and keep its citizens free and prosperous. It paid off its debts and was without debt to the international bankers. Destined to become prosperous beyond precedent in the history of the civilized governments of the world that government had to be destroyed or it would destroy every monarchy on the globe."

"You know, Lance," Monique stopped me, "my favored pursuit

while I attended the University in Europe was to study the United States Constitution. No other country has ever come close to composing a political document that addresses the needs of all the peoples, like the Constitution of the United States. And only those with devious motives would try to change it."

"And that's exactly what they did, Monique," I countered. "Men of genius were selected, only those endorsed by mentors dedicated to the cause of the Elite. These men were groomed from early childhood—learned scholars specially trained at distinguished universities—to understand the affairs of the world. Various tax-exempt foundations, trusts, and endowments, all overt and covert influences that opposed the fundamental principles of the United States, funded these scholarships.

"The recipients of these scholarships were instruments of precision that believed that the first duty of any man was to serve the State. Between one and two thousand of these men were scattered all over the world in various key positions of authority. Many of them were prominent businessmen, the heads of large industrial firms and major newspapers; many were television, movie, and radio producers. Many were placed in government bureaucracy as advisors, aides, and specialists. They remained in these positions indefinitely while elected political officials came and went.

"Like a giant octopus, they infiltrated city, state, and nation. The executive offices were overwhelmed, as well as the legislative bodies, courts, newspapers, and every agency created for the public protection. By clutching the reins of government they secured enactment of legislation favorable to their cause.

"Large contributions were made to both political parties, carefully screening leading personalities picked well in advance of Election Day, which allowed an alternation of the two parties in public office. They wrote the political platforms, used the leading men of private organizations, and resorted to every device to place in nomination for high public office only the candidates that were amenable to their dictates.

"Candidates with great personal ambition and conceivably vulnerable to blackmail for some past occurrences were preferred; consequently, someone not likely to become too independent in time. This also concealed their own influence, inhibited any exhibition of independence by politicians, and allowed the electorate to believe that they were exercising their own free choice.

"The Elite believed that force was the conquering factor in political affairs, especially if it was concealed in those talents essential to statesmen. Violence was the principle, cunning and make-believe were the rule for governments that didn't want to lay down their own power at the feet of the agents of a new power. They believed that this evil was the one and only means to attain their end; therefore, they didn't stop at bribery, deceit, or treachery as long as these served to attain their end. Merciless severity was their greatest factor of strength in the government, not only for the sake of gain but also in the name of duty for the sake of their victory."

"Lance," Monique interrupted, "I could clearly see that kind of attitude and those types of horrible behavioral patterns developing over the years. But never before have those evil traits been so blatant in America as in the most recent Congress, Senate, and White House administration under the last President."

"What puzzled me more, was to witness such gullibility from the people. This President and his administration maintained the highest majority of favor throughout his term than any other President in American history."

"America" I continued "was also a prospering country that caused the Elite tremendous difficulty in controlling its development, since redistribution of wealth was a necessity. The international banking system and the international industrialists had dominated the European setting for decades through the establishment of Central Banks. By this method the Elite gradually absorbed the wealth of the world and used it to fulfill their objective. All previous efforts to palm off a Central Bank on the American public had ended in failure. The United States Constitution gave Congress alone the authority to create money and govern its value.

"With planned precision, every ploy was used to accomplish this end. The adoption of a Central Bank in the United States had to be sneaked into the Republic. It had to be a financial institution that performed all the functions of a Central Bank, and yet, the American public had to be misled into believing that it operated on their behalf. Subsequently the Federal Reserve Act was passed through Congress.

"The Federal Reserve (Fed)—no more than a Central Bank privately owned by the International Bankers—created a financial power independent of and above the Government of the United States. Under the Federal Reserve Act, private bankers were allowed to create money, actually credit, out of nothing and loan it to the United States at a high rate of interest. The Elite had finally devised a means of emptying the coffers of the United States Government, while simultaneously emptying the pockets of every American."

"I've always thought the Federal Reserve was a part of the Federal Government. I had no idea it was a private institution," Monique exclaimed.

"Most people don't," I commented. "That's exactly why this Act transformed the United States from the greatest manufacturing nation into a consuming and importing nation with a continuous balance of trade against it. The United States' national debt mounted to over 30 trillion dollars, which was a greater burden of debt than all other nations of the world combined. Payments toward this debt were paid through a heavy yoke of graduated taxes that was permanently fastened to the backs of each American at birth.

"A Central Bank was needed to consolidate all central banks, so the Bank for International Settlements (BIS) was established. This Central Bank was privately owned and controlled by the world's central banks, all of which were private corporations. Through the BIS, and its American counterpart, the Fed, the Elite was able to shift billions of dollars and change the direction of economics by simply raising or lowering the interest rate one fraction of a percentage point. Collectively, each central bank dominated its government by its ability to control treasury loans, to manipulate foreign exchanges, to influence the level of economic activity in the country, and to influence cooperative politicians by subsequent economic rewards in the business world.

"Another destructive organism cleverly grafted into the structure of the United States was the Council on Foreign Relations, or CFR. The CFR was the American branch of England's Royal Institute of International Affairs, a shoot of the Round Table Groups, and a front for the International Bankers. The CFR was dedicated to the destruction of America's sovereignty and the establishment of a New World, Humanistic, Socialist State. Although the Council on Foreign Relations wasn't a secret organization, each member had to be invited and pledge secrecy on all that transpired within the meetings. Every Chairman of the Board of the Federal Reserve was also a member of the Council on Foreign Relations.

"Once the ruling members of the CFR decided that the U.S. Government should adopt a particular policy, the very substantial research facilities of the CFR were put to work to develop arguments, intellectual and emotional, to support the new policy, and to confound and discredit, intellectually and politically, any opposition.

"This group of Elitists believed that their earthly duty was to shape a New World Order with them at the helm. The slackened reins of government had to be caught up and gathered into their hand. They believed that the blind might of the nations were incapable of existing for one single day without guidance, and their new authority would merely fit into the place of the old, which was already weakened by liberalism.

"To the Elite, political freedom was an idea but not a fact. The political had nothing in common with the moral. The ruler who is governed by the moral is not a skilled politician, and is therefore unstable on his seat. A ruler had to be cunning and able to employ make-believe. They felt that the best way to govern was by violence and terrorization, not by academic discussions. They believed that from the temporary evil they were now compelled to commit, the good of an unshakable rule would emerge. The earth would then be restored to the regular course of national life, which had been destroyed by liberalism, and this result would justify the means.

"Erecting global governance had to be done from the ground up, not the top down. It couldn't be accomplished at one big leap, it had to be erected one piece at a time. So the Elite consolidated their efforts in order to centralize the four centers of power in all its dimensions—political, economical, social, and ecclesiastical.

"Ecclesiasticism was a concession utilized to help direct the minds of the people to further their goal. Religion had to fulfill the spiritual void within humanity; it had to frustrate the fundamentalist Judaic-Christians with their creeds and dogmas while establishing a new culture in society.

"New Age was the product of a strange mixture of environmentalism, pantheism, and humanism. Forged on a universal scale, this humanistic, secular religion—non-theist, void-of-God and centered on nature and the environment not deity—proved to be the answer.

"The fundamental component of this New Age religion was its universalistic character. While it embraced the humanistic teachings common to all great religions of the East and the West, it disposed of the theistic concepts. Synthesis dictated a trend of all the evolutionary processes today; all had to work toward larger unified blocs, toward intermixture, international relationships, global panning, brotherhood, interdependence, fellowship of faiths. Ethnic cultures of all variances had to be blended into one subculture; humans had to become one with nature.

"One major strategy used to forge this subculture was the environmental movement. This New Age religion taught that humans were members of a universal community that included plants and animals as well as rocks, springs, and pools. People were members of a community of beings—living and non-living. Thus, rivers were viewed as mothers, while animals were treated as kin.

"Nature had an integral set of different values—cultural, spiritual, and material—to which humanity had to conform. Human beings were just one strand in nature's web and no more important than any other living creature. Therefore, the natural way was right, and human activities had to be molded along nature's rhythms."

"I see nothing wrong with this, Lance. In order for people to be able to live on this planet together, we have to have some kind of comradery between us," she added approvingly.

"Apparently the majority agreed with you, since the Global Biodiversity Assessment (GBA) treaty was cast in this view. Howeve the treaty itself was nothing less than a plan to reorganize western civilization around nature. Property rights and other resource management practices and uses were limited to only those that would do no harm to biodiversity. Property rights were restricted to *usufractual* or *user rights.* Harvesting quotas, emission permits, and development rights were only some of the rights that were controlled by strict regulations. Since any human activity could threaten biodiversity, all human activity was tightly regulated.

"The treaty's GBA framed biodiversity as a *public good* and part of the *global commons* which no one can own. Value equivalent to human life was placed on a landscape, a species of bird or fish, and of an undammed river—everything became tightly coupled ecosystems.

"The Elite, however, were inspired solely by a demonic lust for power. Theirs was not a system of compassion, humanity, peace, and kindly care, but one of will-to-dominate. Their authority was the crown of order, which included the whole happiness of man. The aureole of their authority demanded a bowing of the knee and a reverent fear of all the peoples. They truly despised having to relinquish any dominance to a religious concept; but this New Age religion, with its philosophy that mother earth was being threatened by global warming and pollution in a way that could jeopardize her survival, was an excellent catalyst to further their plan."

"Lance?" Monique interrupted. "I've believed this all of my life, and I don't believe that its a fabrication. You're saying, just because its written in *The Master Plan* there's no truth to it. When it comes to protecting the environment, I simply don't agree with you."

"Well, Monique," I replied, "there's one thing I've learned about this demonic group of elitist and the governments they control, everything they tell the people is a lie; and every law they make, no matter how much it appears to be in our behalf on the surface, its always another link in their chains of enslavement. In all of my studies of the Elite and their master plan I've kept that idea in mind, and in every incident it has proven correct."

"Well, I sure hope you're wrong, Lance. Go ahead and continue."

"Prior financial dealings with the United States proved that America would not be easily penetrated. The original founders of the United States Constitution had masterfully erected individual, separate institutions to guard against an assault. These independent institutions made it difficult for the Elite to attach their mechanical linkages and frail bridges that were designed to weaken a country's structure and force its collapse. The only recourse was to directly confront the U.S. Constitution and dismantle it piece by piece.

"Through the establishment of the Fed and the CFR the road was paved for the organization known as the United Nations, or UN. At a meeting in Washington the representatives of 26 nations issued the United Nations Declaration. A huge campaign that spared no effort was orchestrated to misinform the American public regarding the direction and purpose of this new organization. Senate opposition was rendered so impotent that there was no significant support against the UN Charter and the treaties that would inevitably follow.

"Subsequently, representatives of 46 nations and 42 members of the U.S. delegation who were or would later become CFR members adopted the Charter of the United Nations. The UN represented the idea of a universal morality, superior to the interests of individual nations. The UN and its Charter was a monstrous destructive mechanism that was now permanently attached to the foundation of the United States Constitution.

"The Soviet Union insisted that the headquarters of the UN be located in the United States. This later proved to be a Trojan horse. The 17-acre site for the UN headquarters in New York was donated by one of the International Bankers at a cost of $8,500,000. The $65,000,000 cost of the UN building was an interest-free loan paid for by the American taxpayers. The U.S. Congress opened a bank account in the name of The United Nations. They gave authorization to the State Department to pay annually, out of the Treasury, whatever amount the General Assembly of the UN felt necessary to cover the United States' share of the UN expenses.

"The UN published a Human Development Report with objectives to establish a global tax and form a strong UN military. The UN was given authorization as the principal custodian of our global human security. And by the establishment of an Economic Security Council they held wide-ranging decision-making powers in the socio-economic field.

"Other objectives included closing our military bases, reducing our military spending, and the initiation of a Social Charter pledging a new global civil society based upon global governance. The United Nations Organization was the installation of a world government with an international control of armies, a universal system of money, and the authority to implement and eliminate tariffs and quota restrictions on trade.

"The ability to make treaties is an extraordinary power that opens the door for subversion. Treaties create international law, and they also make domestic law. They are superior to ordinary laws since congressional laws are invalid if they don't conform to the Constitution, whereas treaty law can override the Constitution.

"Under the Constitution, treaties become the supreme laws of the land. Treaty laws take power away from the branches of Congress and give them to the President. They also take powers from the States and give them to the Federal Government or some international body, and they can cut across the rights given to the people by their constitutional Bill of Rights.

"The World Trade Organization, the North American Free Trade Agreement, the General Agreement on Tariffs and Trades, the Economic and Financial Organization, the Trans-Atlantic Free Trade Area, the Asia-Pacific Economic Cooperation, the Chemical Weapons Treaty, these and all other treaties embrace Trade, Development, and Migration Commissions, and a Central Bank. The introduction of these treaties helped to demolish our sovereignty—economically, militarily and territorially. These institutions were formed to equalize the power-base of all countries through the redistribution of wealth, by regulating the production and distribution of raw materials and food, and controlling the flow of inter-regional investment and migration throughout the world.

"An equitable distribution of income had to be established. And there had to be a dilution of sovereignty, to the immediate disadvantage of those nations that possessed the preponderance of power, chiefly the United States of America. The establishment of a common money had to be vested in a body created by and responsible to the principle of trading and investing peoples, which would deprive all governments of exclusive control over a national money.

"The manufacturer had to be regulated through national planning. Waste in distribution was to be eliminated through a system of department and grocery store chains. The individual farmer would be told just what and how much he could plant. And huge tracts of land were to be acquired by the Government.

"Liberalizing trade in goods and services opened the borders to other countries pursuing their own personal agendas, which created the need for a world governing body to supervise the affairs of the world. By merging into a one-world economic system, the World Trade Organization was the authority to administer arrangements and to resolve global disputes.

"The comprehensive, multilateral, dispute-settlement mechanism was agreed upon in the framework of the World Trade Organization, or WTO. One of the Articles specifically stated that each member had to ensure the conformity of its laws, regulations, and administrative procedures with its obligations. The Dispute Settlement Board was the final judge as to whether the World Trade Organization's global rules of trade and tariffs were met. All nations had to abide by these judgments, and financial penalties and sanctions would be imposed if these rules were not met."

"I can see where they gradually, one right at a time, usurped all of the power from the America people. Why couldn't they see it at the time, Lance?" Monique asked.

"Most of these decisions were made without the public's awareness. Many were kept in the dark through misinformation and lies. But some, like my parents, refused to accept the truth, even when confronted with it," I answered, before continuing.

"They drafted a World Government Constitution, or WGC, established a Chamber of Guardians to enforce world laws, with the United Nations as the global, governing body. This included disarming all nations while simultaneously creating a super military power that no country could challenge.

"For decades the Elite's military specialists had categorized the world into two distinct groups, the oppressors and the defenders. The Communist giant was goaded to conquer, forcing the Capitalist giant to defend, while the smaller countries hastened to unite with one of the two major powers.

"Wars aren't fought to defeat an enemy but to bring about a condition. Enormous changes take place in the organization of society as a result of war. Expenditures of men and wealth during wartime require a tremendous mobilization of resources throughout the world, causing adverse effects on the thought patterns and actions of people forced to undergo these strains.

"War is instigated and then financed by the international bankers. Prolonged wars proved to be very beneficial financially, politically, and conditionally. Changes that would normally take place over a thirty or even fifty-year period in peacetime were brought about in five years during war, creating enormous debt.

"There were other declarations of war that allegedly threatened the American people: the war on poverty, the war on drugs, the war on crime, the war on inflation, and so on. Condemning and then combating these enemies took huge expenditures of both manpower and finances, with none of these wars ever being defeated. In fact, all of these wars were tremendously expanded, increasing the national debt, creating an immense loss of personal freedoms, and contributing in the systematic destruction of America.

"The more I learned about the Elite and the their creation of a New World Order, the more I wanted to learn. I began compiling information on all areas of life; economics, politics; trends, books, the educational system—past and present.

"I always knew that the Elite had direct control of most printed material, but I also knew they allowed truths to be printed next to lies. With the information that I now possessed, I was able to discern the truth from the lie.

"One of their most powerful weapons was the media. Manipulation of opinion was carried out through the press, newsmagazines, radio, and television. Media sources were the force that created the movement of thought in people. These sources were also used to point out requirements, to give voice to the complaints, to express and create discontent. They served to excite and inflame those passions which were needed to serve political parties and selfish ends. The aim was to impair people's ability to think independently without an implanted suggestion by one of the media sources. Corruption, violence, depravity, and endless futility was the constant diet being pumped into the people's minds.

"The most influential newspapers in the United States were selected and emissaries were sent to purchase the national and international administration of these papers. An editor was furnished for each paper to properly supervise and edit the information. They saddled and bridled it with a tight curb; and they did the same with all productions of the printed word.

"People exist by the ideas they absorb through learning. By cleverly manipulating science, theory and verbiage, people were indoctrinated with new ideas. Gradually, these new schools of thought became the established way of thinking.

"Not a single announcement reached the public without their control. All news items were received by a few agencies, in whose offices they controlled from all parts of the world. These agencies gave publicity only to what was dictated to them. Through the press was gained the power to influence; to create, and then manage major crises and resulting chaos; to maintain and increase control of populations and governments while always remaining in the shadows.

"Once the people were thoroughly indoctrinated they were incapable of reaching a conclusion; everything was politically correct. With the media's daily barrage of new ideas people became mental and emotional cripples feeding on worthless theories and senseless philosophies.

"Entertainment wasn't enjoyable it was morbid. Jokes weren't funny they were stupid or degrading. The molded structure of life was to pit one against another. Once completely desensitized, life was only a warped illusion of reality.

"Stupendous amounts of monies were paid to memorize lines and act out parts, throw balls straight, drive cars at death-threatening speeds, and write eloquently phrased words of witless grandeur. Trendy art was but a canvas filled with multi-colored scratches from the painted feet of scampering chickens; music had degenerated to a noisy pulsation of incoherence.

"In sheer madness people flocked to movie houses and entertainment halls to pay homage to their idols. Programmed to idolize people with enormous egos and overly inflated self-images they would frequent any locale that afforded an escape from the reality of being mere human beings. They followed their heroes and heroines like they were pied-pipers, imitating the behavior of these cinematic icons that drove around in sparkling new automobiles, lived in luxurious homes, dressed in the most exquisite attire and expensive jewelry, and falling hopelessly in and out of lust with one another.

"Laws were written with contradictory interpretations. Everyone believed they had a right to something, a right *for* something, a right *against* something or someone, when actually, all of their rights were being taken. Courts degenerated into a morass of petty pursuits. Defense lawyers strove for acquittals at all costs, arguing over every point of law no matter how trivial as long as there was a significant gain. These petty lawsuits resulted in new laws that gave the courts legal authority in every matter of life. And with every new law a measure of freedom was lost.

"The justice system drained the economy of billions of dollars annually. Truth and justice had been bought with lies and greed. Many of the innocent were condemned while the guilty were liberated.

"That's exactly our case!" Monique exclaimed.

"Yes," I replied, while continuing, "individual rights were subverted. Narrow ideals of national sovereignty and United States citizenship were widened into world citizenship. National independence was surrendered and regulated by international authorities. American attitudes and institutions were gradually replaced with a new, global vision. Global governance transcended national boundaries and eliminated nationalistic solutions. Old doctrines of absolute individual rights were surrendered for universal rights and equality for all. Individual entitlements for food, health, and education were exchanged for a broader dimension of global rights. One brick at a time the centuries-old doctrine of absolute and exclusive sovereignty was dismantled.

"Newspapers and magazines were used to club into submission or drive out of office public officials who refused to do their bidding. Whether in politics or business, in our social conduct or our ethical thinking, the Elite directed almost every act of our daily lives. They pulled the wires, which controlled the public mind, and contrived new ways to constrict and guide the world.

"They triumphed by capturing the culture via infiltration of schools, universities, churches, the media, and other societal and religious institutions. In every area, rather than a direct assault, they advocated a process resulting in an evolutionary transition by transforming the consciousness of society.

"Absolutely nothing eluded their contaminating touch. In less than a hundred years the United States of America had fallen into such a dark hole it was virtually nonexistent. I got the Democratic Party platform and laid it out beside that of the Socialist Party. I scratched out the word Democrat and the word Socialist and then studied the record of the present Administration up to date. Afterward, I picked up the platform that most closely matched the record and it was the Socialist platform. I discovered a collectivist one-world State comprised of a socialist democracy.

"The more I learned, the more I abhorred the Elite.

"The Communist Oppressor was the first to fall; it couldn't sustain itself any longer.

"It took communist Russia twenty-one years of unrelenting terror to completely subjugate its people, to break their will and to bring them to a state of near mindless conformity. The horrifying gory details of Communism is written in the blood of at least thirty million defenseless human beings whose only crime was that they lived in Russia, and stood in the way of the Elite's plans to bring about a One World Order.

"The free, Constitutional Republic held on as long as she could. Written into the pages of *The Master Plan* was a cruel trick that even the United States of America couldn't withstand. The Elite deteriorated and drained her from within, while attacking and draining her round about. Finally, she too, staggered in drunken stupor, with nothing to stand on, or stand for.

"Equally as strong as my loathing for the Elite was for those who did their bidding. And the poor, deceived people were like dumb sheep, joyfully rushing to their slaughter.

"I'm going to rest, Monique. Maybe tomorrow night I'll tell you more."

"I understand, Lance. That was the same way I felt about what they were doing to my country."

The next morning Monique roused me before the buzzer sounded. I showered, dressed, and we ate breakfast together. We talked until it was time for me to leave for work.

From the steps of my cabin I watched the procession of men as they filed past. When the guard gave the order, I joined the column at the rear. The daily instructions given from the recorder on the platform were the same. We marched to the fields and irrigated the fields.

During lunch, while I was talking to Haile, one of the men on our crew fell to the ground holding his stomach in pain. Haile jumped up and rushed to his aid immediately. A couple of the guards made their way through the crowd that had gathered and demanded an explanation from Haile for his unsolicited assistance.

Haile was kneeling beside the man holding his head and looking him directly in the eyes. Whatever Haile was doing appeared to comfort the man considerably. Haile had apparently hypnotized the man.

"What's wrong with him?" one of the guards demanded.

"He has a ruptured appendix," Haile answered, his eyes never breaking contact with the injured man who was now lying still, staring into space as though in a trance.

"I don't see nothin' wrong with him. He just looks crazy to me," another guard shouted.

"The man will die without proper treatment," replied Haile.

"Well, what do you want us to do?" responded the first guard. "It'll take at least 30 minutes to get a helicopter out here to take him to the infirmary."

Haile said something to the injured worker and stood up to face the two guards. "Then I would suggest that you do it while there is still a chance to save his life."

The guard gave Haile a disgusted look and turned toward the guard beside him. After a few words, he produced a small two-way radio that had been clipped to the belt around his waist. "This is guard number 29 with the irrigation crew, Camp 1100. Over."

"Go ahead number 29. Over," squawked the voice from the radio's speaker.

"We have a possible appendicitis. Send an emergency unit to cross points six and twelve. Over."

"We'll be there in about fifteen minutes. Over, and out."

Haile had resumed his position beside the man. When the guard finished his radio transmission, he walked over to Haile and the man lying on the ground in front of him. "Who're you?" he demanded, looking at Haile with a scowl on his face.

"Haile Kalef, number 2409, Camp 1100, Cabin 21."

"All right, Haile Kaff, or whatever your name is, you can move away from him now!"

Haile didn't say a word. He continued ministering to the injured man, who was beginning to move about restlessly.

The guard's face grew red, his neck swelled, and his voice became shrill. "I said, get away from that man. You'd better do it *now*, before I have you layin' there next to him!"

Haile didn't move, and the guard raised his club to strike him. Still in a crouched position, Haile pivoted to one side, avoiding the club as it whizzed past his shoulder. He now faced the guard who was drawing the club back for another swing. As Haile rose, he delivered a straight jab to the guard's groin. Almost simultaneously, he hit him with his other fist in the solar plexus. The guard doubled over in pain. Haile stepped to the man's side and administered a sharp chop to the back of his neck, accelerating the guard's fall to the ground.

Instantly, Haile spun around to face the other guard who had watched the entire assault in disbelief. The guard fumbled for his whistle and was able to get off a single blow before Haile attacked him. With uncanny speed, Haile gripped the guard's trachea, terminating his ability to breathe. With all that he had, the guard desperately tried to break the vice-like grip in which Haile held him securely bound. Slowly the guard began to drop to his knees, and then he fell to the ground unconscious.

Without hesitation, Haile whirled around to ready himself for the approaching danger. Five goons rushed toward Haile in reaction to the guard's whistle. Haile began flaying his arms with powerful blows, striking the charging goons in non-stop succession. I had never seen the technique Haile used, performed so effectively. The goons were jolted backward by the power of Haile's blows, but none of them seemed to show any signs of pain.

Everything happened so fast, all I could do was watch in awe. I knew that Haile couldn't continue his onslaught much longer. The goons were fighting as hard as Haile, and yet they appeared refreshed. Haile, aware that his strength was ebbing, slipped between two goons and was off running.

The goons were in a state of confusion. At first I thought they were going to attack one another. They regained their senses once they realized that their victim had gone.

As a fox released from a box, Haile scampered across the fields and out of sight. Moments later a helicopter arrived with three medical aides, two more guards, and four more goons. After a quick assessment of the situation, the pilot radioed in a description of the scene, as the aides placed the injured men inside the craft.

The guards and goons gathered the men together, who were now milling around like children lost at a carnival. Once we were all accounted for, they marched us back to the barracks.

When I returned to the cabin, I told Monique the whole story. She told me, "When they catch him, they're going to either kill him right then, or torture him to death in the Square. And everybody in the labor camp has to be there anytime they have an execution."

I remembered Haile's words: *"Above all, remove hate from your being. Hate is a debilitating sickness that does nothing but destroy the very principles upon which life is based."*

"Lance," Monique interrupted my thoughts, "you're going to see a lot more killings, so you had better get used to it. The only thing that's important is that we stay alive."

She was right, I thought to myself as I left the room.

The cool shower relaxed me. I lay across the bed trying to clear my mind of the thoughts and feelings that engulfed me. Monique came into the bedroom and sat down in the chair by the window. Evidently sensing my depression, she started telling me about the coming changes in our lives.

"Tomorrow, the authorities are going to call you before a special board. They'll tell you that you're going to be transferred to the Main Complex for reassignment as an architect—I confirmed it, you are the new architectural engineer they've been talking about."

"How were you able to confirm that it was me?" I asked, still skeptical.

"Today I programmed your transfer, along with your new assignment, the complex where you'll be working, and the quarters where we'll be living. They also told me that I'm going to be transferred with you. I'll continue my daily classes for a week, then start my new assignment working with the computers."

Relieved that we would be leaving these depressing surroundings, I told her, "Things seem to be looking up. If I had a bottle of champagne, I'd propose a toast."

"Since I've already cooked, and we don't have any champagne, will you settle for supper?" she offered with a smile.

While eating, Monique explained the upcoming schedule. "Saturday we can sleep in, the alarm doesn't go off until 9:00 a.m. At 10 o'clock, we have to be on the porch ready to attend the general assembly in the Main Square. If they schedule an execution, we have to attend."

"If they catch Haile, I don't want to watch his execution!"

"If they catch him, you don't have to watch, but you will be there," she said responding to my statement. "Lance, finish telling me about how you got here?"

"All right, Monique," I complied

"The invasion of our educational system was the most contemptible segment of my discoveries. The teacher was the biggest asset in preparing the hearts and minds of the children for global understanding and cooperation. To the Elite, education didn't mean teaching people reading, writing, and arithmetic; it meant teaching them to behave, as they wanted them to behave.

"The subject that was of most importance was mass psychology. They knew that in time, with money and equipment, they would be able to persuade anybody of anything if they could reach the person young enough. When the technique was perfected, every government that had been in charge of education for two generations would be able to control its subjects securely without the need of armies or policemen. Educational propaganda, with government help, could achieve this result in two generations.

"At the very top of all the agencies that assured the coming of global governance stood the school, the teacher, and the organized profession. Delegates to international organizations, public officials, men and women of the press, teachers and educators—all realized that they had a part to play in molding the minds of children for a New World Order.

"With military precision, encompassing every area of learning, they positioned themselves to get control of the education of the children. The United States joining the United Nations Educational Scientific and Cultural Organization, UNESCO, marked the pinnacle of a movement for the birth of an international agency for education. Any nation that became a member of UNESCO accordingly assumed an obligation to revise the textbooks used in their schools. Each member nation had a duty to see to it that nothing in its curriculum, courses of study, and textbooks was contrary to UNESCO's aim.

"The National Education Association's sole intent was the total transformation of life, with a profound commitment to social duties. They strongly emphasized that the dependability of a labor force and how well it was managed and trained was not based upon its general educational level. There were, however, allowances made for a small force of highly educated, creative people, which they felt was essential to growth.

"This new educational system aimed at destroying individual incentive by forming a society with everyone being equal. Competition was replaced by cooperation, trust in divine guidance by careful planning, and private capitalism by some form of socialized economy. The competitive principle gave place to the principle of cooperation, and the major function of the school to a social orientation of the individual. The purging of ideals were geared around ambition, competition, and individualism. Motivation toward personal achievement was sacrificed for the equality of all.

"The parents, religious leaders, and schools in America taught concepts of right and wrong, facts and certainties, morals and principles, truth and knowledge. This old order of thinking proved to be more revolutionary than any conspiracy to overthrow the government.

"To bring about profound social change, submission to parental authority could not be permitted. In order to expedite these changes a vigorous attack on the family was mounted, lest the traditions and values of past generations be preserved.

"An artificial chasm between parents and children was necessary to insulate the children and make it easier to indoctrinate them with new ideas. They had to be taught not to respect their tradition-bound elders, who were tied to the past and only knew what was unproductive in accomplishing the aims of the Elite.

"What they called *good teaching* was the teacher with the ability to attain affective objectives through challenging the students' fixed beliefs, and offering illustrative objectives. A single hour of classroom activity under certain conditions could bring about a major reorganization in affective behaviors. The affective domain contains the forces that determine the nature of an individual's life and ultimately the life of an entire people.

"By using *values clarification techniques*, students were led to particular value changes through a series of leading questions and systematic doubt. They continuously exposed students to information designed to make them consciously aware of inconsistencies within their own value-attitude system that they learned from their parents. This created an influence that caused students to critically examine their beliefs. They developed a critical attitude within the students that made them disbelieve any claims by their parents that went beyond their own reasoning or their own experience. *Critical thinking* turned out to be lessons in criticizing authority, parents, clergy, and other adults.

"The unsuspecting, gullible parents couldn't begin to fathom the reason for this rebellious attitude amongst the youth, which systematically emerged throughout the country. And those insiders, who were aware of the cause, blatantly denounced the truth when the sources were publicly revealed.

"The fact that children were raised in families meant there was no equality; children raised in families were taught to believe that they could excel on an individual basis. The cultural inequality of homes and environments had to be remedied to fulfill the mandate of equal educational opportunity for all. In order to raise children with equality, they had to be taken away from families and then communally raised. The belief that families were private, non-political units whose interests subsume those of children had to be totally expunged.

"In order to achieve the future goal as a socialist society, children had to be viewed as superior to their parents, since they were the ones who would bring about this new socialist order. With this objective at hand, the UN Convention on the Rights of the Child was unanimously endorsed and adopted as international law. This established universal legal standards for the care and protection of children against neglect, exploitation, and abuse.

"Once the Elite's educational system was firmly entrenched, it took only two generations to change the form of our government by educating the children along their lines. Education was the power tool to alter fundamental values of sexuality and the traditional household, and to control the direction of that change."

"I must admit," Monique confessed, "I was indoctrinated under these ideals. How drastically it's molded my life I'll never know."

"None of us will," I agreed. "But now we have to employ this information to avoid digressing farther into this pit of deception.

"I learned that their first requisite to incite liberation was to force the whole female gender back into public industry. Living standards were raised dramatically—through crisis manufactured by the Elite— so that both spouses were forced to enter the work force just to maintain their standard of living. This in turn liberated the wife and demanded the abolition of the monogamous family as the economic unit of society. With the transfer of the means of production into common ownership, the single family ceased to be the economic unit of society.

"Harsh laws threatened traditional women who still chose to remain home and rear their own children. Social service workers were granted immunity from liability for seizing children from homes on the basis of alleged abuse or emotional neglect. A report by a social service worker or an informant claiming that a child had Oppositional Defiant Disorder, or ODD, could result in the child being seized. Children that were argumentative with adults, frequently lost their temper, swore and were often angry, resentful and easily annoyed by others, and frequently actively defied adults' requests and rules, were considered to be ODD children. The symptoms of this disorder were widely and scandalously abused.

"As influences in home and church declined, public schools began to provide for the emotional and moral development of children. The public schools acquired the direct responsibility for the attitudes and values of child development. Social science and social engineering were the tools to solve the problems of human relations. The child advocate, psychologist, social technician, and medical technician all reached aggressively into the community by sending workers out to children's homes, recreational facilities, and schools. Often, without parental knowledge or permission, young girls were given full female examinations at school; any hint of abuse resulted in the child being taken from their parents. The State subtly acquired full responsibility for all education, health and welfare of the children.

"Schools were no longer addressed as academic centers but social service centers. Social service centers replaced the old-time home environment. School offices contained cumulative information concerning pupils and their parents. They also acquired the responsibility for feeding students all 3 meals a day since children were in the school building most of the day. These social service centers were the hub of the community.

"State departments were tied to a miniature substructure rooted in school, home, and work place. This assured that from the cradle to the grave the people would be continuously indoctrinated with ideals that furthered the goals of global governance with the country taking possession of every individual at birth and never letting him go until death.

"That certainly sounds familiar," Monique inserted, "from the cradle to the grave. Until now, I didn't realize exactly what that saying meant."

"Nor did I. At the time, I thought it was a generous gesture. When in fact, the main emphasis was aimed at learning how to live and work collectively, since the primary function of school was to establish productive workers. Thus, efforts made to take the public into account were supplemented by efforts to take the public into confidence and, finally, into partnership.... Are they learning to be fair and tolerant in situations where conflicts arise? Another phase was to learn a series of skills, for the first set of jobs.... Are they acquiring skills? Since jobs were rotated, learning would be repeated periodically.... Are they becoming more skillful in doing some type of useful work? Education was not just for the young alone, something to be gained in a few years in school; it was a permanent feature of life, with an ongoing process of transforming ideals, thoughts, and wills.

"*The well-being of children* was the postern used to establish an international health system. The first duty of the State was to see that every child born therein would be housed, clothed, fed, and educated. In order to fulfill this, the government had to have complete control over the people.

"The State Board for Children and Families, or BCF, included a new affirmative duty for the State to assure the health and nonacademic well- being of each child until age 18 or graduation from high school. This grew into a State-controlled health system, with health meaning a state of complete physical, mental, and social well-being. This health system provided treatment not only for the children but also for the entire community.

"To prevent the possibility of children eluding indoctrination via the public educational system, the NEA adopted Resolution C-34. The National Education Association stated that home-school programs could not provide the child with a comprehensive education experience. If parents preferred to home-school their children, these students were still required to meet all State requirements.

"Enrolling in college or entering the work force required a Certificate of Initial Mastery, which was only issued through schools that followed the Outcome-Based Education, or OBE, procedures mandated by the State. Accreditation and certification requirements were inaccessible by private and home-school students seeking college admission or trying to enter the work force.

"Parents desiring to have children needed a license of certification from the State. A genetic scan was required prior to becoming pregnant. If it was discovered that the couple was capable of producing superior babies and they weren't well-suited to rear them, the pregnancy was denied or the child was taken away after birth.

"American families were arranged in a neighborhood according to a chart laid out upon social engineering principles. A key family was strategically located so that its influence would have far-reaching effects in molding the attitudes of the entire community.

"The world became a society in which individual freedoms and choices were controlled within very narrow alternatives. Children were numbered at birth and followed as a number through educational training, required military or other public service, tax contributions, health and medical requirements.

"Those who objected to this new way of thinking were described as having mental health problems and were referred to State-approved psychiatrists, psychologists, and social service workers for permanent treatment. Those preaching intolerant salvation-religion rather than socialism were labeled insane, extremists, dissidents, and criminals in an attempt to discredit them. Correspondingly they were denied work from one end of the country to the other. Many were locked into institutions and used for psychological and neurological experimentation.

"Progressive politicians, medical experts, and genteel women's groups most energetically pushed sterilization. Sterilizing the unfit, among who were included all fundamentalists, was the call of the day.

"This was the exact program being implemented in Africa and around the world when your father became involved, Monique."

"Yes, I realize that now. Only if I'd had this information then, I may have been able to save my father's life."

"Well, if this is any consolation, through my in-depth study of *The Master Plan* I did discovered there were two powerful forces that boldly opposed these policies: one was Christianity; the other was nationalism.

"This secret society of social elitists possessed a strong aversion for nationalism and the Christian faith. Nationalism, along with the Biblical profession of Christianity and its way of life were completely adverse to the society the Elite was introducing. Consequently, there was a vigorous crusade to undermine, degrade, and completely dislodge nationalism and Biblical teachings from the minds of the people.

"The teachings in the schools and colleges, the editorials, even the plays and motion pictures were skillfully and influentially molded to accomplish this goal.

"They dismantled and destroyed every national and Christian monument; they seized and then destroyed all national and Christian artifacts; they removed and then destroyed any historical writings that depicted the Christian heritage and the patriotism of our forefathers. By this they eventually erased from the human memory all historical facts of previous centuries and how this country was founded and progressed to become the most powerful nation on earth. These truths proved undesirable to their cause; only those things that represented the errors of the governments in the past remained.

"The Elite-controlled media also spurred a vicious campaign of hatred that was carried out by the homosexual activists, the women's liberation movement, cultic and occult organizations that were all bent on eliminating the Holy Bible and its intolerant and dogmatic creeds from the face of the earth.

Vicious verbal and physical attacks were executed by the youth. Over the years children had been spoon-fed a magnitude of abhorrence for nationalism and Christianity until this ideology had totally consumed them. Their textbooks and lessons, their music and lyrics, their computer games and toys, their conversations and thoughts were all saturated with a blatant hatred for Jesus Christ, patriotism, or anyone who confessed their allegiance and adherence to such beliefs. Unheard of acts of violence and cruelty that were associated only to maniacs were being carried out by children of all ages against Christians and nationalists.

"One afternoon before lunch," I continued, "Isaac called me into his office. He came directly to the point: 'Lance, you've been working here eight-and-a-half years. I consider you a friend and highly respect you as one of the most brilliant architects I've ever worked with, so I'm not going to beat around the bush. I have no complaints with your work, but Lance, your attitude has changed! It's also affecting the morale of your staff.

"'I'm not going to ask what the problem is; it doesn't matter. What I am going to do is give you a two-week vacation to straighten it out, starting today.'

"I had thought about this day for almost a year. From the instant I began studying *The Master Plan*, I knew it would drastically affect my life. I was sure that he hadn't learned of my findings, if he had, we would have been discussing more than a two-week vacation.

"I told him thanks, and that I would be back in a couple of weeks.

"I wondered if I was willing to throw away everything I had worked all of my life to attain, in exchange for the truth. The truth I embraced now was as real to me as the truth I believed when I first started my career. The difference being, now I had all the facts, and therefore I was capable of making a knowledgeable assessment of my future.

"After my discussion with Isaac, I gathered my belongings and left the building. While driving home I spotted a news stand and pulled over to the curb, got out of the car and glanced at the headlines of the daily newspapers glaring up at me from their neatly stacked piles. The headlines of one of the major papers proclaimed: *NEW COMPUTER*

CREATES CASH-LESS SOCIETY! I reached in my pocket and pulled out enough money to buy a paper from each of the stacks, handed it to the newsman, returned to my car and began to read.

"The first article described a computer capable of processing over a trillion financial transactions per second. The International Banking system had engineered what was called the smart card. This lasercard was an updateable, credit-card-sized, multi-megabyte, data-storage card that could accommodate up to 2000 pages of information. It was capable of storing a DNA code, a digital photo, a signature, voiceprints, fingerprints, hand geometry, retina scan, and virtually any form of personal biometrics or biographical data.

"A person's entire history, including statements from any adversary were all centrally accessible and could be instantly displayed on a computer screen at the touch of a button. This smart card preformed a constant updating of data every time a transaction was made or service provided.

"Wages were accredited and stored for access through an international electronic networking grid. To make a purchase, an individual's identification number was scanned—this could take place at four feet away without having to be placed into a reader/machine—and the account automatically accessed. Via the computer chip located on the card, all transactions were instantly debited or credited to each personal or business account as they transpired. This technology instantaneously determined the state of the economy as each transaction transpired around the world.

"The idea was accepted by merchants, bankers, and the public as a lucrative way to maintain accurate records. This system proved to be an automatic bookkeeper for merchants, while linking them with other businesses around the globe. The smart card allowed no room for error, fraud or theft; and in 90 days this smart little card would render currency obsolete.

"When I finished reading the article, I pulled away from the curb and started for home. While approaching the driveway leading to my house I pressed the remote control to open the gate. After taking the mail out of my mailbox, I set it on the seat beside me, and then continued up the driveway. Once I had parked in the garage, I glanced at one of the other newspaper headlines in astonishment: *MILLIONS JOBLESS!* Gathering the newspaper and mail, I rushed inside to study the next article thoroughly.

"My fears were being confirmed. By interlocking international treaties, which produced thousands of regulations under the International Union for the Conservation of Nature, state and local government had shifted significant sovereignty to the WTO. This ultimate power was delegated through a series of various levels of bureaucracy consisting of ten international and regional forms of government that were headed by Non-Government Organizations and unaccountable to any citizenry.

"Through treaty laws such as NAFTA and GATT the United States had significantly shifted state and local government sovereignty to the WTO. This made huge concessions of national power and compromised national sovereignty. Goods were being imported from other countries while jobs were being exported to other countries.

"These treaties, while making huge concessions of national power and compromising national sovereignty, opened the borders of America to foreign products—often produced by slave labor—without sufficiently protecting American jobs. It wasn't free trade, but controlled trade. To avoid the constant bombardment of U.S. regulatory laws and still meet the global competitive demand, corporations merely moved their businesses to other countries that offered cheaper labor. Goods were being imported while jobs were being exported.

"This transition into global production could not sustain the number of people in America who needed jobs. And those that were fortunate to have a job found the pressures from equal trade were pushing wages down. The flow of money, coupled with the ease with which companies were able to move jobs around the globe, shattered the ability of the United States and all national governments to control their own economies. This course resulted in massive unemployment, massive loss of jobs and capital, while increasing corporate profits.

"I sat there contemplating the vast, adverse effects these events would have upon society. Without a warning one-third of the population was forced into the unemployment lines. The people, whose lives were now being controlled by great impersonal forces, would inevitably rebel.

"I suddenly remembered that Greta was due in from Paris that evening. She had been gone for three weeks. Before she left we had made prior arrangements for me to pick her up at the airport when she arrived.

"I realized I had to share my new discoveries with Greta and my parents. No matter what my decision, it was sure to affect all of our lives. I wanted them to understand my position, but I also knew that unless they perceived the Elite's Master Plan as I did, they would never accept my explanation for the calamity I was certain would affect us all.

"These thoughts cascaded through my mind while I was on my way to pick up Greta from the airport. Yes, it was my duty to tell her and my parents. Although I desperately wanted them with me, it was their decision to make.

"Greta was happy to see me. She overflowed with messages and bits of gossip from abroad. The company she worked for had made her an offer to run one of their most prestigious modeling agencies in Paris. She had one week to accept or decline the offer.

"As we rode home, I asked Greta what she felt about the state of our country. 'Well…,' she pondered, 'our economy's as strong, the stock market's up and unemployment's down. I must admit, the behavior of some politicians leaves a lot to be desired, but I don't believe that a person's private life and personal preferences have any reflection on their ability to do their job. Anyway, whatever people do in their private lives is their personal business, not anyone else's. Why do you ask, Lance?'

"Even though I knew the headlines I had just read proved her wrong, I simply replied, 'I just wondered if you've ever considered the possibility of some international group of financiers behind the scenes pulling the strings of global affairs.'

"'Oh, Lance, please! Next you'll be telling me about Big Brother and a conspiracy to take over the world; with black helicopters patrolling the skies, hidden surveillance cameras on every corner, and concentration camps filled with nonconformists.'

"Although this may have been my response a year ago, with what I knew now, my perception had changed a hundred and eighty degrees. Greta's reply was the typical response of the liberal left. It would be fruitless trying to explain my discoveries derived from studying *The Master Plan*. I was certain Greta wouldn't accept what I had to say, because she didn't want to, no matter how credible the evidence I presented.

"I felt it best that I encourage her to accept the job offer in Paris. If my conclusions were correct, the preliminaries were complete, one major catastrophe was all that was needed to usher in the New World Order. Greta would be better off in Europe, where the public was unarmed, than in America, where firearms were kept in seven out of ten homes.

"At my urging Greta accepted her new job offer and was leaving for Paris in two days. I went to great lengths in order to make everything as pleasant as possible for her departure. I planned a bon voyage party and invited all of her friends and family.

"Bright lights sparkled from the hanging chandeliers that filled the large hall I had secured for the occasion. Greta was ecstatic. She maneuvered her way throughout the hall, intentionally spending quality time with each of the quests. I forced myself to appear happy, certain that I would never see here again. I wanted our last occasion together to be a memorable one.

"I handled the situation with my parents differently than I did with Greta. I felt obligated to tell them everything. To my amazement they reacted with indifference rather than defiance toward the Elite, as

I had expected. They didn't disbelieve what I told them, they just didn't care. It was as if I was the perpetrator for telling them the truth; as if I forced them to see reality and spoiled their world of contentment.

"Resentment turned into denial. They acted as though I was at fault for discovering the Elite's scheme prematurely. They challenged my sources and dismissed my suggestions and warnings as absurd. The evidence, however, was overwhelming, and eventually they resolved, 'What will be, will be. And, besides,' my mother sighed, 'who are we to question the judgments of such influential people. After all, there is only one world, we must all learn to live together in harmony. From what I can see, they are only trying to make this a better, more peaceful world to live in.'

"The more I insisted that we prepare for what was ahead, the further they retreated into their state of resignation. Finally, I stopped all attempts to convince them that a catastrophe was coming. Resolving the fact that all hope was lost, I kissed and hugged my parents and wished them the best, for I loved them dearly.

"My parents' attitudes caused me to reflect on one of the Elite's boastful claims: *'We stand above this race of men as an immense and tutelary power, which takes upon itself alone to secure their fate. After having thus successively taken each member of the community in our powerful grasp and fashioned him at will, the supreme power then extends its arm over the whole community. The will of man is not shattered, but softened, bent, and guided. It does not tyrannize, but it compresses, enervates, extinguishes, and stupefies a people, till each nation is reduced to nothing better than a flock of timid and industrious animals, of which the government is the shepherd.'*

"I held no illusions that the Elite could be stopped, that possibility had long passed. Yet, I wanted the truth known so that anyone willing to listen would have the opportunity to prepare for what was ahead. The question I asked myself was, if I convinced someone of the truth, would they be willing to hold to their convictions regardless of the opposition?

Monique interrupted me, "Lance, with the information my father and his colleagues complied, along with your knowledge of *The Master Plan*, do you think we could have turned this thing around for the good?"

"I doubt it, Monique. For more than a century the Elite has insidiously labored to bring about a New World Order. There's no power on earth that can stop them from accomplishing their goal now."

"You're probably right," she signed in resignation.

"The Elite," I continued, "were masters at contriving financial schemes that reaped enormous profits. One of these schemes was the insurance business. Here was a business that required a relatively small initial investment, yet produced enormous monetary returns, with a minimal risk. Seventy-five percent of those insured have paid double the amount of benefits due them before ever receiving a penny. And in the case of automobile insurance, most States had been lobbied so heavily by the insurance companies that auto insurance was a requirement by law.

"Another financial scheme was the International Monetary Fund, or IMF. The IMF was formed to administer loans to a contributing IMF-member-nation with a deficit, thus preventing devaluation of that nation's currency and a possible international economic crisis.

"Nations seeking a loan had to allow the IMF investigators to examine its books and come up with an austerity plan capable of restoring that nation to favorable balance of payments position. The Special Drawing Rights, or SDR's, was the pool of money the IMF maintained from which nations could borrow in order to cover short-term balance payments deficits. SDR's were valued according to five currencies—the US Dollar, British Pound, Deutsche Mark, Japanese Yen and French Franc. Quotas or membership fees paid by the subscribing nations determined the total amount of the loan available. A nation's quota was determined by the size of its economy. The higher a nation's quota, the more it could borrow from the IMF.

Consequently, the IMF imposed strict financial reforms, prescribing governments to increase tax and raise interest rates, creating an even heavier burden on the people of that nation. At any time the IMF could withhold its own loan installments, while influencing other international organizations not to lend money until the nation agreed to the terms of the IMF. This also gave the IMF, an outside institution, dictating policy to a sovereign government while placing it in the position of restructuring failed economies.

"Devaluing currencies diminish the value of local assets, normally due to speculative excesses and unwise government ventures. In essence, governments taxed the people and squandered the revenue. The reason nations faced financial difficulties was because they imposed bad economic policies on themselves. Bailouts by the IMF only shielded financiers and politicians from the results of bad financial practice and encouraged bad investments; the governments and lenders were rescued while the people were left with an ongoing debt.

"As nation after nation fell behind in its obligation to its creditors, a new International Credit Insurance Corporation was formed with the taxpayers as underwriters. This new institution operated in collusion with the IMF and guaranteed international loans up to a point equal to the countries ability to pay.

"Over the years foreign investors had invested heavily in the United

States. Collectively they owned more than half of America's enterprises. Because of the inflated economy, stock market, and the high deficit, investors pulled their finances out of the US market. This demand upon our already failing economy compounded the present loss of jobs.

"Since the beginning of time gold has backed the monetary systems of the world and determined the value of money and its equivalent in goods and services. To create a cash-less society, gold had to be extracted from the public. An edict was issued requiring that all form of gold bullion and coin be surrendered to the local banking institutions. The gold was exchanged for its equivalent and credited to the person's account.

"I had fifty thousand dollars' worth of South African Kruger Rands locked in my safe deposit box. For some reason I was skeptical about relinquishing my only financial security, so I placed them in a small, metal container and buried them in a safe place. I was content, knowing that if my prediction of a black market came to pass, the coins could be very useful.

"While attending school, I had discovered a ridge on the side of a mountain overlooking a beautiful valley that proved to be ideal for hang gliding. Whenever I had the opportunity I would go there to clear my mind and practice my favorite sport. Nestled in the valley below was a small, peaceful community, the only indication of citizenry for a hundred miles in either direction. The only way into the valley by vehicle was a pass just wide enough for two cars. It was in this general vicinity that I had buried my gold coins.

"It was close to a year since I had my last vacation. So when Isaac gave me the two weeks off I decided to take a trip to make sure my coins were secure and enjoy my favorite sport. Not wanting to be seen, I parked a sufficient distance from where my coins were buried and went the rest of the way on foot. Satisfied that they were safe, I reburied them in the same spot.

"It was mid-afternoon by the time I reached the crest of the pass leading into the valley. Pulling my binoculars from the glove compartment, I got out of the car to look over the familiar valley below. The town may have grown some since I was there last, but nothing else had changed.

"I drove down the hill to the gas station where I normally purchased my gas before returning home. The same proprietor and his wife were operating the station. The tall, lanky man wearing a pair of denim coveralls came forward to pump my gas. His wife walked over to wash the windows and while doing so asked if there was anything else I needed. Suddenly a thought struck me and I decided to respond to her offer. I stepped out of the car and introduced myself. 'How are you both?' I asked, looking each of them square in the eyes. 'My name is Lance Roberts. I'm interested in buying some land in this valley. Would you know of anyone wanting to sell a piece of property?'

"They looked at one another first and then turned to me. The man wiped his hands on a rag he pulled from a pocket and reached out to shake my hand. 'Pleased to meet you, Mr. Roberts. My name's John Freeman. This here's my wife, Mary. Yes, we know of two families who're sellin' property, but I don't believe you'll be able to meet their requirements as a buyer.'

"I told him I didn't understand, so he began to explain. 'You see, Mr. Roberts, we're Christians here. One of the requirements is that anybody who buys property in this valley has to be a born-again Christian.'

"'A born-again Christian...?' I repeated, unsure of what he meant.

"'Yes. You see, Mr. Roberts,' he continued, 'there're a lot of activities you folks have out there in the world that we don't want in Peaceful Valley—that's what we call it here. But now, there're also a lot of activities we have here in Peaceful Valley that you folks in the world don't want out there either. For instance, there's no stealing here; there's no robbing, murdering, or anything of the kind. But there's respect and kindness, peace and joy, and we put forth our best effort to see to the needs of others, in the same way we see to our own needs.'

"When Mr. Freeman finished his speech, he nonchalantly asked me, 'Are you a Christian, Mr. Roberts?'

"I had read about clans and cults that lived secluded lives so that they could practice their strange rituals without being disturbed by outsiders. I had also read about cults that lived on large estates expecting a super natural event that would project them into a life of utopia, with some of them committing mass suicide to hasten their end. And I had also heard tales about people who lived in the mountains in utter fear that doomsday was approaching. Although I didn't think these people were cultic, Mr. Freeman's statements caused a slight suspicion.

"'No, Mr. Freeman,' I answered honestly, 'I'm not a Christian. But I would like to know more about your town. It sounds like what I'm looking for. I've made a point to visit here quite often since I went to college. I have always thought it is one of the most beautiful valleys I have ever seen.'

"'Well, I tell you what, Mr. Roberts, Sara, my oldest daughter, and little Jenny, my youngest one, ought to have supper ready in about four hours from now. Between now and then, you do some looking around, maybe from that place where you usually fly that kite of yours. And we'll meet you at our place for supper at five-thirty. Here, I'll write down our address and draw you a little map of how to get there.'

"I accepted his invitation, thanked him and his wife, and drove to my favorite spot. It was a 30-minute drive from the Freeman's station to my favorite location for hang gliding. I removed my gear from the car and climbed the path that led to the ridge where I normally jumped. Nothing had changed. I put on my suit and assembled my glider. I barely raised my foot when the wind lifted the wing and picked me up. I quickly found a short lift from a thermal, but they were small bubbles and inconsistent. I smelled it before I felt it, a combination of earth and grass, and then I started up fast. I'd found a good thermal and kept on going, finally topping out at about 6500 feet.

"An occasional spray of condensation, the coldness at cloud-base, and the forces in the last thermal all contributed their part to a gratifying experience. I sailed around for awhile, feasting on the extraordinary view. With the mountain range on one side and the skyline on the other, the picturesque patterns of the valley below presented an incredible sight. I checked the time, saw it was getting late, and started looking for a landing zone. Once I located my landing zone I came in for a smooth, no-step landing. After unhooking my gear, I walked to the car and prepared to go to the Freeman's for dinner.

"As I drove along the streets I noticed a peace I had never experienced before. People even waved as I passed, which was unheard of where I came from. Mr. Freeman's point was well made, what was going on here wasn't happening in the rest of the country, and this was where I wanted to live.

"The houses were medium sized, solidly constructed farmhouses, nothing extravagant but sufficient for my needs. Most of the houses were sitting on a few acres of land with pastures, fruit trees and livestock. I saw a Ma and Pa grocery store, a hardware store, and one store with a sign that read: Men's And Women's Apparel. I hadn't seen one liquor store, bar, or cocktail lounge.

"Keeping my dinner engagement, I pulled in front of the Freeman's house. Mr. Freeman was standing in the front yard watering the lawn. While coming to greet me he said, 'I thought you had lost your way for a minute there, Mr. Roberts. Glad you were able to make it. Welcome to our humble home; I believe dinner's ready.'

"I appreciated his respectful manner but felt that it was I who owed him the honor of being called mister. So I insisted, 'Please, Mr. Freeman, call me Lance; I'm very grateful for you having me.'

"I followed Mr. Freeman into a living room that was comfortably furnished. A partition wall separated this room from the dining room, but through the archway I could see a table covered with food.

"Mr. Freeman had five children, ranging in ages from eight to twenty. Sara was the oldest, John Jr. was sixteen, Mike was thirteen, Jenny was nine, and Mark was the youngest. All of them came over and politely shook my hand.

"While we were eating Mr. Freeman explained their belief. They were Christians who believed in the Full Gospel of Jesus Christ. They believed that the Holy Bible was the inerrant Word of God, dictated by God, and written by His holy prophets and apostles. He professed that the Bible didn't have any errors, contradictions or falsities; God said what He meant and meant what He said.

"'If you want an answer about anything,' he assured me a number of times during our conversation, 'God made sure to address it in His Word, the Holy Bible.'

"The food was delicious and I complimented Sara and Jenny more than once during the meal for being such good cooks. When we finished eating, Mr. Freeman invited me into the living room. Once we were comfortably seated he asked, 'So why would a man like yourself want to live in a place like Peaceful Valley?'

"I pondered his question and concluded that he sincerely wanted to know why I wanted to move to Peaceful Valley. Almost impulsively, I told him everything I had learned while studying *The Master Plan*.

"Mr. Freeman listened attentively to every word. When I finished, he smiled. 'Son, the Bible mentions everything you've just told me. You know, it amazes me to think that most of the Bible was written over 2000 years ago, and yet it's still more accurate than newspapers reporting information that just took place yesterday.

"'What you just described are some of the very reasons we're living here, and not out there. We're not saying we won't get hurt, that's up to the Lord. But we're not gonna put ourselves in harm's way, either. And we're just not gonna worship anybody or anything except the Lord! If we have to, we'll just move up into the mountains, above that place where you used to fly that kite of yours. My grandparents, along with a few other grandparents of folks living here, bought a couple thousand acres in those mountains over a hundred years ago.

"'Here, let me show you something.' I followed him into the barn behind the house. Stacked from the floor to the rafters were rations, sleeping bags, medical supplies, butane heaters, lanterns, a couple of small generators, ammunition, and arms. He stressed that the arms were specifically for hunting food or protection against wild animals and not to be used on human beings under any circumstances. There was nothing lacking to sustain his entire family for at least six months in the wilderness.

"'All of us have provisions like these to take care of our families in case something like you described were to happen. We've been expecting it for some time now. We just didn't know how close it was.'

"It was getting late so Mr. Freeman asked me to stay overnight. I gladly accepted his invitation and was shown to a guest room connected to the back of the house.

"'We get up early around here,' he said. 'I'll wake you at six, Lance. Breakfast is always on the table at six-thirty.'

"'That will be fine with me, Mr. Freeman,' I replied. 'If I leave right after breakfast, I could be home by noon tomorrow.'

"The next morning after we ate, I asked Mr. Freeman about purchasing a parcel of his land, since he had twenty acres.

"'Son,' he replied, 'here's what I'll do. You come back and spend three weeks with us. After three weeks, and you've had time to see how we live, then we'll discuss selling you a piece of land here in the valley.'

"I assured him that I would be back the following Monday prepared to spend whatever time they would allow me to stay. As I was about to leave, the Freeman family gathered around me. They said a prayer specifically for me, and then the children bid me farewell. Since it was approaching the time they normally opened the station, Mr. and Mrs. Freeman offered to accompany me to the edge of town. There was a bond between us, and I felt I had just met the most trustworthy family I had ever known.

"On the way home I couldn't help thinking about the events of the past day. The inhabitants of Peaceful Valley were plain, ordinary people. To most, their lifestyle would be considered dull and boring. The life they lived was all the life I needed, or wanted. And I was willing to trade everything I had in the world to prove it.

"As I pulled into my driveway I sensed something was wrong. An uneasy feeling came over me when I entered the house. Two men dressed in suits were waiting for me.

"'Good afternoon, Lance,' one of them greeted as though we had been friends for years. 'We've been waiting since early this morning for you to return.'

"What can I do for you?' I asked, trying to appear unshaken and in control of the situation.

"He reached inside his inner jacket pocket and pulled out a wallet containing a badge. While displaying it he said, 'My name's Fleming. This is Davis. We're agents with Internal Affairs. We investigate information concerning treason, espionage, and the like. We've received reliable information that you're involved in treason against the United States. Your copy of this, uh,' he pointed to my photocopy of *The Master Plan* laying on my coffee table, 'looks like a strong piece of evidence to me.'

"'That's ridiculous,' I retorted. 'Every treasonous act written in that document has already taken place, and none of it involved me. I assure you Mr. Fleming, your information about me attempting to overthrow the government is erroneous. However, I will gladly give you the names of some of our congressmen and senators, and even a president or two who through their unpatriotic deeds have committed high treason against these United States of America!'

"It was Fleming who read me my rights and gave the official address: 'Mr. Roberts, you are under arrest for espionage and conspiracy to overthrow the United States government. Please come with us.'

"I was denied bail and my trial, for what it was worth, lasted a little over a year. During the litigation my parents came to visit me in the detention facility on one occasion. In tears, they begged my forgiveness for turning me over to the authorities. I recalled words from *The Master Plan* pertaining to situations such as this. *'The people are obliged at their own risk to denounce to the authorities apostates of their own family or members who have been noticed doing anything in opposition to our cause. So, in our kingdom over the entire world it will be obligatory for all to observe the duty of service to the State in this direction.'* There was no consolation in causing them more grief, so I forgave them and let them know I still loved them.

"While awaiting trial I kept abreast of world events by reading the daily newspapers. I looked at one of the headlines in astonishment: *STOCK MARKET CRASH CREATES AN ECONOMIC DISASTER!*

"For years an enigmatic bull market had defied all logic. Regardless of the rise or fall in interest rates, unemployment and the dollar, the Dow mysteriously continued to climb until the market reached over 900% inflation in a 16-year period.

"The Fed, by intentionally keeping interest rates low, lured tens of thousands of formerly cautious savers and retirees out of the security of bank deposits, CDs, and money market funds into the stock market and equity mutual funds. That influx of capital continued to pump billions of dollars into the market and stock futures index.

"On many occasions when the market would decline sharply or was approaching a technical breakdown point, certain big buyers would mysteriously appear at the last minute to make an investment that would frustrate the shorts. These large orders of Dow Jones Industrial stocks from certain large institutions with close government connections would appear and turn the market up again.

"All of a sudden, this procedure was brought to a halt. Without these government affiliates sustaining the market, a meltdown was inevitable. After years of inflating the stock market the Elite simply pulled the plug.

"Stockbrokers would dump their stock on the market in order to pay their loans. Simultaneously there would be an order to sell and a call for 24-hour broker loans. Banks involved in broker-call claims would quickly exhaust their currency to meet the excessive demand by the brokers, which in turn would cause a banking collapse around the country.

"The stock market crash would create a domino effect that would panic the business world. Tens of thousands of companies would fold, millions of people would lose their jobs, and hundreds of thousands would lose every penny they had. An international financial crisis would cause a total meltdown.

"After reading that article, I was drawn to another article typed in bold print halfway down the page: *THE DREADED Y2K STRIKES!*

"According to the article, mainframe computers first became prominent in the 1960's. In order to save valuable time and space two digits were used for the month, two for the day, and two for the year. The two-digit year became an excepted procedure with the assumption that later replacement systems would be upgraded to rectify the problem. As technology advanced and space was no longer a crucial factor, the omission was never corrected.

"Finding this a little hard to swallow, I obtained all of the material I could on the Y2K problem. I learned that on November 1, 1968 the National Bureau of Standards issued federal Information Processing Standards Publication 4, which specified the use of 6-digit dates, instead of 8-digit dates, for all information exchange among federal agencies, and, the computer industry complied with that Government directive. So apparently, it was known for over twenty years that the mainline computers were programmed to crash with the arrival of the new millennium.

"Date-sensitive information was essential to determine when something was to be disbursed or received. Since the last two digits were the only way to determine the year, at the turn of the century the last two digits of the year 2000 would be read as 00, and interpreted by the computer as 1900. Thus was created the Y2K or Millennium Bug.

"On midnight of December 31, 1999, all date-sensitive computers could suddenly malfunction. Systems such as Social Security, pensions, Medicare benefits, driving licenses, voter registrations, tax payments, tax refunds; trucks, planes, ships, trains; banking systems, credit cards, interest due dates, delinquent accounts, mortgages, loans, stocks; AT&T, Pacific Bell, Water and Power, PG&E, were only a few operations that depend on dates to function properly.

"While precious time was running out, many still believed that someone would find a quick fix or silver bullet. However, computer technology was advancing so rapidly—companies were too busy trying to compete with their competitors—no one was willing to take a loss by regressing to the foundational stage and starting over again.

"The problem wasn't technical, it was managerial. There remained only two solutions to this problem. One, a programmer had to sit before a computer screen and decipher the 30,000 to 200,000,000,000 lines of code, the typical number of lines of code for a business, determine which combination of twos were two-digit dates, and then correct them. Or two, save all existing data, create a new system that's year 2000 compliant, and then reprogram the existing data onto the new system. Either way was extremely time-consuming and very expensive.

"One million lines of code wasn't uncommon for the average company. A programmer looking at a million lines of code at a line per second would take more than 26 years to fix the problem. To make matters worse, there were only 500,000 Cobol programmers qualified to address the problem nationwide and twice that many were needed. Qualified Cobol programmers were literally writing their own tickets.

"When a programmer finished a system and sanctioned it to be year-2000-compliant, a full year of testing was needed to assure no two-digit dates were missed. Another concern was that the systems that were already year-2000-compliant, couldn't communicate with systems that weren't year-2000-compliant; one overlooked date could crash all of the systems on a network.

"Embedded chips created even greater complications. Billions of date-sensitive computer chips were embedded in communication apparatus and mechanical devices that intersected the world. The locations of most of these embedded computer chips were unknown or irretrievable, such as telephone cables or oil rigging lines buried under the ocean, or those date-sensitive mechanical devises used to operate the satellites in outer space. To further complicate matters, the year 2000 was a leap year.

"The truth about Y2K was concealed from the public as long as possible. After becoming widely known, programmers began writing programs to solve the Y2K problem. Private businesses welcomed these new programs and many were able to take advantage of the solution. These programs, however, were still incapable of detecting and rewriting date-sensitive embedded chips.

"Companies writing programs, practically guaranteed to fix the Y2K problem, ran into extreme opposition when they offered their wares to government agencies. Not one branch of the government would agree to accept the programs, even on a trial basis.

"Politicians either avoided the issue entirely or used the media to disseminate inaccurate information about the government's progress in relation to the problem. With elections approaching, the motives of politicians proved to be self-seeking.

"Through non-conventional sources such as the Internet, the public became aware of the severity of the Y2K problem and pressured the government to address the issue. With valuable time lost, the government's major problem was coordinating its fix with the Defense Department and Internal Revenue Service. The next undertakings were in the financial telecommunications, health, transportation, and power-generating industries.

"Public Utilities and International Telecommunications were the first to address the problem. Once the immensity of the predicament was learned, they began to prioritize. Their foremost concern was to procure a method of maintaining a limited but reliable system. As technology and costs would allow, normal service would be gradually restored to the general public.

"As the year 2000 drew near, major systems began to fail, even the election process was aborted. For the first time in American history, the president, who had already served out his full two terms, remained in office.

"In one day, the world was hurled back into a primeval condition. Food, clothing, medical supplies, hospital respirators and life-supports, gasoline, kerosene, and diesel fuel would be consumed within days. It wouldn't be long before all forms of transportation accessible to the people would come to a halt. People, whose lives were controlled for decades by unscrupulous politicians, would rebel. Riots, looting, and mass killings would surely ensue.

"All of this fit snugly into the plans of the Elite, *'Abuses of power will put the final touch on preparing all institutions for their overthrow, and everything will fly skyward under the blows of the maddened mob.*

"*'All people are chained down to heavy toil by poverty more firmly than ever they were chained by slavery and serfdom; from these, one way and another, they might free themselves, but from want they will never get away.'*

"Just as I had suspected, there was total insurrection. When all sources of income were drained, the people went on a crazed rampage that triggered chaos throughout the country.

"Insurrection started in the inner cities and quickly spread in an ever-widening circle. Like locusts devouring the fields before them, crazed mobs plundered, burned, raped, and murdered. After devastating the inner cities, the mobs ravaged the countryside and foothills. Food, water, and personal possessions were open game for those with the power to take them.

"I recalled more of the Elite's boastful atrocities: *'Assemble a mob of men and women previously conditioned by a daily reading of newspapers, magazines, and every other type of verbosity. Treat them to amplified band music with strobe lights flashing at alpha-wave frequencies; or the television's extra-low frequency waves, with their quickly changing highlighted moments of unusual images swirling at them, and in no time you can reduce them to a state of almost mindless subhumanity. Fools, maniacs, or criminals are what they will be.'*

"Crises were customarily created to consolidate power. People then chose willingly to trade their freedom for security. Social crises were proven to be just as effective as military crises. These created crises were *straw men* to establish and empower a government agency to destroy the created crises. They were merely convenient schemes for government expansion.

"Funded by the UN was the Commission on Global Governance. This Commission was headed by the previous IUCN president and comprised of known promoters of global governance and key officials of the UN. The global commons include the atmosphere, outer space, the oceans beyond national jurisdiction, and the related environment and life-support systems that contribute to the support of human life. Its functions included the administration of environmental treaties in such fields as climate change, biodiversity, outer space, and the Law of the Sea. The Elite now regulated direct control of the entire universe and everything in it.

"The Commission on Global Governance appointed an economic Security Council to oversee the world economy, set up a new court of criminal justice having binding verdicts and superior to all national courts. They also established a permanent UN standing army in order to disarm all nations and civilians, set up an independent taxation system, and establish a new world ethic based on a set of core values to unite people of all cultural, political, religious, or philosophical backgrounds.

"Before a standing army could rule, the people of the United States had to be disarmed as they were in almost every kingdom in Europe. The supreme power in America could not enforce unjust laws as long as the whole body of the people was still armed.

"Executive Orders, or EOs, cover every imaginable facet of American society. EOs guarantee that no event takes place without bureaucratic supervision from Washington. Under the Emergency Preparedness Order, an order given by the President is as valid as if passed by the Congress and approved by the Supreme Court. The Office of Emergency Preparedness is responsible for assisting the President in all emergency preparedness activities. Its director is a member of the CFR.

"Under the terms of EO 11490, the President of the United States can order, for whatever reasons he determines necessary, that a national emergency exists. A contingency plan, within this same EO, allowed the suspension of the American Constitution. These standby provisions and the statutory emergency plans are there whereby he could, in the name of stopping terrorism, apprehend, invoke the military, and arrest Americans and hold them in detention camps. He can then order the takeover of all communications media, seize all sources of power, and control all food resources. He can seize all forms of transportation, control all highways, seaports, and railroads. He can commandeer all civilians to work under federal supervision and register every man, woman, and child in the United States. He can also order the transfer of any segment of the population from one locality to another.

"Presidential Decision Directives, PDD 13 and 25, put U.S. troops under foreign UN commanders that were in charge of military troops from practically every country around the world. This Planetary Police Force of inherently striking proportions was perfectly capable of subduing any revolt.

"For years United Nations Peacekeeping Forces were stationed and trained at American military bases throughout the United States. The global army, strategically positioned throughout the world, was specifically trained to carry out the terms under EO 11490.

"When the President declared a National State of Emergency, he invoked military action. All troops were under the absolute authority of UN Commanders not U.S. Commanders. Martial law was immediately put into effect. Private homes and businesses were besieged; homes and buildings that were deemed useful to the cause were commandeered. Arms, ammunition, and items of value were confiscated; any resistance resulted in the person being sent to detention camps or eliminated.

"Journalists, writers, politicians, religious and other leaders known to oppose the cause were removed from society and detained indefinitely in detention camps. Any unauthorized movements by civilians without a special travel permit were also hurled into detention camps indefinitely. Survivors of the insurrection were rationed limited amounts of food, water, and clothing on a daily basis. Black markets involving every necessity of life ran rampant.

"Although video surveillance was initially started under the pretense of monitoring traffic violations and protecting the public from crooks, the uprising opened the door to start a process to set up surveillance cameras on buildings, billboards, telephone poles, and street signs on most corners. Audio and video screens were to be placed inside buildings and public areas; they were also to be installed on phones. Televisions would be adapted for 2-way viewing with the video images relayed to police substations for surveillance.

"The Treaty on Open Skies allowed low-altitude and high-altitude photographs for screening nations' and individuals' activities, and no area of any country would be off-limits. High-powered satellites were capable of photographing practically every inch of the earth's surface. Once the necessary apparatus was installed, there wouldn't be any location hidden from the all-seeing eye of the Elite. Insurrection was the crisis—created by the Elite—which sanctioned World Law.

"Another article I read was precisely what you had described earlier, Monique. The State, under what they termed the Global Commons, was issuing a Biochip with the same information contained on the smart card. Everyone's personal records, along with an access number, would be programmed onto their personal Biochip. Anyone who wanted to pledge his or her allegiance to the New World Ruler would receive a month of credit with the privilege to buy and sell.

"Yes, Lance." Monique interjected enthusiastically. "That's the project we'll be working on next. The Biochip is injected under the skin either on the back of the hand or the forehead. They originally experimented with United States Armed Forces. All servicemen were required to take the mark for identification purposes. Everyone will be given a choice to receive the mark and pledge their allegiance to the UN."

"Is there a deadline when we'll have to make this decision?"

"Not yet. I overheard the conversation yesterday. From what I understand, it all depends upon how long it will take us to transfer the data from each smart card to a Biochip. They will also present the offer to everyone in the labor camps."

"According to the article I read while in the detention facility, it's voluntary," I said in response to her last statement. "Of course, everything they claim to be voluntary is always within constricted perimeters, with negative alternatives if someone refuses. In this case the negative alternative to receiving the mark is the inability to buy or sell.

"The article also said that the people who accept the mark will receive sufficient credit to sustain them for a month. According to *The Master Plan*, no one will be allowed to remain poor. If necessary they'll be forcibly fed, clothed, lodged, taught, and employed whether they like it or not. And if they don't demonstrate the necessary character and enterprise that merits their worthiness, they'll be susceptible to elimination."

"How are they going to enforce these demands on a free society?" Monique asked.

"The United Nations Peacekeeping Forces have been thoroughly trained to openly intimidate public displays of discontentment and if any unnecessary disturbance is discovered it will be quickly silenced. The troops are indoctrinated not to show pity, and they're less inclined to demonstrate charity. They've all been brainwashed with ideals that will make killing worthwhile, so they will not be squeamish in either facing or inflicting death.

"The appearance of peace and stability is their main objective. And to prevent discontent, the teachings in the schools and colleges, the sermons, the editorials, and even the plays and the motion pictures will be skillfully and influentially molded to accomplish this goal.

"The Commission on Global Governance had for some time concluded that politicians would not yield their power gracefully to allow the solution of major problems. The principal challenge from that point on was to mobilize political will; the overall objective was an effective system of world law.

"At the appropriate time for overt rule, they plan to remake all legislation. All of these new laws will be brief, plain, and stable, without any kind of interpretations. Anyone will be in a position to understand these new laws perfectly. The main feature is submission to orders, and this principle will be carried to a grandiose height. Every abuse will quickly disappear when the consequences are felt from the lowest unit of responsibility to the highest authority that represents power.

"Monique, very shortly the condition of the people will be pitiable. All their old liberties will be gone. They'll be labor-slaves and denied their choice of work. Everyone will be machine-serfs and labor-serfs for the Elite. In the New World Order there will be one common language, and everyone will be submitted to one common rule under a totalistic system with one autocratic ruler.

"During my trial I often thought about the Freeman family and the small community in Peaceful Valley; I wonder if they were able to escape in time. Well, that's my crime and how I came to Camp 1100."

It was Saturday and we were able to sleep in; Monique served me breakfast in bed.

"You should get up, Lance," she urged after I finished eating and climbed back under the covers.

"I'll get up in a while," I responded, turning over and fluffing the pillow comfortably under my head. "I just want to relax my first day off from work."

"If you don't get up now, we won't be ready when they come to get us for the meeting in the Square!"

Upon hearing her warning, I quickly scrambled from beneath the covers and made my way into the bathroom. After showering and dressing, Monique and I went to the porch to await our escort to the general meeting.

A massive crowd of men and women marched through the narrow street past our cabin toward the Main Square. A guard ordered us to join them at the rear. With every cabin we passed, another couple joined the marchers. Upon reaching the Square we were at least a thousand in number.

We gathered before a platform 8 feet high and 100 feet square, with a staircase through the center, and surrounded on three sides with lights. It was completely enclosed underneath and there were two doors allowing access to the stairs that ascended the center of the platform. A dark velvet curtain hung from a brass rod partitioning the stage, revealing the front half while concealing the back half from the crowd's vision. Near the front, a microphone rested upon a podium. Two enormous amplifiers positioned at both ends of the platform helped give the appearance of an outside theater.

There was a rope that kept us from advancing closer than 50 feet. A company of guards and goons compassed both the stage and the throng of people who were now growing impatient.

Finally a middle-aged man wearing a fully decorated military uniform parted the curtain and stepped up to the podium. "Silence!" he commanded. Immediately the roar of voices dimished to a hush.

"For those of you that do not know me," he continued in a strong German accent, "I am Commander Gustoff of Labor Camp 1100. Today we are forced to confront the behavior of three criminals who have shown no regard for the State, or you, their fellow workers. Being fully aware of the consequences, they deliberately committed unpardonable transgressions. Behavior that threatens the security or tranquility of this camp *cannot*, and *will not* be tolerated! Therefore they *must* be sacrificed for the betterment of us all.

"I would also like to remind each of you that in order to maintain the peace and tranquillity that exists in Camp 1100, your full cooperation is mandatory at all times! All of you are familiar with the security buttons located in each of the rooms in the cabins. There are also note boxes positioned throughout the barracks, and guards are always prepared to receive any information regarding an infraction. Do not hesitate to inform the authorities about the slightest mention of a security breach, plans to escape, or any display of violence, which is exactly the charge against this couple about to come before you today.

"We have unveiled their plans to escape and we are *certain*, had we not discovered their plot, they would have attempted their escape by now. So, let us commence with the execution that has been sanctioned for today."

The curtain parted, and a huge glass tank approximately fifteen feet high, ten feet long, and ten feet wide loomed beneath the bright lights. The water level of the tank extended about five feet from the top. Directly above the tank was a platform slightly larger than the mouth of the tank. Standing on top of the platform above the tank, with their hands and feet securely bound, was the couple Monique and I had seen being taken from their cabin the night I arrived.

Because the platform was positioned exactly over the tank, they were unable to see what was beneath them. Although they heard the gasps from the crowd, before they realized what was about to happen, the platform collapsed. The couple plunged into the tank of water, going directly to the bottom. With their hands and feet bound securely they were unable to swim. As their feet touched the bottom of the tank, they projected themselves upward, desperately trying to make their way back to the surface for air. The top of the man's head was the first thing to emerge from the water; seconds later the woman's head emerged. With all their strength they frantically tried to position themselves to breathe, but they continued to sink with every futile attempt.

At first I wasn't able to interpret the crowd's reaction. But I quickly realized that what I thought to be compassion was actually excitement. I couldn't believe what I was hearing; they became ecstatic and started to cheer and applaud as if they were watching a sports event.

The woman was now desperately trying to maneuver herself to the top of the tank. She was only able to take one breath of air before she drowned. The man was now fighting with all he had, only to have his hopes dashed when water filled his lungs. They both slowly sank, floating about the tank until the curtain dropped.

I felt Monique's hand clutching mine tightly. I bent down and consoled her.

The crowd was in an uproar. They acted as if they were at a Roman coliseum watching gladiators defend themselves in an arena for their amusement.

The first of the two exhibitions was over, and the crowd seemed smugly satisfied that justice was served.

The Camp Commander took his place at the microphone and repeated his opening command for silence. Looking into the crowd, he tossed his head upward and shouted, "*Justice has prevailed!*" Responding, the crowd roared with approval.

"But justice is not complete," the Commander continued. "There is another who must receive his just punishment!"

"A guard and two aides have been murdered, and another guard and five more aides were severely injured before this criminal was apprehended. I will say no more, other than to give my respects to my fellow comrades who have fallen in their honorable line of duty. May they rest in peace knowing that their lives were not taken in vain, nor without retribution!"

When the curtain opened, we saw Haile bound to a thick wooden board that was elevated at the head, giving the crowd full view of his body. Leather straps secured his neck, arms, wrist, thighs, and ankles. Two men appeared from behind a partition. One of them pulled a cart that contained a wrought-iron stove and a small shovel. The other man was holding a poker in one hand and bellows in the other. Wearing welder's gloves, he opened the door to the stove and placed the poker into its opening. He began working the bellows until the fire was blazing and the poker was red-hot.

Haile remained motionless. Although his eyes were open, he appeared to be unaware of anything that was taking place. I wondered if he was in a self-induced trance. If so, it was the same as being unconscious, his nervous system would be suspended and he wouldn't have any awareness of feelings.

Whether Haile was capable of pulling it off, I didn't know. My conclusion would have to be based on his inability to experience pain. This likelihood certainly relieved my heaviness.

The poker was glowing as the man wearing the welder's gloves drew it from the stove and walked toward Haile. He thrust the poker into Haile's right eye. Smoke emerged, the sound of searing flesh sizzled and an awful smell floated into the crowd, but Haile never flinched. In frustration, the man rammed the hot poker into Haile's other eye; there was still no reaction.

At this point neither of the men knew what to do. They acted as though Haile had cheated them out of their pleasure. After discussing the matter, one of them snatched the shovel from the cart and began removing coals from the stove and spread them across the length of Haile's body. When the coals were gone the men were at a loss.

The Camp Commander appeared from behind a partition. Without a word, he walked over to Haile, pulled his pistol from its holster and emptied the gun in Haile's head.

The speaker hurriedly dismissed us, and we were marched back to the barracks to resume our normal functions.

Monique locked her arm in mine as we joined the throng of men and women being marching back to their cabins. The only voices were those of the goons demanding that we: "Shut up and keep moving!"

I wanted my freedom now more than ever. Once I was transferred to my new assignment, I would have liberties unavailable to me here in the labor camp. I would also have access to information that would help me find the best way to escape.

When I explained this to Monique, she agreed, assuring me that her new assignment would also place her in a position to help.

The next morning a guard escorted me to a single-story building outside the barracks. There I met Mr. Hal Copeland, my camp counselor. He told me I had to be ready at seven o'clock sharp the following morning to be escorted to his office. He would then transport me to the Main Complex for a meeting with my new counselor, Ms. Amanda Rourke.

He asked me if I had any complaints about Monique. I assured him that she was working out fine, and whatever complaints I had didn't include her. After he had sufficiently briefed me on all the changes, he directed me to a room to await an escort back to my cabin.

I told Monique what Hal Copeland had said. She seemed pleased to know that her information was correct.

Later that day, a company of guards and goons escorted fifty of us to an enormous temple a mile from the barracks. I couldn't help admiring the exquisite architecture as we approached the huge building. The architect had cleverly designed stained glass within metal frames as the exterior of the structure. Utilizing stained glass, each window portrayed a unique graphic design. When combined, each exterior wall revealed a picturesque scene of Gaia arrayed by all existing life forms. The interior walls, pews, and altar consisted of intricate metalwork displaying superb craftsmanship. It was truly a magnificently designed structure.

A strong, pungent smell of incense overcame me the instant I entered the temple. A hundred rows of pews were positioned on both sides of the main aisle and stopped 20 feet shy of the altar. We were ushered to our seats, filling the temple to its capacity. Our group sat amid the others, while the guards, who were positioned about the temple, also remained through the hour-and-15-minute service.

At the far end of the temple stood a luxurious altar. I had never seen anything like it. The main attraction was an exquisite throne fashioned from pure gold and covered with jewels of every kind. Surrounding the throne, including the entire wall behind the altar, were replicas of a variety of species; all of them were fashioned from silver.

Suddenly a male voice started singing. It was accompanied by music that filled the sanctuary, surrounding us from every angle. The singer encouraged us to join him and become a spiritual participant in what was taking place. For 20 minutes he sang a variety of songs; many were familiar to the crowd and they joyfully sang along with him.

"Don't miss this opportunity to receive your blessing," he exhorted the crowd in between songs. "The prophet wants to bestow a blessing upon us all!"

Directly in front of the altar, a large motion picture screen began to rise upward from the floor 15 feet high. With all the effects of 3-D, a life-like image appeared on the screen. High above an altar a man sat upon an elaborate throne identical to the one in the temple. He wore a shimmering black and white robe with a long train that almost covered the altar. The lights were positioned in such a way that as he turned in a certain direction he seemed to disappear and then he would suddenly reappear in brilliant splendor before our eyes.

He was extremely articulate and an excellent orator. In correlation with the emotion he desired to induce and the thought he wanted to implant, he raised and lowered his voice with the proper inflection at the precise time. His words conveyed authority and commanded our full attention. He spoke to all of us collectively, and yet, to each of us individually. I felt he was talking to me, and me alone.

His eloquent mannerisms and his persuasiveness captivated the audience. Before long, shouts of praise and echoes of worship resounded throughout the temple. The atmosphere was electrifying. The people were entranced; they feasted on every word the prophet spoke.

Within, my intellect and emotions struggled to dominate the other. I was tempted to suppress what I knew to be sound judgment and give reign to my irrational feelings by joining in with the crowd.

He masterfully painted a picture of utopia; a world designed to meet every need and every desire. He claimed that utopia existed in every sector of the world where people were in harmony. And, by our faithful prayers and worship, together we could gain the support of the spiritual forces of the universe and convince all living beings of the great plan for peace. Our combined prayers would empower the prince and him to usher forth a global utopia for all creation.

Suddenly, as if struck by rage, he began to curse the God of heaven and all of His heavenly hosts. Simultaneously, the lights brightened, and for the first time I noticed woven within the strains of his garment the words, THE MOST HOLY.

Before any of us realized what was happening, in one clean swoop the prophet removed a large canvas, revealing an enormous, full-length statue of a man. The workmanship was superb, almost lifelike. Although I wasn't positive whom the statue represented, his aristocracy emanated powerfully from the image. "Here is your ruler!" he shouted. "Here is your savior; the savior of the world!"

The instant he finished his charade, I was overwhelmed with anxiety. When we left the building I took a deep breath of fresh air, relieved to leave the dancing shadows, dimming lights, and pungent odors that lingered inside those cryptic walls.

Monique explained later that the Sunday services continued throughout the day from 6:00 a.m. until 6:00 p.m., with varied sermons every week. She also told me that the image we saw was the prince, and then she described the service as being in the presence of a divine, spiritual holiness. I held back from telling Monique what I really thought; that the ordeal was spiritual, but it certainly wasn't holy.

The following morning I was escorted to Hal Copeland's office to be transported to the Main Complex. We drove for miles through beautiful, unpopulated countryside.

"We are going through one of our buffer zones surrounding a World Heritage Site, Lance," Hal Copeland proudly informed me. "Altogether we have over a hundred million acres of American soil in 140 sites. They're Biosphere Reserves, Core Wilderness Areas, and World Heritage Sites. If we include the buffer zones, it's more like a hundred and fifty million acres. Only authorized personnel, none of the public, are allowed to travel the thoroughfare going through a buffer zone or a designated site. The sites and buffer zones are strictly reserved so that there won't be any disturbances to the environment by man's destructive influences."

Although I understood the hypothesis, I wanted to hear what he personally felt about the loss of Americans' inalienable rights and the freedoms once afforded to every citizen under the United States Constitution. "So, Mr. Copeland, where does the populace live now that all their liberties and their rights have been usurped?"

"They live within the island areas, where they can't destroy the natural habitat. They're like kids. They need someone to tell them what to do, where to go, and how to think. No, the environment's better off, the animals are better off, the world's better off; it's a lot better place for everybody this way," was his unconvincing reply.

Suddenly a massive cluster of connecting structures appeared. "Now this," Hal Copeland proclaimed, "is the Capitol of the World State. It houses the computers that run not only this city, but pretty near the whole world. Can you imagine a machine that can hold the personal history of every human alive in the world today...? Boy, that's mind boggling. The rest of the buildings are offices, living quarters, and recreation facilities for the workers of the State."

All of the structures were multilevel, some reaching two hundred stories high. I noticed that there were no windows under ten stories. "They place the windows at least ten stories from the ground," Hal Copeland explained, "to deter escape attempts."

This was an ultramodern city with no streets or sidewalks on the ground level. The Peacekeeping Forces that patrolled the perimeter of the city used the only roadway. Only the tops of the buildings appeared above the surface, since the heart of the city was underground.

Buildings connected to one another formed a mass of compact structures of different heights, shapes, and sizes. Four roads, one each from the East, the West, the North, and the South provided the only entrances and exits into and out of the Main Complex. All the structures above the surface were an off-white color.

The road upon which we traveled suddenly sloped downward. After descending a few feet we approached a steel door enclosed within concrete. Above the door was a sign with instructions on entering the city.

Hal Copeland took the telephone receiver from its cradle under the dashboard. He dialed a number, and then spoke into the receiver: "This is number forty-two, Camp Counselor for 1100, entering under code eight with one passenger, a Lance Roberts, number 3900. Access, please."

After a brief silence a voice responded, "Access granted, number forty-two." Simultaneously the thick iron door began to part and we entered the tunnel. The incandescent lamps provided light equivalent to the brightness of any sunny day.

"What is the distance from here to the complex?" I asked.

"The tunnel's only 4 miles long. What's visible on the surface only constitutes a fourth of the city, the rest is underground. From the surface you can't detect that there is a world down here. That's another reason there aren't any windows under ten stories. This place was designed for security and efficiency!"

"How big is the complex, and what's the population?" I asked, trying to get an idea of what lay ahead.

"The Main Complex is 160 square miles underground. Everything's electric, and the temperature is maintained at 65 degrees; you can adjust the degrees inside each building to suit your taste. There are six million, six hundred, eighty-four thousand people... excuse me, eighty-four thousand and one, with your entry.

"There's a hydroelectric transportation system that moves at speeds up to 350 miles per hour. You can reach any point in the city in about 20 minutes. Each building has its own incoming and outgoing transport cars, both two-seater and multi-passenger vehicles. There's also an Open Transport System able to seat 35 people.

"This system was originally designed on the same principle as a spider's web. Just like a spider is able to travel along its web and reach any point, so can the hydroelectric cars. Like everything else here, they're all computerized, which makes them accident free. As soon as I park, we'll take one of the cars and I'll show you what I mean."

Exiting the tunnel, we pulled into a parking garage. Hal Copeland drove up to a booth manned by a guard. They exchanged information and the guard handed him a plastic key-card, which he had programmed with all the data necessary to reach our destination. We parked in the space designated by the guard and caught an escalator that connected us with a conveyer-driven walkway. The walkway took us to a transportation station that overlooked rows of hydroelectric cars.

The cars resembled clear plastic, egg-shaped capsules with two seats inside. All of the cars were contained inside plastic see-through cylinders extending in any given direction. As Hal Copeland had just described, the cylinders were designed in a pattern similar to a spider's web, transversely at the highest points of the city. Ample reserves of these hydroelectric cars sat geared to reach any destination within the complex. The power source was hydroelectric, and the destinations were programmed into key-cards, like the one given to Hal Copeland by the guard.

We stepped through the cylinder opening and into an awaiting car. Hal Copeland inserted the key-card into a slot and a computer screen lit up on the dashboard. A voice asked for a verbal verification of the destination. "Main Complex, intake department, office 32, Amanda Rourke," Hal Copeland responded. After the confirmation, we were given a warning that the doors were about to close to secure our safety.

The screen lit up and a map appeared. A blinking yellow light displayed the location of our car, while a constant green light displayed the destination Hal Copeland had requested. The proper connections, including the arrival time for each stop, appeared upon the screen for our information.

"See," Hal Copeland exclaimed, "the information that just appeared on the screen shows us exactly what number sidewalk, escalator, and elevator we have to take. It also tells us the exact time of all the connections for reaching Amanda Rourke's office. The computer has already made all of the calculations in order for us to reach our destination."

The more Hal Copeland talked, the more I realized that World Construction was responsible for designing this complex. Although it had been some time, I was certain I had worked on the plans. If I was correct, finding an escape route would be less complicated than I had originally feared.

Instantly we were on our way. I expected the pressure from the speed to force me back into my seat, but to my surprise we had total freedom of movement the same as being stationary. As we zipped through the cylinder, the blinking yellow light continuously displayed our location. In a few minutes we reached our connection point ninety-five miles away.

Far beneath the cylinders containing the hydroelectric cars were the moving sidewalks. These sidewalks ran along steel cables supported by steel beams. Transversely in every direction these sidewalks created a continuous flow of people.

The cylinder in which we traveled swooped downward, leveling off at a platform station. The car stopped instantaneously. The door on the cylinder parted and then the top swung open, allowing us to disembark so that two more passengers could take our place.

We exited the car and stepped onto a platform station. Individual, square, metal plates formed a long line beside the platform station. Forged around the perimeter of each metal plate was a barrier with a gate. Attached to the barrier were seats, a computer screen, a keyboard, and a communication device. These plates, sized to carry one, two, or a group of people made up the platforms for the moving sidewalk.

Hal Copeland scanned the plates looking for a two-man platform. When he spotted one he opened the security gate and stepped onto the plate. "Come on aboard," he encouraged in jest, "we're going for a ride."

Comparable to the hydroelectric cars, once the key-card was inserted into its slot all the calculations for any connection points were instantly computed. A graph displaying these connection points and the estimated times of arrival appeared on the screen.

Three lanes of traffic traveled the moving sidewalks in different directions. A switch labeled *Enter* enabled you to enter the closest lane of people-traffic moving in the direction that you desired to go. The center lane was for high speeds, and more extended travel. The last lane only carried uniformed guards and Peacekeeping Forces. Security forces were able to control their own speed, or connect with another plate and control its speed, and they constantly patrolled the moving sidewalks.

After inserting the key-card into its slot, Hal Copeland pressed the switch marked *Enter*. The speaker under the computer screen cautioned us to remain seated and hold on to the barrier at all times. As the sidewalk moved past us, two platforms automatically separated, creating a space for our platform to slip into a connection. By moving into the fast lane we advanced our speed. Before approaching our destination, the platform automatically disconnected itself from the fast lane and moved into the slow lane. When we arrived at our designation, the platform automatically disconnected itself from the moving sidewalk and entered into the next available space at the platform station. The speaker under the computer screen cautioned us to hold on to the handrail, since we were about to stop. We stepped off the platform and onto an escalator that took us to the second level of an immense plaza.

The administration building was a large, sleek, ultramodern structure. Hal Copeland stopped in front of our designated elevator and looked into a camera with an intercom beneath it. The pleasant voice of a female asked us to state our business. Hal Copeland pushed the button on the intercom, "This is number forty-two, Camp Counselor for 1100, traveling under code eight, escorting Lance Roberts, number 3900. We have an appointment with Amanda Rourke."

"Your presence will be announced. Elevator nine, please," was the reply.

Elevators provided the only access into the building. When we reached our floor, the door opened into a reception area. Seated behind a desk was a pretty receptionist. The instant she saw us she stood to her feet and smiled. "Mr. Copeland, Mr. Roberts, please follow me." She directed us to a hallway and opened the first door on the right. "Ms. Rourke is awaiting you both. Please, go right in."

At the far end of the room, Ms. Rourke was sitting behind a desk. I looked around curiously. To the right was a peach-colored, leather sofa with two matching chairs arranged around a walnut coffee table. Sitting on the table was a lovely jade vase. On both sides of the couch were end tables with matching jade lamps. On the opposite wall was a walnut bookshelf with a wet bar in the corner. Throughout the room were various plants. The office was nicely arranged, and I appreciated her taste. I felt very much out of place dressed in dirty khakis and work boots.

We crossed the room and approached Amanda Rourke. While looking through a file in front of her, she gestured in the direction of the two chairs standing before her massive marble desk. "Both of you, please be seated," she offered. I glanced at the file and saw my photograph attached to the cover.

She was a handsome brunette, dressed conservatively in a dark pin stripe business suit. After reading the last page she closed the file, removed her glasses and set them on the desk. Looking up, she greeted

Hal Copeland, and then turned her attention to me. "I am Amanda Rourke, your new counselor. From now on I will be personally in charge of you. Your records show that you are a good architectural engineer, so we have decided to take advantage of your talents. That is, unless I've made a mistake? I'm assuming that you prefer an office to the irrigation fields."

Before I was able to comment, she continued, "How do you want to be addressed by staff?"

I didn't like her attitude and something within compelled me to challenge Amanda Rourke, just to see how far I could go. "I prefer being called, *Mr.* Roberts, it commands respect not afforded otherwise. First names are reserved for relationships with friends."

My irony didn't affect her in the slightest, "All right, Mr. Roberts it shall be. I'll have a nametag made accordingly.

"I want to show you where you'll be working and introduce you to some of the staff you'll be working with. I also want to show you your new living quarters. Would you follow me, Mr. Roberts."

She glanced at Hal Copeland. "You can relax, Hal. Rose will get you whatever you would like."

As we passed Rose's desk, Amanda stopped, "Rose, I'm taking Mr. Roberts on a tour of his working and living quarters. Page me if I'm needed. And see if Hal needs anything."

The elevator opened as we approached it. "Sixty-fifth floor," she announced to an undetected receiver. Turning to face me, she began, "We have been awarded the contract to build a new Complex. It's also been decided that you would be the head architectural engineer. We made this decision based upon your experience. I hope you'll apply yourself *here*, in the same manner you applied yourself at World Construction.

"Life can be very pleasant here, Mr. Roberts. However, I think you should know that I could also make it very, *very* uncomfortable for you. Before we continue, I'd like to know your feelings on this matter?"

"Ms. Rourke, you know my history. Therefore, you also know I'll do whatever is necessary to survive, comfortably."

"Very well, then!" she retorted, with a smug look of accomplishment.

The elevator door opened into a large, well-lit drafting room. The sight brought back old memories. The excitement from the men and women going about their various jobs motivated me. There were draftsmen sitting at tables and in front of 32-inch computer monitors; messengers were running errands and supervisors were giving instructions. There was also a uniformed guard seated at the far end of the room.

Other than the guard, these were the kinds of conditions I considered challenging. A life of training prepared me to excel in this kind of environment. I knew what was expected of me, and I was capable of handling whatever came my way.

"Your personnel supervisor is John Phillips. He's a special director from the Region, in charge of the Development Department. All plans, revisions, and reports must be submitted and approved by him. I'm the only other person that has authority over you. My authority constitutes the security of this Complex, and security supersedes everything else."

As we walked through the room, Amanda introduced me to various personnel. I noted the working conditions, observed the people and studied their faces closely while being introduced. I searched for any sign of discontentment, but I was unable to detect even one.

At the end of the room, on the right, was a small office. Bent over a drafting board was a lanky man with graying, curly hair toppled upon his head. As we entered the room, Amanda asked, "What are you working on, John?"

"Hi, Amanda," he replied, peering over the top of his glasses. "Just a meager project for a friend."

"John Phillips," Amanda said, gesturing in my direction, "this is Mr. Lance Roberts. He is the new architect we've been discussing. Mr. Roberts, this is John Phillips, the director from the Region."

"Hello, Mr. Roberts. I haven't had a chance to go over your file thoroughly yet, but judging from what I have read, I'm sure we'll get along just fine. By the way, Amanda, when are we going to get Mr. Roberts a more appropriate attire?" he asked, while giving me a hardy handshake and a pleasant smile.

"He'll be dressed appropriately when he reports for work tomorrow," she concluded, as we left the room.

While riding the elevator down to the main floor, Amanda's voice pager sounded. She removed the receiver that was clipped to her inside jacket pocket. "Yes," she responded, after pressing a button.

"This is Rose, Ms. Rourke. There is a Mr. Cabe on the line requesting your whereabouts. He claims he must contact you immediately, regarding the Hershey matter. Shall I tell him where you are?"

"No! As far as I am concerned, we have concluded the Hershey matter. Tell him I will contact him when I find a free moment. And by the way, contact Max at the garage, give him our destination, and let him know we're on our way."

"Yes, Ms. Rourke," Rose replied.

Stepping off the elevator we faced an information directory that filled a billboard. Amanda scanned the board for the quickest route to our destination. Turning, we went toward a conveyor-driven walkway. "Watch your step, Mr. Roberts. I wouldn't want anything to happen to you."

"I've come too far to be done in by a moving floor," I retorted.

People were passing us in both directions, and many knew Amanda. Some of them addressed her formally, while others were intimate. Everyone gave her the utmost respect. She responded to some by name and to others she merely nodded, but she was polite to everyone.

"What is your position with the State, Ms. Rourke?" I asked.

"I wear a number of hats, Mr. Roberts. I am the chief counselor for transferees from the labor camps and I am the head in charge of human behavior for the Main Complex. There aren't many people with qualified skills to graduate from labor status to resident status; and I've only seen one person graduated from resident status to an official member of the State.

"I also have a case load of non-residents. These are State officials with slight problems in their past, but can be of great assistance if handled properly.

"We will get off here, Mr. Roberts."

We walked over to a metal door with the number 60 written in bold white letters. Amanda opened the door and we walked down a short stairwell that took us to a travel station. At the bottom of the stairwell was a glass-enclosed booth with a uniformed guard sitting inside. To the left of him was a group of hydroelectric cars with cylinders branching out in different directions. As the guard saw us coming, he stepped out of the booth. "Good afternoon, Ms. Rourke. Here's your key-card for a two-seater. Rose called and gave me your destination."

"Good afternoon, Max. Thank you very much."

After Max handed her a key-card, he pushed a button and one of the hydroelectric cars moved forward from the group. The glass capsule automatically opened and we stepped inside the car and took our seats. I couldn't help noticing that these cars were much better maintained. They were deluxe compared to the one that Hal Copeland and I had traveled in. The compartments were larger and the seats more comfortable. There was also room for the seats to swivel around so that the occupants were able to face one another by simply pressing a button.

Amanda inserted the key-card, confirmed our destination, and we were off. "I'm going to show you where you will be living. You are very fortunate. The computer recommended one of our best housing complexes, normally reserved for State officials. You were also given the top floor, which is one of our best locations, due to the outside terrace and scenic view. The interior was reconstructed according to a set of plans we found in one of the drawers in your office at World Construction. They were marked, *A Bachelor's Dream House*, by Lance Roberts."

"It seems that the State has gone to a lot of trouble on my account."

"Not particularly, we try to please everyone, especially those who serve the State well."

"If that's the reason, aren't you taking a lot for granted?"

"No, not really. Everything we know about you is compiled from your past thoughts, and your reactions to various situations. The computer compiles this data, and then categorizes it. There are always exceptions to the rule, but we can nearly predict a person's response to just about anything. It's almost like two plus two equals four."

I turned from facing Amanda and looked ahead. In the distance I could see a guard's booth. We were there in an instant.

From there we took an elevator up to the 196th floor of a stately apartment complex. The elevator opened into an entryway with closet doors on both sides. A short hallway led into the large circular living room. In the center of the living room was a huge, round fireplace. Encircling the fireplace were curve-backed sofas and matching chairs. The sofas and chairs rested against a 3-foot high wall that supported a floor, which also encircled the living room.

Upon entering the living room, on both sides of the opening were short staircases that led to an elevated floor, enabling you to circle the living room from either side. The 3-foot high wall that supported the elevated floor was also the wall upon which the sofas and chairs rested.

On the far side, directly across the room was another staircase leading to the elevated floor. From this elevated level we could look down into the living room as we walked around, which gave the living room a sunken effect. And there was an assortment of various accessories that helped beautify the room.

The elevated floor was fifteen feet wide and extended to the outer walls on each side of the room. On one side were a baby grand piano and a spiral staircase leading up to the master bedroom. On the other side were a wall bookcase and an open reading area.

On the far wall, directly across from the entryway, was an open dining area. To access the dining area, you could walk directly through the living room or around the living room by taking the elevated floor that encircled it. The dining area was partitioned by a wall that separated it from the kitchen and maid's quarters.

"I'm truly impressed," I told Amanda as we toured the living quarters. "It's difficult to admit, but this is exactly how I would have arranged it."

"I'm glad you are pleased. Considerable effort was put forth to make sure it would suit you. It took Rose two weeks of searching the files containing the information gathered from your memory banks. Once the data was compiled, I utilized the information to determine the choices you would make if confronted with the same situation. I also gathered information pertaining to your taste in decor. Let me show you the master bedroom, and your wardrobe."

We climbed the spiral staircase. The master bedroom was also round. One half of the room suspended directly above the elevated floor that encircled the living room. The master bedroom was directly above the inner circle of the living room, like two half circles facing in opposite directions and connecting at their circular edges. This caused the bedroom floor to form the ceiling of the elevated floor beneath it. Looking through the glass wall from the master bedroom allowed us a full view of the living room below. A button opened and closed the drapes, revealing and concealing the bedroom from the living room.

There was a fireplace, a wet bar, and a solid glass wall on the far side of the bedroom, which opened onto a terrace that duplicated the average backyard. Since the building was located on the outer perimeter of the main complex, the exceptionally large terrace stretched the full 75-foot length of the quarters and extended 25 feet out from the building. The terrace included artificial grass, patio furniture, a barbecue pit, two hammocks, and provided a panoramic view of the mountain range a span away.

"Very well done, Ms. Rourke," I reluctantly, but honestly complimented. "I couldn't have done better myself."

Amanda picked up the remote control off a nightstand. "This will operate any gadget in the house, including the projector and screen over the bar. There are also similar controls downstairs."

When she pressed one of the buttons, a wall began to withdraw into another wall, gradually revealing a wardrobe closet, a dressing and vanity area, and then a bathroom containing a huge, sunken tub.

"To stop the wall, you simply release the button," she instructed.

Amanda quickly thumbed through the suits until she found the one she wanted. It was a black double-breasted tuxedo. She pulled a white, formal, ruffled shirt from its place, slipped them both over her arm and reached for a pair of black patent leather loafers.

"These are what I would like you to wear Saturday, Mr. Roberts. The State is having a banquet to celebrate the new contract. It would be impossible to celebrate such an event without giving honor to the head architect. Wouldn't you agree?"

"A banquet on Saturday... Well, I guess... Uh, certainly." Amanda caught me off guard. Without my knowledge or consent, she had made social arrangements that involved me. I wasn't sure *what* her ulterior motives were, but I knew that some existed.

"Is there some kind of a problem, Mr. Roberts?"

"You have to excuse me, Ms. Rourke. Things are happening rather fast."

"Maybe you've grown overly fond of that shack you're living in?"

"Of course not! When do I actually start my assignment in the department?"

"Hal Copeland will escort you back here tomorrow morning, which is the official date for your permanent transfer," she answered hurriedly before making another accusation. "Or maybe it's the *female* staying with you.... Who *is* the female staying with you, Mr. Roberts?"

"Her name is Monique Duval. But what does *that* have to do with any of this?"

"Duvall. Monique Duval..." she reiterated thoughtfully. "Yes!"

I noticed her expression changing; she apparently recognized the name. "Yes, she's also graduating from laborer to resident status. I recall now. I did her paperwork last week, and she'll be working on the new computer. I also recall hearing her name mentioned with relation to her attitude regarding the men. *Yes*, Mr. Roberts, I understand. Come!"

After our conversation about Monique, Amanda's attitude changed. She was no longer intimately charming; she was curt and indifferent. Realizing that Amanda Rourke could be treacherous, I felt a tinge of fear. My future plans for escape; in fact my life itself could depend upon the favorable development of our relationship.

When Hal Copeland dropped me off in front of my cabin, Monique was anxiously waiting for me to return. She bombarded me with questions as I entered the door. "Well, what did they say? When are you being transferred? Isn't the Main Complex a fantastic place to live?"

"In answer to your first question, there was a lot said. After all, I was there all day. In answer to your second question, we're being transferred tomorrow. And the answer to the third question is 'yes'. The Main Complex is an unusual place, and it certainly provides better living arrangements than these," I concluded with a smile.

"You know, Lance, I've been thinking. This is probably the best thing that could happen to us.

"Speaking of living arrangements," she continued, "were you shown our living quarters?"

"Yes. It happens to be a house I had designed when I was a kid in college. I called it A Bachelor's Dream House. Amanda had the interior constructed exactly as I had designed it. I was really impressed."

"I can hardly wait to see what it's like. I'll let you know if you are the master architect that they claim you are."

"I'm hungry, Monique. Is there anything to eat?"

"Of *course*, there's something to eat. Have a seat at the table, Lance," she answered affectionately.

The following morning Hal Copeland transported me to Amanda's office. My resident status was now official. Monique's transfer and change of status would become official when she was transported to the Main Complex for her training session in the afternoon.

"Good morning, Mr. Roberts," was Amanda's greeting. "I took the liberty of picking your attire for the day. You'll find them hanging in my private lounge; the door behind me on your left."

"Thank you," I retorted. "Anything would be an improvement over what I'm wearing."

Amanda Rourke was an expert in the observations of human behavior. I was certain she was attempting to devise a stratagem that would substantiate a reason for me to need on-going therapy. If I expressed my dislike for her parental behavior, she could easily dismiss my valid reaction as immaturity. If I flatly refused to play her game, she would assuredly respond with more drastic measures. A violent reaction on my behalf would only confirm a need for therapy; or worse, provide her with an emotional button to push whenever she felt like provoking me. This was going to be a deadly game of wits. In order for me to win the game, I would have to play according to her rules.

It was ironic that everything she selected suited my taste perfectly. She held a definite advantage, since she was drawing from a recorded account of my preferences. It was as though I had shared my opinion about the matter, and yet in reality we had never discussed it.

"What should I do with these old clothes?" I asked, exiting the lounge with the worker's outfit over my arm.

"You can hand them to Rose on our way to the drafting department.

She'll dispose of them for you."

"By the way, Ms. Rourke," I said, turning to face her. "I wear my haberdashery in a variety of designs, whether they be solid colors, polka dots, stripes, or paisleys. However, when I select a tie and pocket scarf, I never match the patterns. It would be helpful if you remembered that in the future. Better yet," I added as if having second thoughts, "I'll relieve you of that obligation entirely. I'll manage it myself from now on. Thank you."

John greeted us as we stepped off the elevator into the drafting department. "Now that's more like it," he exclaimed, brushing an imaginary piece of lint from the lapel of my navy blue blazer. "Come on, I'll show you your office," he beamed, leading the way.

It was an exact replica of my office at World Construction. My oak desk, my leather chair, the paintings, the sofa, the matching love seat and chairs, even the wet bar brandishing my preference of liquor were exactly what I had in my previous office at World Construction.

"Well," Amanda asked, "how do you like it?"

"Ms. Rourke, you simply relocated my former office. Of course I like it, it's my arrangement." I knew I was pushing my luck. But I had to keep her off balance; otherwise, her dominating personality would be impossible to withstand.

John led us into my drafting room, but it was not the same as the one I had at World Construction, and yet the surroundings looked familiar. Two of the walls were solid mahogany; one contained the door through which we entered, and the other was lined with computer furniture and a bookshelf. The two remaining walls consisted of tinted, unbreakable glass from ceiling to floor. Since this room was on the top floor, the entire ceiling was also tinted with unbreakable glass to utilize the maximum amount of daylight.

In the far corner where the two glass walls met stood my drafting table and stool. On the left, halfway across the room, facing the glass wall and a striking view, was a leather chair beside a small leather sofa. These furnishings were arranged around a small coffee table that held a plant. The only other furniture was a chair in the area of the bookcase, and the desk the computer sat on.

I suddenly realized why it looked familiar. I had designed it myself some time ago, but never got around to having it constructed. Evidently Amanda discovered the plans and made the necessary arrangements, the same as she had done with my living quarters. It was immensely effective, and I sincerely complimented John and Amanda on their superb job.

Seemingly Amanda was only interested in hearing my opinion, because she turned to leave immediately thereafter. "I'll talk with you later, John," she stated before reaching the doorway. "And I will *see you* at the end of the day, Mr. Roberts. Report to my office before retiring to your living quarters," she commanded while leaving the room.

John showed me around and introduced me to the personnel. My assistant was Fred Feinberg. Fred was a short, handsome, and amiable man in his mid-to-late thirties. I learned that he lived in the quarters directly beneath mine, and I looked forward to our becoming friends.

Most of the day was spent with John and Fred briefing me on the current project. When left alone in the blueprint room, I located the plans of the Main Complex and searched for an escape. I examined the boundaries, the tunnels, the drainage systems, the aerial views, everything and anything that might help me formulate a plan to get out. However, I didn't find anything that would assist me in an escape, other than a photograph of the surrounding area and its terrain.

At the end of the day John escorted me to Amanda's office. "Have a seat, Mr. Roberts," she offered, pointing to the chair before folding her hands upon her desk. "I reviewed Monique Duval's file. Judging by its contents, she's a troublemaker. Would you care to add anything to my evaluation?"

"No," I answered. "As of yet, I haven't had any problems."

"I want to be certain that she will not be an interference to your work. She will stay with you another week, and then you can make a selection from one of our catalogs. The females offered in our catalogs are more refined than those offered to the laborers. Due to Monique's new status, she will not be displayed in a catalog unless she requests it. Since she is presently assigned to be with you for another week, I will not arbitrarily remove her. That is, unless you request it..."

"She hasn't presented a problem, so I don't see any reason to remove her." I interjected, hoping to conclude the matter.

"I have assigned you a guard. He will pick you up at seven tomorrow morning." She pushed the intercom button on her phone. "Rose, please summon guard-28 to escort Mr. Roberts to his quarters."

By the time I walked out of Amanda's office, guard-28 had arrived. The elevator door opened into the entrance of my quarters, and I stepped into the entryway, while guard-28 remained on the elevator.

As I approached the living room, Monique jumped up from the sofa and ran to greet me. "Oh, Lance, this is the most eccentric home I've ever seen. How did you pull it off? I mean, it's unbelievable. And look at *you*; my, aren't *you* handsome."

I knew Monique had already explored the living quarters, but I wanted to personally give her a tour. Afterward, I went over to the bar, picked out a bottle of champagne, and we toasted our good fortune.

I learned earlier, while studying the different sets of blueprints that all living quarters were bugged. However, the rooms in my quarters were spacious, and I knew the location of each receiver. If we spoke in a whisper and maintained a high volume on the radio, it would be difficult to understand what was being said, even with the most sophisticated listening device.

I directed Monique to an area of the house I knew was safe. I told her about the hidden transmitters and pointed out each of their locations. I also explained my new assignment, and confessed that I hadn't yet found a way to escape. I felt it was necessary to recount the conversation Amanda and I had, and I explained the importance of having her photo placed in a catalog. She told me that she would make a request for placement in the latest edition, if I promised to choose her for the next session.

That night I couldn't go directly to sleep. I wasn't sure if it was due to my change of surroundings or anxiety because of my new assignment. Long after Monique was asleep, I lay in bed thinking about Haile and then the Freeman family. They believed so differently, and yet they were prepared to die for what they believed.

Hopefully the Freeman family was still alive and the beautiful, peaceful valley they lived in was still habitable. When Monique and I escaped, that's where I wanted to live.

Maps, substantial rations, and the proper clothing were items that were easy to get. The problem was reaching the outer perimeter of the buildings and getting away from the Main Complex undetected.

I spent the remainder of the week working on the design for the new campsite and complex facility that would be similar to the Main Complex and Camp 1100. It would be larger, however, with state-of-the-art equipment, and far more precocious than anything I had previously endeavored.

While studying the specifications, I realized that this project was similar to others I had worked on while at World Construction. At World Construction, however, no one ever imagined we were designing underground complexes and labor camps. Isaac Burgess was able to disguise these projects by allocating individual sections as though they were separate jobs. I would work out the calculations, write specs, draw sketches, and then assign a section to a draftsman. As each job was completed, I submitted them to Isaac for approval and, if approved, that project would be closed. None of us ever saw all of the sections of the project compiled, and therefore could not have realized its finished state. I was certain that this project would have gone to World Construction had it not been that the State was benefiting from my free labor.

Realizing that I was a vital entity in fulfilling their plans helped to calm my fears. Being eliminated was unlikely without a thorough inquiry; and it wouldn't be based on one person's opinion alone, not even Amanda Rourke's.

My spare time was spent compiling a list of the filing sequences for maps of the surrounding area and the distant terrain. I needed their filing sequences in order to go directly to them when I needed them.

The highlight of the week was the upcoming Awards Banquet scheduled for that Saturday. Our department was receiving the highest award of the evening: the actual contract for designing the new Complex and Campsite was being awarded at the banquet.

The advice given by the seasoned personnel was for everyone to come prepared for a gala affair. We all looked forward to the big night out. It would be a welcome relief from the formalities and pretenses that prevailed under our imposed working conditions.

Although Monique was my guest, her department was also receiving an award. The decision to award the Main Complex of Camp 1100 the design contract was contingent upon my expertise as a designer and manager. Likewise, the privilege of housing and maintaining the world's largest computer was contingent upon Monique's expertise in computers. Prominent State officials would distribute these awards.

Due to our transfer and change of status, we weren't required to witness the Saturday morning torture killings. Those functions were designed only for the laborers.

We now had access to clothiers, hair salons, exercise and recreation facilities, spas, and social events. Being Saturday and our day off, Monique and I had the whole day to prepare for the banquet.

Leaving our quarters for any reason—unless requested by an official—required a detailed weekly schedule submitted to our counselor at least one week in advance. The form was called a Schedule Request. The counselor considered each request, made a decision accordingly, and then returned them by the first day of the week. The guards were also given these weekly schedules for escorting purposes.

Guards and State officials, like Amanda and John, were the only ones in possession of card-keys. Card-keys contained code numbers for unlocking doors and compartments. The key-cards were different, they contained destination data and were only used for operating vehicles. Thus, a *key*-card containing the desired destination data was essential for operating a vehicle, and an escort with a *card*-key was essential for any movement by residents.

I had just returned from getting a haircut and shave when the intercom announced an incoming call. I pushed the button and greeted the caller. It was Amanda Rourke: "Mr. Roberts, guard-28 is on his way to accompany you to my office. Please be ready."

When I arrived she was sitting behind her desk looking over my file. "Please, be seated," she offered, handing me a catalog containing females. "You can choose three females, one for each of the next three months or one for the entire quarter, whichever you prefer."

I quickly searched the photographs for Monique. "Number 12, page 43, for the entire quarter," I replied after finding her picture and returning the catalog. She made a note of the number and page. To my surprise, she refrained from making a comment about my choice.

"Something puzzles me, Mr. Roberts. Except for possessing an unauthorized copy of Manual IV, your record is unblemished. I'm assuming that your arrest took place before you were able to discuss your ideologies with anyone other than your parents. As you know, they willingly informed the investigators about your convictions.

"But what about your girl friend, Greta? We questioned her extensively. She convinced us that she knew nothing. Did you discuss anything with her?"

"Ms. Rourke, you have my file there before you. You know exactly what happened. So why are you asking me questions when you obviously know the answers?"

She slowly closed the file and leaned upon the desk. "I'll tell you why. Because we don't know what you did the day before or the day of your arrest. We know you were gone for at least 48 hours, but the memory-scan only revealed ambiguous traces of your activities during that period. Those 48 hours were interpreted as a *dream state*. Because dreams are not real, we don't have a definite chronicle of what took place those two days. We both know that you weren't asleep the entire time, so where were you Mr. Roberts? Who were you with? What did you do?"

"You're wasting your time, Ms. Rourke. If the memory-scan can only pick up abstract traces of the events of those two days, how do you expect me to remember? I can only tell you I went on a two-day drunk."

"I intend to waste a little more of *my* time. Since you don't intend to cooperate, I am going to make an appointment for you to have another memory-scan. This gives you six months to voluntarily disclose what happened during those two days. You are very fortunate; due to the tremendous influx of those receiving the mark, our technicians are presently overburdened transposing data, so that is the earliest appointment I could arrange. If you decide not to divulge the details of those events, and we discover anything to indicate that you were not inebriated for those two days, I am going to have you returned to the labor camp or placed in solitary confinement as a security risk.

"The banquet starts at eight. This is a very important occasion.

You and Monique Duval are going to be honored. Be sure to wear the tuxedo I requested."

It was quite obvious Amanda was going to pursue this matter to the end. My only leverage was that my services were needed. I also realized that I wasn't expendable, but without confirmation from a memory-scan, Amanda didn't have sufficient evidence to convince her superiors that I was a security risk.

Whatever her intentions, I couldn't withstand another memory-scan. The reason for the first one failing was beyond me. If I was going to escape, I needed to find a way out within the next 6 months. If I didn't, the Freeman family and the location of Peaceful Valley would become public information.

I returned to my quarters to find Monique dressed for the banquet. Her silky hair glowed under the lights. Her large hazel eyes sparkled as she turned to watch me enter the room. She was more beautiful than ever. Her full lips glistened and her perfect figure constrained by the gorgeous gown only enhanced my desire to escape from this tyrannical existence of which I remained a captive.

Amanda had requested that I wear a black tuxedo, a white ruffle shirt, a black cummerbund and a large, black, bow tie. Together with Monique's exquisite white lace gown, we made a lovely couple.

Guard-28 accompanied us only as far as the banquet hall. The elevator opened into a lobby. Straight ahead of us, standing behind a counter was a pretty young woman checking hats and coats. She smiled graciously and offered to take Monique's shawl in exchange for a token.

Doors on either side of the counter led into the main hall. Tables arranged end to end extended to the center of the large banquet room where the dance floor began. Fine china, crystal goblets, and silver settings sparkled atop embroidered linen tablecloths, exemplifying the arrangement throughout the room.

Two steps up from the main floor were private tables ceremoniously grouped for dinner by candlelight. These tables lined the outer walls, encompassing the banquet tables and dance floor.

On the back wall directly opposite the entrance was a platform large enough to hold a quartet, two tables, a podium, and the microphones and speakers.

After being asked our names and numbers, a waiter escorted us to a table prepared for two couples. Live jazz set the mood. There appeared to be over 300 guests present, with sporadic groups of late arrivals.

A waiter dressed in tails made his way through the guests and handed us a menu. He politely asked if we preferred drinks before dinner. I told him we did, and he handed me a wine menu to make a selection. On the front side of the menu was a note in bold print: *Only One Bottle*

Per Couple. I requested a bottle of their best champagne, and then Monique and I ordered our meal.

When my eyes grew accustomed to the candlelight, I spotted Fred and a gorgeous blonde sitting at one of the tables not far away. It was apparent, even though they were seated that she was at least four inches taller than he was. I beckoned a waiter, and asked him to invite them to our table. I also suggested that he make the necessary arrangements so that the couple scheduled for our table would be rescheduled to sit at Fred's table instead.

Fred recognized that it was I extending the invitation, but it wasn't until he noticed Monique that a smile filled his face. He reached for their drinks, the hand of the blonde with him, and headed our way. I rose to my feet as he introduced the girl accompanying him as Suzann. I, in turn, introduced them to Monique.

"She's gorgeous, Lance," he complimented, never breaking his stare. He hadn't taken his eyes off Monique, even while telling Suzann to be seated. "What catalog is *she* in, Lance? She really *is* lovely, pal."

"She's in my *personal* catalog, Fred. Suzann is lovely, too.

"We just arrived. Have we missed anything?" I asked, hoping to change the subject.

"Naaaw," he responded, finally breaking his gaze from Monique for the first time. "We've been here about thirty minutes. My experience with these banquets—this is my third year attending these functions, ya know—is that things don't get started for almost an hour; we can kick back until then."

The waiter brought the champagne I had ordered earlier. After thanking him, I turned to Fred. "We have time for a toast. Let's see... Here's to the, uh, State."

"State, my eye!" Fred countered. "Here's to Monique and Suzann; two of the *loveliest ladies* here tonight. And here's to us, two of the luckiest *guys* here tonight. Now that's a toast worth remembering."

As we were about to toast, Fred looked over my shoulder. "Oh, no!" he exclaimed, not allowing his expression to portray his feelings. "Don't look now, but here comes the wicked witch of the Main Complex."

Instinctively, I turned in the direction Fred was looking. It was Amanda Rourke, and she was coming directly toward our table. As she approached, Fred and I both stood briefly to acknowledge her presence.

"She nodded to everyone at the table and then looked at me, "How are you, Mr. Roberts?"

"I'm fine," I answered. "Monique, Suzann, Fred, Ms. Amanda Rourke." Amanda gave a slight nod to each of them, but quickly turned back to me. "I would like a word with you, please."

I stood reluctantly and followed her to an isolated area. "I just wanted to remind you that tonight you will be honored by a prominent State official. Please make sure that you stand when your name is announced.

"You look very nice," she complimented, catching me somewhat off guard.

"You look very nice, too," I responded, not knowing what else to say.

"If you'd like, after the banquet you could join me for a nightcap. I can arrange an escort."

"I'm enjoying myself, Ms. Rourke, for the first time in a *long* time. Thanks, though, maybe another time."

"There won't be another time. It would be to your best interest if you took advantage of my invitation, tonight."

I turned to leave, and then paused for a moment before turning back to face her. "I'll tell you what... In six months, after the brain scan—that you've so graciously scheduled with intentions of having me removed—I'll take you up on your offer. Until then..."

Before I finished she raised her hand to slap me, but I caught it, holding it fast until I finished, "Until then," I repeated, "I'm not interested in your offer! Excuse me, I've kept my guests waiting long enough."

I was playing with fire and knew it. The way I saw it, I was in a no-win situation anyway. By submitting, I'd be the loser when she tired of the game. By not submitting, I'd just lose a little sooner that's all. The fact that prominent State officials were honoring my presence was in my favor. I knew that Amanda was working her scheme alone, that she also had to abide by the bureaucracy; therefore, she wasn't able to unleash the full force of her wrath upon me.

As I returned to my seat, the first speaker stepped to the microphone. Instantly, silence fell throughout the hall. With every introduction, Fred had a comment.

"*Hey*, that's Horowitz. He's been the Labor Camp Commander since the camp opened."

"Yes, Monique and I have had the displeasure of seeing Camp Commander Horowitz at his best," I asserted.

Fred continued his personal analysis of each speaker.

"*There's* Johnson. He's as dumb as he looks, but he's got plenty of juice with the heavyweights.

"Here's Moorehouse. Don't get in *his* way. *Strictly* by the book, he is.

"Would you look at Fitzpatrick...*an Irish genius*...only with figures, though. No *common sense* whatsoever. But he's second in command to big Hendricks himself.

"*Hey, Lance,* they just mentioned your name. You'd better stand up, pal. It's spotlight time."

I stood and forced a smile for the crowd. As I was about to sit down, Hendricks announced Monique's name. He explained that she would be in charge of operating the new supercomputerized system that was just awarded to the Main Complex of Camp 1100. Her surprised expression turned into a smile just as the spotlight shifted her way.

Fred was impressed, "Man! Where did you get her, Lance? She's got brains, too!"

After the ceremonies, the speaker encouraged us to enjoy ourselves. The band began to play again and couples moved onto the dance floor.

Fred turned to me, "What did you do for recreation before you came here, Lance? Did you have any hobbies, or play any kinda sports?"

"Well, let's see... I play a pretty good game of racquetball, and my tennis game isn't too bad either. But my *favorite* hobby was hang gliding."

"*Oh, really,*" Fred responded enthusiastically, setting his drink on the table. "I happen to be one of the best racquetball players in the entire complex. I just recently lost my tennis title to a young kid who could play like a whirlwind. And gliding was my *life* for about ten years. Have you ever flown from Lookout Mountain in Chattanooga, Tennessee?'

"No," I answered with resignation. "I sure haven't, Fred. But I've heard about it and the incredible thermals and awesome wave lifts all around that area."

"Between you and me," he leaned closer to me, lowering his voice, "I have a glider and all the gear. It cost me, too! One of the guards has family in the free world, and I still have a few solid connections with the aristocracy, so I fixed them up. I paid a big price for that glider, Lance, and all I can do is look, and dream."

My mind started reeling like a VCR stuck on fast forward. We were on the top floor of one of the tallest buildings in the Complex, using the terrace would give us all the height we needed. Greta and I had flown double on many occasions. Depending on the kind of glider it was, it could be risky with two of us, but Monique was a smart girl and I could teach her all she needed to know. By working the thermals and flying at night we could fly hundreds of miles before being missed by anyone.

"What kind is it?" I asked, curious as to whether an airlift or a downhill slope would be needed

"It's called a Klassic. Just a little something that provides world class performance, with leisure class handling. Only 13 feet in the case, about 42 feet when I set it up on my terrace. I had it custom made with a 3-layer Sandwich Mylar sail. It's incredible. You should check it out, Lance."

"I would love to see it one day, Fred. You wouldn't happen to have two, would you?" I asked, hoping that he might be willing to part with one.

"Two! Be serious, Pal. It was hard enough getting *one*. But you can check it out for a day or two—it really is a beauty. Hey, just don't get too attached to it and forget who it belongs to," he added with a chuckle. "Since my quarters are right under yours, I could pass it up to you from my balcony."

"It's a deal, Fred," I told him. "How about a game of racquetball tomorrow? It's Sunday; there won't be anything to do after service."

"Eleven-thirty will be fine with me. I feel it's only fair to warn you, since you're my supervisor and all, I *play* to *win*. You have to promise me that you won't take it personal. I don't want any retaliation, like giving me a massive work load at the office just because I whipped you in racquetball."

"Okay, Fred," I promised with a smile. "This deserves a toast."

Monique and Suzann were deeply engrossed in their own conversation and hadn't paid any attention to ours. But when I lifted the bottle to refill Fred's glass, Suzann's eyes followed my hand. "Another toast?" she questioned with a slight slur in her speech and reaching for her empty glass. Monique also reached for hers, which was still partially full.

I was confident I had secured our means of escape, but for some reason I didn't want to tell Monique yet. I wanted to work out the details before I let her in on the surprise.

It was truly an enjoyable evening. On a number of occasions I danced with Monique and also Suzann. We all left the banquet content.

I couldn't help but notice that in the Main Complex, the workers were pampered; comfort and pleasures were exchanged for the slave's technology. However, even in the labor camp the workers were pacified; basic necessities were provided in exchange for slave labor. We had all become labor slaves with the Elite as our masters.

Everyone was required to attend service on Sundays. We had our choice of the time we attended, but we chose the early service so that it wouldn't interfere with other activities scheduled for the rest of the day. Monique and I attended the 6:00 a.m. service.

The prophet gave a stimulating message. He strutted, disappeared and reappeared, and then strutted some more. This time he magnified the image, even above himself, and encouraged everyone to worship the prince and his image. He referred to this prince as being the savior, the messiah, even God. He spoke astonishing things against the God of heaven, while profaning His name in every conceivable manner. I never knew that someone could hate with such vengeance, particularly since

I remembered when most people considered God to be the Creator. As usual, I left the temple vexed.

It was different with Monique. I witnessed her gravitate with every word. I felt it was pointless to try to dissuade her now. She had been too thoroughly domesticated; I would have to wait until we escaped.

At ten-fifteen, the intercom buzzed. Monique was closest to the receiver, so she answered it. "Lance," she called from the bedroom, "it's Fred."

I pressed the button on the receiver, "Hey, Fred. Are you ready for your racquetball lesson?"

"Am I *ready*?" he exclaimed. "I expected Monique to tell me you'd taken a canoe to China *just* to avoid having to play me.

"I'll meet you in the elevator in a few minutes, Lance," he concluded.

I had dressed for the game earlier, so I went downstairs to catch the elevator. The blinking red light above the door alerted me that the guard was on his way. When the door opened, I stepped in. We stopped at the next floor, picked up Fred, and then proceeded to the floor that held the Recreation Activities Center or RAC, as they called it.

I noticed the guards mingling freely with the residents. Fred seemed to know most of them on a first name basis.

Whatever sport you desired was available at the RAC. The different types of sports were listed in alphabetical order on the computerized electronic directory. A light indicated whether a particular sports facility was available or not. Any facility could be reserved for up to two hours. A blinking light beside a facility indicated its availability. No light indicated the facility had been reserved, and also gave the time it would be available. The same directory also had a list of available saunas and Jacuzzis, with masseurs and masseuses listed by name.

Located beneath the directory board were a number of computer keyboards and screens. The number of the facility being requested, the desired time, and each name and I.D. number were typed onto a form displayed on the screen.

There were four racquetball courts available. Fred picked number four. "I've played on all of them, Lance. Trust me, this is the best of the three."

We were playing the best three-out-of-five games; the first player to win three games was the winner. Fred was an excellent player, and played all six walls, either forehand or backhand, expertly. He won the first three games easily.

After a short rest, I asked him to play one more game. "Fred, you're one of the best I've seen, and I've witnessed a lot of competitive matches. I wonder if you'd give me some pointers on my backhand?"

Fred was also an excellent instructor. He showed me how to strengthen my backhand with a simple twist of the wrist.

He was naturally a happy-go-lucky person who got along with everyone. He was a good listener, and made it his business to show a sincere concern for everyone that he met. Even the guards gravitated to Fred, and many confided in him. I couldn't help but notice that Fred never talked about himself, or his past.

After the sauna, Fred requested two of the prettiest and most efficient masseuses I'd ever experienced.

I witnessed another side of Fred when I asked him about his offense against the State; his whole attitude changed. "That's *my* business! The only reason the State knows anything about me is because they've tapped my brain!" I apologized and quickly changed the subject.

While we were dressing, I asked Fred when would be the best time to send up the glider.

"Well, Lance," he answered almost apologetically, "the upcoming month is out of the question. I'm scheduled for a meeting every single night. But how about that following weekend, after work...around eight o'clock?"

"No rush, Fred. Whatever's convenient for you is fine with me. It's not like I won't be here." I replied with a grin, not wanting to appear anxious. "Hey, I'll give you a better game next time. After all, I am out of shape, other than working in the fields. I haven't played racquetball in a couple of years," I added, trying to justify my poor performance.

Fred had an entirely different attitude the next day at work; I was his friend now. John and Fred instituted the drafting department. He had personally trained everyone, and he was therefore able to give me invaluable insight. Personal motivations, capabilities, and shortcomings were all a part of Fred's mental reportage for each staff.

He understood the procedures, and his opinions were priceless to me as a supervisor. He openly communicated vital information that would have taken me weeks to ascertain otherwise. I learned to trust his judgment, his ability to make snap decisions, and his discernment regarding the staff. Because Fred knew his job and liked what he did, he was one of the best assistants I had ever worked with.

John was different. He was a seasoned, efficient director that knew every phase of the department's operations like the back of his hand, and he was an excellent engineer. He was confident of his abilities and didn't need any approval or reassurance from others. Unlike Fred, John was a private person who remained personally unattached to the people he worked with. When asked for help, he willingly offered his assistance; if never asked, he would never volunteer. He gave you your space but was there when you needed him. He preferred working alone;

not that he was unfriendly, because he wasn't; he simply valued his solitude.

John also knew his subordinates, and he possessed an ability to exhort them in such a manner that caused them to produce to their maximum capacity. Because of his gentle, easygoing personality, John was a pleasure to work for.

My urgent desire to escape quickly fell to the bottom of my priorities. I was finding it impossible to give serious thought to an escape plan. My heavy schedule filled my days, and most evenings and weekends were spent escorting Monique to one social event after another. I relished my free time, and spent most of it with Fred at the RAC.

On three different occasions I canceled arrangements I had made with Fred to get his glider. The last time I was unable to keep our appointment, I apologized and told Fred I wouldn't ask again until I was certain I was able to receive it. I felt as long as I had access to his glider when I needed it, that was all that mattered.

Monique had become quite a celebrity within the Complex, and understandably so. She had developed a computer language for reading her unique mathematical equations that only she and the computer could comprehend. She started working on this theory of integral calculus long before her incarceration, but she wasn't able to develop it until she was given access to the supercomputerized system.

As a result, she was being considered for State Official status. Monique was given freedom of movement, the authorization to request any materials she deemed pertinent to her assignment, and direct accessibility to any location within the Main Complex.

One day Amanda ordered me to report to her office after work. "I understand that you are making exceptional headway on the plans for the new Complex and Campsite. Have you finally recognized that effort exerted for the benefit of humanity is the ultimate attainment in our existence?"

"Well, no. I hadn't realized that, yet," I answered honestly.

"Mr. Roberts, you had reached your crest at World Construction. Your only hope for advancement was to replace Isaac Burgess, which was impossible because of your status at the time. Under our New Age New World Order, the interests of all are fused into a single whole. Burgess has pretended to be a part of our cause for years, but he also insisted on his individualism by refusing to relinquish control of World Construction. Although he professed equality for all, his actions proved him to be no different than any other bourgeois Capitalist.

"There are only two cultures in this world, Mr. Roberts; the bourgeois culture and the socialist culture. The demand for individualism is no more than a reactionary demand of the bourgeois. Individualism can only infect the minds of the people with the virus of nationalism, and that would take us back to the dark ages. World Construction is sinking, and Burgess is begging us to throw him a lifeline in order to keep it afloat."

I listened to her Marxist philosophy without a word; I was very familiar with this revolutionary propaganda. I also knew what she didn't know, that the Elite sought power entirely for its own sake, and that they were priests of power for enslavement of *all* humanity.

"The airspace," she continued, "and the Earth's moon, the oceans and the seabeds of Gaia are the common property of *all* residents of Mother Earth. *All* are included within the World Federation. Ownership is lodged on behalf of humanity in the Federal World Government organized under the Constitution for the Federation of Earth. Every man's life is at the call of the State and so must be every man's property. The State is all; the individual is of no importance unless he contributes to the welfare of the State; he must hold his life and his possessions at the call of the State."

Although she concealed her true motivations, as she rightly accused Isaac Burgess of doing all these years, the same force motivated her. She would never admit to her abusive actions against others for her personal advancement; these kinds of actions were always falsely ascribed to benefit the State and the betterment of all. The motivating force for power was egoism and greed, which included the Elite and their pawns, such as Amanda Rourke, Isaac Burgess, and all individuals that prostrated themselves to bring about the New Age New World Order.

"Come to your senses, man!" she said. "Can't you see that I'm offering you an admirable appointment within the Order?"

Her last words compelled me to respond. "I'm sorry to disappoint you, Ms. Rourke, but I've never considered an alliance with this totalitarian system that has been sold to humanity under the pretension of utopia. This system that you worship was designed and orchestrated decades ago by a small group of men determined to enslave *all* humanity. My accepting their lie means I would have to denounce what I know to be true."

With degrees of facial expressions that ranged from surprise, to anger, and then restraint, she retorted. "Maybe this is a good time for us to reconsider your position here. Tell me exactly what happened during those days surrounding your arrest, Mr. Roberts."

"We've been down this dead-end road before. I told you, I was drunk and can't recall a thing."

"You have one more month to remember, and then *I* will tell *you* what you did on those days in question!"

"*One month*? I don't understand," I questioned, revealing the fears I had suppressed since her first mention of a memory-scan. "You said it would take *six* months for you to arrange an appointment for a memory-scan? It hasn't been but four months."

"I have advanced your appointment one month. If you have nothing to hide, there is nothing to worry about. But if there *is* something to hide..."

She purposely left the rest of the sentence hanging. Turning, she pressed the intercom, "Rose, summon guard-28 to escort Mr. Roberts to his quarters, please.

"Oh, by the way, Mr. Roberts," she mentioned casually while

turning back to face me, "before you go; are you aware that I have recommended Monique Duval for the highest status ever permitted a laborer? If it's affirmed, and it will be, she'll be the first to advance from laborer status to a full-fledged State Official. Her new number system has rendered common arithmetic obsolete. And her revolutionary *False Reality* has made her well known around the globe. Even the prince has agreed to allow her into his presence."

"I knew that she was being considered for a status advancement, but I didn't know a laborer could become a State Official. I also knew that she had perfected a mathematical system that outdated all other forms of calculation. But I'm not aware of this False Reality."

"You must ask her to explain it to you; you will find it most interesting. Irrespective of Monique's situation, *you* are the loser. Just as I recommended Monique's advancement, I could do likewise for you. Your chances of becoming a State Official are as good as hers are. Think about it, Mr. Roberts. I could even dismiss this business about the memory-scan."

Amanda was shrewd and relentless. At the moment I was useful, but I was just another stepping stone. Her indication to forgo the memory-scan was sheer deception. However, my response to her offer was crucial to my survival. She was asking me to join her and survive, or refuse and be banished to the labor camp forever, or maybe worse.

"What you're purposing is something I need to consider carefully. Give me some time. I'll make a decision before the month is up. If I decide before then, I'll contact you."

"Sure," she answered, "Maybe one day we can discuss it further over lunch. This is to your advantage, you know. There *is* no other way."

I left her office and entered the reception area. Rose and guard-28 were deeply engaged in conversation. Judging by their obvious embarrassment when I stepped out of Amanda's office, I concluded they were closer than casual acquaintances.

That evening when Monique came in from her work assignment I asked her about False Reality. Full of excitement, she began to explain its procedure.

"First, let me say that the idea did *not* originate with me; I merely expounded on the original concept. False Reality, I call it FR, is a technology that fully immerses the operator in an interactive computer-generated environment. The operator in an FR experience interacts with the system through a series of sensors, receptors, and sophisticated output devices. These three devices include the display, worn like a pair of eyeglasses, which gives an illusion to the operator that three-dimensional, computer-generated objects surround him, the data gloves which track hand positions and configurations to an entire body suit which senses the entire orientation of the FR operator.

"I have written a number of programs and copied them onto Compact Disks as demonstrations. You simply don the suit, slip the CD of your choice into a computer, and you're on your way. The CDs also have *Save* capabilities for reviewing the experience later.

"It's ironic that you would ask me about FR tonight. I just submitted an order to produce a number of various suit sizes. I call it a suit because it's designed similar to a diver's wet suit, composed of a very thin, durable rubber that zips up the front."

"If all you really need is the headpiece and gloves, what's the purpose of wearing the whole bodysuit?" I asked, thinking of the possible discomfort of having to wear a rubber suit.

"Let me explain each function individually. I'll start with the headpiece display, which fits securely over the head and houses the monitor's wrap-around glasses. The glasses perform the same function as any common computer monitor, with three additional features. The screen is curved to make allowances for peripheral vision; it has three-dimensional viewing capabilities, and its high-quality resolution produces unbelievable life-like images. In order for a person to interact with a virtual environment, their actions have to be communicated to the FR generator. The transducer converts an action into a form that can be interpreted by a computer. Actions include movements of the head, eyes, hands, and body as well as speech and brain activity.

"The measurement of head movement provides signals which allow the image generator to produce an output appropriate to where the head is pointing. Head movement is measured optically, acoustically, mechanically, and magnetically, or with combinations of these methods.

"The data gloves fit over the fingers and hand and are measured using ultrasonic transmitters and receivers and triangulation technique. Body movement transduction causes a person to move naturally through the virtual environment.

"Complex technology combined with the speed of the new computerized system capacitates the computer to interpret physical movement, and then reconstructs that exact movement. The computer instantly determines the visual direction of movement and simultaneously creates the appropriate scene. The reconstructed scene is displayed on the screen in the form of three-dimensional images.

"The suit and gloves are theoretically the same. The electronic sensory receptors are capable of transferring data from the operator to the computer and from the computer to the operator. Stimulating impulses located throughout the gloves and suit receive and transfer the data, which produces the appropriate response. When the operator moves, the computer instantly produces a similitude of the events as they transpire, and the sensors enable the operator to interact with the images displayed on the screen. Being a participant rather than just a viewer gives the operator the concept of being virtually immersed into the computer-generated world of FR."

"So what's the big deal about moving images on a computer screen and hearing sounds that correspond with those images? They accomplished that over fifty years ago with video cards, sound cards, and joysticks."

"It's a lot more complicated than that, Lance. The electronic sensory receptors are capable of reacting to the slightest human impulses, simultaneously applying impulses to the appropriate nerves to produce the desired effect. It's through these electronic sensory receptors that the operator can *feel* an image displayed on the screen when it's touched."

Monique hadn't yet convinced me that her apparatus merited her being promoted to a State Official. "My idea of *reality,*" I interjected, "is being able to smell the coffee, taste the honey, and feel pain from the rock that just fell on my toe. If my senses can respond naturally, *then* I would consider calling it reality, whether false or otherwise."

"You're right, Lance. Our five senses make life real to us. The most powerful sense-gate we possess is our *sight*. In order to create a sense-orientated environment, I've linked authentic 3-D sound, actual aromas, and genuine tastes to the visual 3-D images seen on the screen. You can feel pain and induce pleasure. You *can* smell the coffee and taste it if you would like. You could also feel pain from the rock that just fell on your toe. Collectively, these effects produce a computer-generated world that the operator can enter into and become a partaker of through interaction.

"You can take a plane ride, a train ride, or fly across the Grand Canyon like a bird. You could visit the Alps in Switzerland and ski down the slopes. How about dancing in New York, or dinner in Paris? Simply slip the CD into the computer and you're on your way."

"It seems to be based on the Air Force's flight simulators used to train jet fighters years ago," I interjected.

"Yes! But much further advanced. This computer is capable of constructing a similitude of digital images taken by cameras, whether still or video. One-dimensional digital images reproduced into three-dimensional images create another world.

"Imagine, a physician diagnosing a patient's problem from the other end of the world. A surgeon can simulate a surgical operation—watchful of complications—and later perform the actual operation problem free. Without leaving the room, a patient with paralysis can encounter numerous experiences never possible before. Students can receive on-the-job training while at home, and when they enter the workplace they are well versed with hands-on experience. And endless explorations can be experienced on the vast Internet highway.

"By networking two or more computers, each operator can utilize the same application while interacting with one another. I call this the *group* category. Each operator can see the image of the other operators on the screen. I've included a catalog of interchangeable features and body parts, which enable the operator to construct human images according to what they like. I've also produced a catalog of existing human images. This catalog includes most of the famous people of today and times past. An operator can also create an image to represent them on the screen, which will be the image that's viewed by the other operators. If you don't like the look of another operator, simply recreate his or her image to fit your preference."

"*Now*, I'm impressed. That's more like *reality*, Monique," I submitted, conveying a sincere compliment. But I could see countless ramifications accompanying this invention, although most of them good, I could also see various aspects of False Reality open for abuse. But many technological inventions carried potential for abuse, I rationalized.

"Isn't it awesome, Lance? The opportunities and alternatives are limitless. And, it can be applied as an amazing instrument for architectural drafting.

"Yes. I can see that," I assured her, contemplating the application of False Reality in Architectural Engineering. Once sufficiently trained, no team of draftsmen could match the speed and accuracy in which I could design a structure. I could inspect the building and make the necessary revisions before the actual construction began. Being able to make the revisions beforehand would cut the cost and time of completion considerably.

My primary concern was to be able to demonstrate the vast accomplishments of False Reality as an enticement to Amanda. I would have to convince her that the advantages of False Reality would more than compensate for the time spent learning the technical aspects of the application. I would also have to convince Amanda that I was capable of achieving what I professed. The benefits would be rewarding for all humanity—particularly Amanda Rourke.

The plans for the Main Complex were presently on schedule, but time was always an essential quality. If the matter was handled discreetly, I would hopefully nullify the threat of a memory-scan and conceivably obtain State Official status. It wouldn't be easy, but it was possible.

"What do you think about the possibility of using False Reality to finish designing the new Main Complex?" I asked.

"No problem, Lance," she answered with a sudden look of expectancy. "Architecture can probably reap more benefits from False

Reality than any other field."

"I have a twofold question. Can you write a program that is comparable to the CAD program we presently use; and how long will it take you to teach me to sufficiently operate False Reality?" I asked.

"With your help, I can rewrite the language for the CAD program, and teach you the basic necessities of FR in two weeks. We'll have to work together while I'm writing the program because I'll have a lot of questions about specific drafting techniques. While you're helping me, you'll also be gaining a working knowledge of how to maneuver within FR," she answered.

"Do you think two weeks will give us enough time, Monique?" I asked skeptically.

"It's really simple to learn, Lance. Once you give me a copy of the top program you use, *we* will rewrite it so that it will perform smoothly in FR.

"When I originally wrote the basic program for False Reality, one of my objectives was to make it so simplistic that a child could easily learn to operate it adequately. The two of us will have to systematically work our way through the technical aspects of architectural design. That's the reason it'll take approximately two weeks. I've devised each program to walk the operator through one step at a time. Once you're familiar with the techniques, there's no end to the capabilities of what you can render. In no time at all you'll be able to function more than adequately."

"If I understand you correctly, the only obstacle I have is convincing Amanda Rourke that the time spent learning False Reality would expedite the completion date of the Main Complex considerably."

"How do you plan to go about that?" Monique asked.

"I'll make an appointment with Amanda and convince her to give me a transfer to your department so you can train me. Knowing her propensity for prominence, and considering the circumstances involved, I don't think she'd hesitate approving a temporary transfer for two weeks. The question remains, are you sure we can pull it off in such a short time?"

"I know we can. You get the approval from Amanda, and I will arrange my schedule so that I will be free to train you," she replied.

The less Monique knew the better off we both were. She would simply teach me to operate the device. I would deal with Amanda. All I would have to do is show her the amenities and her possibilities for advancement. If I presented the situation properly, she would gladly make the necessary arrangements for the training session.

Monique's department would only have to know that she was training someone in the techniques of False Reality, but they needn't know any of the specifics involved. Once I became competent, I would write my own program. Then, I would be the only one needed for the operation.

I would have to take advantage of Amanda's influence with the heads of the State. Meeting her superiors would hopefully put me in a position to gain their favor; after all, it was her idea that we become a team. At the slightest indication of her causing a problem, I would use my influence to have her stopped. Everything was contingent upon me being discreet; one bad move could result in my detriment.

Taking advantage of the invitation Amanda gave during our last meeting, I made an appointment for the two of us to have lunch. I artfully demonstrated that False Reality could revolutionize architectural engineering, and that the benefits could be limitless. I was rather surprised how readily she agreed to everything.

"So you have decided to come in out of the cold," she stated flatly. "I must admit, you brought an enticing gratuity to secure our alliance. If the possibilities are anywhere close to what you allege, we'll be able to write our own ticket."

Amanda made the arrangements to start my training the following Monday. She also volunteered to cancel the memory-scan without me having to mention it. Had she forced me to approach her regarding the memory-scan, she would certainly presume that I had something to hide. I didn't want the authorities knowing about the Freeman family and Peaceful Valley; if ever I did escape and needed a place to go, they were my only hope.

Monique was elated when I told her about Amanda's decision. She made a wonderful suggestion that Fred, Suzann, she, and I spend a three-day weekend together, one of them being a day at the RAC. We all agreed to reserve a hotel suite, rather than the four of us sharing one of our living quarters. Taking advantage of Fred's insight, we submitted a joint request for the four of us on one form. That made it difficult for Amanda to deny all of us, and being a joint request, she couldn't deny any one of us individually.

Amanda sent each of us a written approval, along with a catalog of the best hotel accommodations available in the Main Complex. We were able to book a double suite in a four-star hotel that featured the Tennis Championship finals.

We all looked forward to this weekend away from the common routine. Early the following Saturday morning, Monique and I met Fred and Suzann in the elevator on our way to the hotel. Although Monique was exempt, a guard was required for the rest of us. Fortunately he was a good friend of Fred's. This gave us the liberty we needed to enjoy ourselves. He was also able to arrange it so that we didn't have to attend Sunday service.

After unpacking, we changed clothes, and then left for the RAC. Three games of doubles on the racquetball court, with Fred and Suzann winning two games out of the three, proved to be plenty of exercise for all of us. Suzann and Monique were average players, which made the games competitive as well as fun. A refreshing dip in the pool, followed by a soothing rest in the sauna and a relaxing massage, helped to raise our disposition.

Earlier we had unanimously agreed to attend the championship tennis match that was taking place in the hotel's stadium. During lunch, Fred took notice of the two finalists. They had both fought their way to the top and were the best tennis players in the Main Complex. They were competing against each other for the title and trophy of the year. Since Fred knew them both, being beaten by one of them earlier in the season, he excused himself to talk with them. After a short time, he returned with four tickets for some of the choicest seats in the stadium.

It was an excellent match. Fred introduced us to Raymond Belgium, the winner. Raymond wasted no time extending us an invitation to join him at the championship celebration party later that evening.

"You know, Lance," Fred stated, leaning around Suzann, who was seated between us, "it's a must that we attend this celebration. During my years here at the Main Complex, I've attended or played in every championship tennis match held; and I must declare, the after-parties are awesome."

"We don't have anything better planned anyway, Fred." I replied. "I'd rather honor this invitation from Raymond, especially since he's a personal friend of yours."

While turning to Suzann, Fred asked: "Would you exchange seats with Lance, honey. I'd like to talk with him."

He turned in my direction as I sat down beside him. "Raymond's a good friend, Lance. I met him about ten years ago in Germany. He's a stand-up guy, probably the best friend I've ever known. We ran together for a few years, partying and hustling tennis across Europe. We didn't allow anything or anybody to come between us. We were inseparable; like identical twins. You'll like him, Lance."

Fred wasn't the kind of person that idolized people. Since he felt obligated to speak up for Raymond, I knew he wanted me to accept him as my friend. The way Fred spoke so highly of him, I had to respect him.

Raymond suggested that we dress casually. The spectrum of dress was broad, ranging from shorts and jeans to tuxedos and evening gowns. Champagne flowed like water, which produced an uninhibited atmosphere. Because this affair included both residents and State Officials, the standard rules for residents weren't enforced.

One of Fred's characteristics was the ability to put people at ease.

When we arrived at the party he had Raymond paged. Raymond insisted that Fred come with him while he greeted the guests. He put his arm around him and they made the rounds together. He took great pleasure in introducing Fred, his old friend, to everyone that came to celebrate his victory.

To Fred, people represented positions of usefulness; or they possessed serviceable skills that could be used to win favor with others; not to enhance his own position, like Amanda did. He simply liked people. For conversational purposes, Fred made mental notes of important names for a time when they could be dropped during a conversation. Although Fred had an uncanny way of manipulating people, he did it in a way that made them feel grateful for being allowed to be of service.

About an hour after Fred and Raymond left, they doubled back and invited me to join them, but I declined. Meeting people for the mere sake of meeting them wasn't my idea of a good time. I was certain there were some important people who could possibly help me, but I came to enjoy myself and I intended to do just that.

Fred and Raymond returned with a very attractive young lady, whom Raymond introduced as Heidi. They could have passed for sister and brother. Both of them had long, straight blonde hair, big blue eyes, keen features, and suntanned bodies. He was toned with rippling muscles, while she was perfectly shaped. They made an attractive couple: Raymond in his white silk shirt draped loosely over his upper body, the pleated white trousers and white loafers, and Heidi in her sheer, white dress and white sandals.

It was early morning when we returned to the hotel. We ordered breakfast and reminisced about the events of the party and the day before. Then we all retired, totally exhausted.

We slept until late afternoon. Fred suggested we go to the RAC for a sauna and massage, but I didn't care to go. I preferred to lounge around the suite, reading one of the monthly digests published for architects, while he took the girls for a massage.

Raymond had made reservations at one of the top restaurants in the Complex, insisting that we meet Heidi and him for dinner. He informed us that the dress code was strictly formal. When Fred and the girls returned, we met him there.

Raymond was a gentleman who portrayed a casual manner, sprinkled with humor, which compelled you to like him. Raymond's charismatic personality, Fred's witty sense of humor, and the interaction with three lovely ladies made for an enjoyable evening.

The following morning brought our mini-vacation to a close. It was time for work. There was a long, hard climb ahead, and I was ready for it.

Monique proved to be an excellent teacher. She answered my questions with clarity and fully explained each aspect of the device and its inner workings. In less than two weeks, I was apt in the functions of False Reality.

The excitement I experienced many times during my ascension at World Construction was back. I knew what was required, and I felt confident I could accomplish those requirements successfully. My position in the Design Department here in the Main Complex was comparable to being transferred to a branch office of World Construction.

I had copies of the notes, the current drawings, and the specifications sent to my office and carefully scrutinized everything we had done to date. I made copies of the existing drawings and examined them carefully, making any necessary changes. My final calculations showed that one-third of the project had been completed. After confirming the results on three separate instances, I formed my conclusion for a prospected completion date. A workable set of plans, confirmed by a tour of the Main Complex could be ready in approximately six months. My rough estimate for completing the project beat the intended date made by the heads of the Design Department by at least a year and a half.

Normal drafting procedures called for a calculated design, producing the plans for that design, and then having blueprints copied for the contractor to read. Once construction was in progress, any errors resulted in costly delays. FR, however, was a device that eliminated all possibility for error.

When I submitted the finished drawings to John, he gave his stamped approval and directed me to continue. I divided the project into sections, giving each section an identification code as to its location within the structure being built. Each piece of material was also given a code and listed under the specified section where it would be used. When each item for a section was coded, I entered the information into the computer. The computer sorted that data and compiled it accordingly. Miscalculations or errors were highlighted, and I was given the option of correcting them by modifying the original floor plan or changing the specifications according to the options the computer gave. When completed, FR provided a 3-D image of each section from the ground up.

FR also gave me the option to stop the process at any time and make a physical inspection of the structure before I printed the blueprint. I could easily inspect the interior or exterior construction of the building. With the maneuverability available through FR, I was able to inspect areas that would be extremely difficult in an actual physical inspection. When I was satisfied, I would move on to the next phase of the project.

I worked ten, sometimes twelve hours a day. After the first month I was given free rein of the Main Complex. Guard-28 would escort me anywhere I needed to go, any time, day or night. This gave me access to the drafting department whenever I wanted to work. It took six months and twenty-one days to produce a complete set of working drawings for the new Main Complex and Campsite.

On the day of completion, I contacted Amanda. "It's finished," I told her when she answered her phone. "Come on over and we'll take a walk into the future."

"I'll be there in 15 minutes!" she replied.

When she arrived, I donned her in the head-mounted display for a guided tour. "Amazing! Fantastic! Incredible! Unbelievable!" she exclaimed while we made our way through the Complex.

After we had finished the tour, I invited her to my office to discuss my intentions. "I'll talk to John, show him what we've got, and make the necessary arrangements for breaking ground for the actual construction," I told her, knowing that I had better take control.

"Until John has given the approval," I continued, "I'm asking you to keep what you've just seen between the two of us. I don't want every Tom, Dick and Harry calling every day demanding me to take them on a tour of the complex through False Reality. In order for you to get your due recognition, I'll let you know in plenty of time when you can go public. Is it a deal?"

"This is not what I had in mind," she said. "I've waited patiently for you to finish this project for over six months; now you want me to wait for an approval from a half-wit. What I have just witnessed is one of the most fantastic works of genius known today. I have no intentions of having it stolen from under my nose.

"This is *my* discovery, Mr. Roberts!" She continued, becoming more irate as she spoke. "*You* are still a ward of the State. And, you happen to be under *my* direct control, *not* John's. Therefore, *I* will tell you what you will do, and *you* will obey! Do you understand?"

"I don't think you fully realize what I'm trying to tell you, Ms. Rourke. It's essential that we wait until..."

I wasn't able to finish my statement before she interrupted. "I have no intentions of arguing with you about this matter. This is *my* discovery. I will handle it as *I* see fit. Don't worry about the details, I'll take care of everything from now on, Mr. Roberts. I am asking you again, do you understand?"

With no other alternative, I answered, "Yes. I certainly do, Ms. Rourke."

Although I hoped otherwise, I had suspected that this might have been her reaction. She was forcing me to make a stand against her. Through *The Master Plan* I knew the Elite's pronouncement against administrative abuse of power: *Abuses of power will be so mercilessly punished that none will be found anxious to try experiments with their own powers. We shall follow up jealously every action of the administration on which depends the smooth running of the machinery of the State, for slackness in this produces slackness everywhere; not a single case of illegality or abuse of power will be left without exemplary punishment.*

Concealment of guilt, connivance between those in the service of the administration—all this kind of evil will disappear after the very first examples of severe punishment. The sufferer, though his punishment may exceed his fault, will be counted as a soldier falling on the administrative field of battle in the interest of authority, principle, and law. These interests do not permit any of those who hold the reins of public coach to turn aside from the public highway to their own private paths.

As soon as she left, I went straight to John's office. He was sitting behind his cluttered desk reading from a folder and eating an apple. As he looked up, I politely asked, "May I speak with you a moment about an urgent matter, John."

"Sure," he answered, looking up attentively from the folder resting before him on the desk. "What's the urgency, Mr. Roberts? Is there a snag in the project you're working on?"

"No, the job is finished. At your convenience, I would like to take you on a guided tour through the entire Complex and Campsite. However you're right, there is a problem. It's Ms. Rourke, John. Before I started this project she made it clear that no one was to know that I had finished until she inspected it personally. She also demanded my utmost secrecy in this matter, knowing full well that your approval was necessary before anyone else was told. In compliance with her command, I contacted her as soon as I finished. Today I took her on a visual tour of the Complex. She was quite amazed. I told her I intended to contact you for your approval before any news was released to the press. John, she went berserk. I tried to explain to her that until your inspection was complete, we weren't certain what we had; and, having to deal with a barrage of reporters and officials would work to our disadvantage. She refused to listen to reason, claiming that this was *her* discovery to do with as *she* saw fit, and no one was going to steal it from under her nose.

"John, I believe this thing is bigger than even I imagined. But, unless its handled properly, it's going to become a political bombshell for every official that wants another step up the ladder."

"May I call you Lance?" he asked.

"Sure," I answered.

"If what you're telling me is correct," he continued, "then it's something that needs looking into."

"My first, and foremost, concern is Ms. Rourke," I interjected. "The problem is, I don't know if what I'm about to request is possible."

"Let me hear what's on your mind, and I'll be the judge of what's possible and what isn't," he quickly responded.

"I realize that Ms. Rourke is the chief counselor and that security has priority over everything else. I'm also aware that one of her functions is to ascertain the potential of her clients and convince them to use this potential for the service of the State and the betterment of all humanity; she is very good at what she does. However, I am certain that Ms. Rourke has used her clients for her personal advancement."

John raised his hand to stop me. "What gives you that certainty, Lance?"

"My roommate, the inventor of False Reality, and myself are at least two individuals I know for certain that are being used for Amanda's personal gain."

"How is that?" John queried.

"The procedures she used in my case were exactly the ones she used against my roommate.

"John," I continued, "if it is possible, I would like to be placed under your direct and sole supervision. I'd also like any affiliation with the project taken out of Ms. Rourke's hands. You are the expert in this field and only you should have the authority in this matter. If that's not possible, then I would like to make a request for another counselor— although I realize there's no guarantee that another counselor would be any different.

"We've just touched the tip of potentiality with False Reality in the field of architectural design. I can foresee so many directions we can take with this new technological device that it staggers the imagination. But if it's not managed properly and falls into the wrong hands the outcome can be devastating to society. Once you experience False Reality you'll understand what I'm saying."

"Let's take one step at a time," John responded. "First, I'd like to see for myself exactly what it is we're dealing with. Then, we can take the appropriate steps."

"I appreciate your reserve, sir," I added. "But since the plans to market this device are being put into motion this very instant, I can't over-emphasize the urgency to act immediately."

"I understand," he replied in the same calm attitude. "Let me take a look at what you have, then I'll be better informed as to what must be done, if anything."

I saw a confident assurance that I hadn't noticed before. John knew his capabilities, his position, and the authority he held. He wasn't about to allow my unsubstantiated accusations against one of his colleagues persuade him to make a rash decision.

On our way to my office, I explained the procedure to John. When we arrived, I dressed him in the full body suit. I wanted him to experience the entire effects of FR, leaving nothing for question or doubt.

As I did with Amanda, I also donned a suit so that I could personally guide him. For three hours we walked through the Main Complex as I explained each phase of the intended construction and he inspected its accuracy.

"It took me six months to complete this project by using the techniques available through False Reality. It would have taken a full staff of ten, working five days a week, no less than a year and a half," I stated confidently, knowing that he was currently experiencing the proof of my claim. When we finished, he expressed his amazement.

"This *is* something to behold, Lance," John exclaimed after inspecting some of the smaller details. He expressed his satisfaction, agreeing that everything was according to the floor plan and specifications I submitted to him.

"I don't think I've ever experienced anything like this before," he began. "I've had a similar idea that I've been toying with for years. Now that I know what this device is capable of producing, I'd like to hear your opinion on some of my ideas. I'd also like to hear the direction you plan to take in the area of exploration.

"Regarding this matter with Amanda and False Reality, I understand your concern about her desire to monopolize this device for her own personal benefit. I believe your concern is merited, and it could be devastating if handled improperly.

"As of this instant, you're no longer subject to the authority of Amanda Rourke, nor is she associated with this project in any manner. I'm taking full authority over your case, the case of your roommate who's responsible for this invention, and the entire matter regarding False Reality.

"By the way, what's her name?"

"Monique Duval," I answered.

"Isn't she due for State Official status?"

"Yes. According to Ms. Rourke, the request was submitted."

"I'd like to see the two of you in my office tomorrow morning," John said, flipping through his daily schedule. How about ten?"

"I don't know if you realize the weight that you've just lifted from my shoulders," I expressed with gratitude. "Thank you. We'll be in your office at ten tomorrow morning."

"Are there any other needs before I go?" he asked.

"What about my freedom of movement, will it remain as it is?" I asked, concerned about being restricted since I had completed the job. I dreaded having to go back to the original policy of submitting a weekly movement schedule.

"Sure. Are you satisfied with the guard who's assigned to you? If he and Amanda are close associates, it may be best to replace him with one of my people," he said, thoughtfully.

"No. I'll keep the one assigned to me now. We know each other pretty well, and he doesn't care that much for Ms. Rourke either," I answered honestly.

I didn't want one of John's men that close to me. Of course guard-28 could be ordered to scrutinize my movements, but I was certain that all of John's escorts were highly trained investigative officers and I would rather take my chances with guard-28.

Being released from Amanda's authority was a sudden turn of events that I hadn't expected so quickly, nor had I expected the change to go so smoothly. Another pleasant surprise was to find John so understanding and agreeable. I wasn't sure if he was sincere, or if he was waiting to see if *I* might be the one with a hidden motive. John was a dedicated executive of the State and his authority came directly from the Region. I didn't know the Region's standing within the global governance, but it was the highest source of authority in the Main Complex. Amanda needed permission to administer punishment to a client on her caseload; John possessed that authority and didn't need permission.

When I returned to my quarters, I explained the situation to

Monique. "We're no longer under the supervision of Amanda Rourke," I mentioned while we were having dinner.

"Oh, really... Why is that, sweetheart?" she asked.

"John Phillips felt that the potential for FR was too great, and everyone involved with it should be handled by personnel from the Region. Since John is from the Region, and he also happens to be my immediate supervisor in charge of the Design Department, he's the one in charge. I've been working directly under him, so we have a pretty good rapport. He'll be our new counselor instead of Amanda. He also inquired about the request Amanda submitted for your promotion to become a State Official. I told him that you're still waiting for an approval.

"He had his first experience with FR today. I walked him through the finished design of the Main Complex and Campsite. He was amazed, and decided to take charge."

"Why the sudden concern about FR?" Monique asked, almost indignantly. "Is John Phillips sincerely concerned about protecting FR, or is he really interested in using it for *his* personal gain? If he is, we're in the same predicament we were in with Amanda Rourke."

"I don't think so, Monique. After he asked me a few questions, he concluded that the entire project was much too significant to remain under the direction of Amanda Rourke. We have an appointment with him in his office tomorrow morning at ten. You can ask him any questions you'd like, that way you can determine for yourself what his intentions are."

"Well, that's okay with me," she replied. "I didn't care for Amanda Rourke, anyway. I hope he is more reasonable, or at least I hope he is fair in making decisions."

The next morning, guard-28 escorted us to John's office. I introduced Monique to John.

"Do you mind me calling you by your first name?" he asked her, before taking the conversation further.

"Oh no," she answered. "Please do."

"Well, Monique, last night I did a background study on you. First, let me congratulate you on your new discoveries in False Reality. The original concept was good, but it was flawed and limited. Writing a language that enabled the computer to read your new number system seemed to explode the possibilities."

"Thank you, sir," she replied to his compliment.

"No, I thank *you*, Monique. Please, call me John.

"The two of you are quite a team," he continued. "As far as I'm concerned, you've both proven yourselves regarding your allegiance to the State. In each of your cases, the potential is boundless. It's my desire that you continue your work with the least resistance possible.

Therefore, I intend to allow you all the liberties you need.

"Monique, these are the changes I have made regarding your job assignment. I want you to have your own office, the freedom to work when you please and how you see fit. If you need personnel to assist you, submit a Request For Staff form. The forms can be obtained from my secretary.

"I'd like for you both to submit a weekly report every Friday. Please turn them in directly to me. That will give me the weekend to review them.

"Lance, you and I will meet at eight every Monday morning. We can discuss your report then. Monique, you and I will meet at one o'clock every Monday afternoon, right after lunch.

"Are there any questions?" he asked, looking to each of us individually. We answered no, and he continued. "Fine, I've already given the necessary directives to the people involved with your cases.

"Feel free to contact me any time you'd like to discuss a matter. The numbers where I can be reached, including my pager, have already been programmed into both your home and work communications systems.

"Dialing the number one activates my phone here at the office. If there's no answer, it automatically transfers to my pager. If for some reason you can't contact me by pager, then my answering service will pick it up. If you don't have any questions, Monique, a young lady is waiting to show you to your new office. Afterward, it would be nice if you took the rest of the day off? Lance, why don't you do the same."

I appreciated John's concern. I was also grateful to him for saving my neck. It was a relief to know that Amanda's fiery threats had been extinguished, at least temporarily. Although I was aware that Amanda was revengeful, I was thankful to be able to live a normal life again. My chances of expanding the field of engineering and design were unlimited. This was the position I had exerted a lifetime of effort to attain, and I consoled myself with these thoughts.

John and I grew very close during the next few months. He invited me to all the official meetings at the Region, along with the social and ceremonial gatherings that were given by those in charge. I attended most of these meetings to stay abreast in the areas of planning and development. Socializing with the decision makers helped to promote the work I was doing. Moreover, it solidified my relationship with those in power.

Fred was my close friend and valuable assistant. He expressed his gratitude for making it possible for him to demonstrate his creativity in the areas he was gifted.

Shortly after my meeting with John, I had my last encounter with Amanda Rourke. I had slipped from her clutches and she took this opportunity to express her desire to retaliate. I was at the office when she came to see me; John had stepped out and was due back at any minute.

"I want you to know that your attempt to ruin me has failed. It could have been you and me instead of you and John. I also want you to know, I'm working very hard to have you sent back to the labor camp, or worse. A little bribe here, a little favor there, a threat or two here and there; it all helps achieve one's objective, you know?"

Just as she started to voice her threats, John appeared in the doorway. He patiently waited for her to finish before he spoke. "Hello, Amanda."

I saw the color drain from her face before she turned around to confirm that the voice she heard was truly John's. Before she could produce a word, he asked, "Please don't say anything. I've heard enough. I'm temporarily relieving you from all your duties; you'll be contacted regarding a hearing date. And please remain in your quarters until you're notified."

Not knowing what to say, I mumbled a few words: "I'm glad you returned when you did, John." He didn't say anything; he simply acted as if nothing had happened.

It wasn't long after that that John, Fred, and I became known as the miracle-working threesome. There wasn't a job too difficult for the three of us to handle, thanks to False Reality.

With access to state-of-the-art technology, I was better equipped to achieve my life's goal than when I was with World Construction. There wasn't an organization that came close to producing with our expeditiousness. Dealing in the outlandish or embarking upon uncharted territories became commonplace in our line of work.

I truly enjoyed what I was doing. My life here at the Main Complex was no different than anyone else's life. Actually, I was better off than most people who had to forge an existence in this socialistic society.

I wanted to make a confession to John about the memory-scan. I believed that he would defend me because of our friendship and my ability to produce; he benefited from my labor as much as I did. But encouraging him to look into a situation that could cause my detriment would be foolish. I found myself reconfirming my belief that John wouldn't allow anything to interfere with what we were doing.

At one time I considered telling Fred about Amanda's threats; he could possibly have my file changed. He knew all the right people in all the right places. But that would mean telling him about the Freeman family and Peaceful Valley. The more people who knew, the greater the chances of it being used against me in the future. I would keep it to myself and take my chances with John.

One afternoon, I received a call from John asking me to come to his office. "Lance," John began in his normal tone, "If this may be of any consolation, Amanda has been demoted to labor status and transferred to the labor camp.

"During her trial she emphasized a matter involving your case that I'm finally forced to address. Because it's strictly a security measure and has nothing to do with your ability to produce, coupled with the month or so you would have to be away from the job, I've hesitated about addressing this matter in the past. But recently, and with some persistence, colleagues of mine have insisted that I rectify the matter. Due to a recent policy, written by Amanda, and just recently initiated, it's impossible to ignore it any longer. This new policy states: *All personnel transferred from a labor camp must maintain a thorough analysis of a memory-scan within his/her file.*

"In your case, I have taken great pains to obtain a special provision to circumvent the policy. Give me your testimony of the days in question, I will enter that information into your file and the matter will be permanently resolved."

I was trying to come up with an answer that would satisfy his request and not incriminate me further. In the few seconds that I had, I couldn't come up with a thing. I finally rationalized that if the memory-scan failed once, I would chance it failing again.

"John, I'm sure you know that Amanda has asked me that question a number of times. She's also threatened me with the labor camp and solitary confinement. I have to tell you the same thing I told her, if the memory-scan failed to reveal a comprehensive account of those days in question, how can I possibly remember?

"Look, John, I can't imagine anything I could have done within a 48-hour period—almost two years ago, mind you—that would be of such a detriment to the State that it might nullify what we are doing now."

"I agree with you, Lance. I also wish your answer would satisfy the stipulations in the new policy, but it won't.

"Here's what I'll do. I'll make an appointment for you to have a memory-scan thirty days from today. Between now and then, if you give me a sworn declaration about the missing days in question, I will resolve the matter forthwith. If you can't, then I'll proceed with the memory-scan. That way, everyone will be satisfied that those days weren't of any relevance."

It was obvious I had misplaced my trust in two dispensable beliefs, my ability to produce and trusting an adversary. Believing that a State Official would forsake his allegiance to the State for me was foolish. I was now compelled to live with the results of my self-deception and there wasn't anything I could do to change it now.

Over the next two weeks John inquired about the two days in question on several occasions. One time while we were alone in an elevator he asked me about the matter. "Lance, there's got to be something you can remember about those days surrounding your arrest. Maybe you were with a girl and she slipped something into your drink? I don't know; but there's got to be an explanation."

I wasn't sure if he was offering me an alibi or simply expressing his disbelief. "There was only one girl in my life, John, and she was out of the country at the time."

A few days later he approached me in the office. "This is beginning to puzzle me, Lance. Last night I studied the results of your last memory-scan and there is no logical explanation for the results it provides. Everything is legible up to the time you went to sleep two days before your arrest. It's from that point on that things become obscure. It picks up again with your conversation between the arresting agents when you returned home, and they firmly testify that you were not intoxicated."

"John, as much as I would like to tell you what happened, I can't remember a thing!" I lied in the most convincing portrayal I could muster, but he was not impressed. He glared directly at me, and without a word, he turned and walked away.

I had done nothing but create suspicion and doubt. Even if I told John the truth, he wouldn't accept it now. He was determined to find out what took place during those two days surrounding my arrest.

I had two weeks left. If I didn't come up with an idea soon, there wouldn't be any time left to come up with one. I had bungled all the tricks in my hat and there weren't any left.

One evening after returning to our quarters from a dinner engagement with Monique I turned on the radio and whispered in her ear: "I believe I've finally discovered a safe way to get out of here." Before I could continue she interrupted me. "Look, Lance," she countered in a voice louder than I cared to discuss an escape plan. So, before she could go any further I asked her to lower her voice. "I don't care to talk about that," she continued in a whisper. "Why are you so hung up on this business of escaping anyway? I have enough on my mind without worrying about that kind of foolishness.

"You should have enough to worry about, too, with all the work they've been dumping on you lately. Besides," she continued, sweetening her tone, "it was such a lovely evening. Please, let's not spoil it with such talk. Okay, Lance?"

I understood what she was telling me but I wanted to be certain: "Do you ever intend to leave this place, Monique?"

"Well, yes. But where would we go? What would we do when we got there? Let's be realistic about this, Lance. I've worked all of my life to reach where I am today. I love working with computers, and I'm naturally gifted with numbers. If I apply these talents, I can truly advance the cause of all humanity; it's my reasonable contribution to Gaia for the life and the talents she's given me. And you want me to disregard everything for a selfish impulse?"

Before I could comment she continued.

"Furthermore, *if* we escaped—and that is a huge if—we would be wanted by the authorities and hounded for the rest of our lives. And if... I should say, and *when* they caught us they would either kill us instantly or bring us back to the labor camp to be tortured to death. *If*—and here is another mighty big if—*if* they allowed us to live, they would never trust us again; we would never be permitted to work in any complex again—I couldn't take it in another labor camp, Lance.

"But that is only my situation, what about you? You're not doing too badly here. I mean, you are *the* number one man in your field. If a building project is desired, no matter how high their greatness, no matter how extravagant, absurd, or frugal their desire, they *must* come to Lance Roberts. The State *needs* you, the same as the State *needs* me. Don't you understand, this is our fate; this is our calling in life?"

I stopped her, "I understand. Believe me, Monique, I understand." And I did understand. I recalled the Elite's words, *Each state of life must be trained within strict limits corresponding to its destination and work in life. The occasional genius will always manage to slip through into other states of life. They will rejoice that we have regulated everything in their lives as all wise parents who desire to train their children in the cause of duty and submission.*

For the first time in Monique's life she realized that she was needed. She was accomplishing her objective and I was asking her to disregard it. I couldn't blame her. Had this been three weeks earlier, and she asked me to escape, I would have argued against it as strongly as she had.

I had deviated entirely from my original plan. Once again I was offering my life as an instrument to further entrench a diabolical system designed, constructed, and sustained by a diabolical force. Until now, I hadn't realized how far I had fallen.

It took this conversation to make me realize that I was the one who had lost direction, not Monique. She hadn't vowed against furthering the destructive forces of the Elite, I had. It took a major threat and Monique's honesty for me to come to my senses. I had regressed to chasing a dream; the same old childhood dream that I thought I had put to rest. If this was truly what I wanted, I should have kept my secure position at World Construction.

There was something Monique didn't understand, though. Even in the case of her father, she never fully realized the grave adversity the Elite was committing against humanity. For decades they had devastated the earth, and every living creature on it. Everything on earth suffered under the vile hand of the Elite.

It was difficult to accept that *I* was the only one aware of what was taking place. I remembered how appalled I was when I learned about the Elite and what they were doing. Ironically everyone I told refused to believe it, or they accepted it as the way of life. Was I the only one right and everyone else wrong? I wondered if taking advantage of others was truly the intended way of life.

Suddenly Mr. Freeman came to mind. "No!" I heard myself shout aloud. There *are* people who understand. The people living in Peaceful Valley knew that the human race couldn't exist by devouring itself, and so they lived their lives opposing everything the Elite's secular system represented. My determination had been revived. Again, I vowed to devote my efforts to escaping and returning to Peaceful Valley.

The next morning Monique and I attended the Sunday service together. It was obvious to me that our discussion the night before had created a chasm between us. We were going in different directions, and because of it, I was at a definite disadvantage. If I angered Monique, or she sought to gain favor with the authorities, she could easily tell them my plan. I would certainly be confined to a cell, or maybe executed.

Suddenly one of Haile's warnings came to mind: *"An accomplice may hinder your escape and cause more trouble than help!"*

I had foolishly taken Monique into my confidence. But now that I was on my own, I wasn't obligated to Monique any longer. Knowing that she wasn't my responsibility gave me a sense of relief. I felt as if a weight had been lifted.

All of this, however, was secondary to the threat of undergoing another memory-scan. The authorities would not only learn what took place the 48 hours before my arrest, they would even know my immediate thoughts.

Again, Haile's words of advice came to mind: *"You have a plan within you. You must search within yourself until you discover the way that is perfect for you. When the time is right, and you will know that time, execute your plan with precision."* When I sensed the time was right, I would make my escape.

Fred and I had made an appointment to play a game of racquetball that Saturday. This had been a long, hard week for me. Accepting my position with Monique didn't help matters any. A good game of racquetball would clear my mind and refresh me physically.

I still enjoyed Fred's company, and the games we played together always brought out the best in me. My game had improved considerably. Fred could only beat me three out of five games. He was still the better player, but he had to vigorously compete to win. I appreciated his skill, and continued to seek his advice to help improve my game. Because we both loved the sport, we were able to enjoy each other's competitiveness on the court without allowing our feelings to become involved.

While dressing in the locker room, I asked Fred if he still had his glider. He told me he did. I asked him if he would send it up to me later that evening so that I could see exactly what he had.

"Why the sudden renewed interest in my glider, Lance?" he asked, taking me by surprise.

"Well, Fred, I've caught up on most of my work at the office, and Monique's been attending a supervisor's training session every night of the week. I thought it would be nice to check it out and reminisce about the good old days. Is something wrong with that?" I asked, hoping to dispel his curiosity.

"No, just wondering. It's been a long time since you've asked to see it. But tonight's not a good night, Lance. I'm scheduled for a dinner party with Suzann and her friends, and I'd prefer she didn't know anything about this. How about Monday evening, after work; is seven o'clock all right?"

"That's fine with me. I'll send the rope down at seven sharp. Attach the glider, give the rope a little tug to let me know it's secure, and then I'll haul it up. I'm looking forward to see what you have, Fred. If you were as good hang gliding as you are playing racquetball, you had to be one of the best."

Before we parted, I told Fred how much I appreciated his friendship, and how helpful he had been the past few months. As I reached out my hand to shake his, he pulled me to him and gave me a manly hug to let me know how much he appreciated our friendship.

The project I was working on needed three maps. I filled out all the necessary request forms to place the order. However, instead of requesting only the three maps needed for the job, I requested five. Three were for the project I was working on, and two were to be used for my escape.

John was the one who approved my request for ordering materials. He had never questioned any requisition I made in the past, but now that there was a rift between us I wasn't sure what his reaction to my requests might be. I filled out the Material Request Form as usual. If the additional maps aroused John's curiosity, I was prepared to give him a valid reason for ordering them. Although I was positive that no one knew what I was doing, fear of being caught kept me in a state of paranoia.

Monique was being promoted to a supervisory position, and she was scheduled to attend a supervisor's training session every evening for the next two weeks. Her advancement to State Official status had also been approved and her superiors wanted to award her the advancement and promotion together.

I had planned to escape Friday, three days before the date of my memory-scan. Fred and I had arranged for him to send me the glider tonight, but Monique hadn't made any preparations to leave for her session. "Aren't you due to attend a training session tonight?" I asked nonchalantly.

Her answer caused me to panic: "I have an awful headache. I believe I'll go upstairs and lie down."

I didn't know what I was going to do. According to our arrangement, Fred was sending up the glider in thirty minutes. I suggested to Monique that it wouldn't be to her advantage to miss a training session, but she shunned my advice. "I don't feel good, and they can wait for me for a change," she retorted.

The thought of her finding out about the glider brought back the same fears I had experienced earlier that day at work. With her in the bedroom, I wouldn't dare try to get the glider from Fred.

I tried to contact Fred a couple of times to cancel our plans until further notice but he wasn't in. Suzann told me that he was due back any time, and that she had an appointment but would leave a message for him to contact me as soon as he returned. Since I had cancelled so many arrangements to get the glider before, I felt if I reneged this time Fred might not give me another opportunity.

At the last minute Monique changed her mind and agreed to attend the training session. As soon as the elevator door shut, I ran up the stairs to prepare the rope. I had to make it out of sheets, by tying them together.

At seven sharp, according to our arrangement, I dropped the knotted sheets over the edge of the balcony. I felt the tension from the weight of the glider as Fred secured it. Without a word, he connected the glider and gave a hard tug to let me know it was clear for me to pull it up.

I hauled up the large black case and set it on the bed. My heart seemed to beat through my shirt as I carefully unzipped the leather container. It was a Klassic glider made of camouflaged Mylar; one of the best custom gliders designed. Included in the case were a weather-resistant flight suit, gloves, goggles, and helmet. A small tool kit containing a special navigational instrument that was capable of telling me how to fly, an air speed indicator, a compass, and binoculars were arranged neatly in a small leather satchel inside. All I needed were the maps I had selected, enough provisions for at least three days, and I could be on my way to Peaceful Valley.

I carefully concealed the glider on my side of the closet along with my sports equipment. Since Monique never looked on my side of the closet, I felt confident she wouldn't detect it. The monthly inspection of our quarters had been the week before and wouldn't pose a threat for another three weeks.

The next morning at work I waited for the five maps to be delivered to my office. Asking for them would only draw attention and I wasn't about to do that. I needed three of the maps for the project I was working on, so all I could do was wait.

The two additional maps I ordered were vital for my escape. One of them showed Camp 1100 and the surrounding area, the other showed the highways and mountain terrain, covering a thousand-mile perimeter all the way to the coastline. While working for World Construction, I designed a home security system that was capable of detecting an intruder within a one-mile radius of a structure. I was prepared to explain to John that the reason I took the liberty of ordering the extra maps was to design a device that would enhance the security system and eliminate the guard patrols completely. After all, I was in this position because I was capable of making competent decisions with the least amount of supervision.

Right before lunch the maps were delivered to my office. Their arrival meant that John approved them. Either he hadn't examined the requisition thoroughly or he was setting a trap. If it was a trap I would have to deal with it when the time came. There weren't many options for me at this point, either I continued as planned or I allowed fear to influence my decision.

After making copies of the two maps that I needed, I carefully folded them and then placed them in my shoes. During lunch, I studied the original maps, making the necessary notes and drawings of the direction I intended to go. I had completed a diagram of a flight plan over the mountains and to my destination. I also hid this information in my shoes along with the maps.

It was mid fall and the perfect time of year for long-distance flying. I had competed in cross-country flying on a number of occasions and was confident I could make it to Peaceful Valley in 3 days or less. I planned to maintain a height of no less than 4,500 feet. If I flew during daylight hours I would be visible to aircraft, even with the camouflaged coloring of the sail. With the exception of launches and landings, I wasn't worried about being seen from the ground.

Flying at night would be difficult and extremely dangerous; however, darkness would eliminate the threat of being seen. I would have to fly all night, find a landing zone at daybreak that would also double for a launch, or at least be close to a location where I could launch. Considering my two options, I concluded that night would limit my chances of being detected, although it wasn't the safest time to travel.

Through the World Wide Web, I downloaded all the information I could find on night flying and studied them thoroughly. I also copied every flying scenario I could find and started using them to make practice flights in False Reality.

Through these practice flights I quickly realized that identifying distinguishing landmarks would be impossible at night and navigating by the stars would be difficult. This would limit me to the special navigational instrument and compass, and so I also downloaded the latest information on this navigational instrument and studied it thoroughly. It was considered to be state of the art in navigating devices. It was actually supposed to think for me and tell me exactly how to fly. That also meant I needed easy access to my flashlight to read the instruments while flying. These kinds of thoughts bombarded me, but with the vast information I was able to extract from the Internet, I was able to solve these problems one by one.

Monique had left a note telling me that she would be working late, and from there she would go straight to her training session, so I ate alone. When I finished, I climbed the spiral staircase, walked through the bedroom and out onto the terrace. Other than a stiff breeze, it was a beautiful, cool, moonlit, starry night.

Being well rested, I decided to watch a movie. Unable to find anything that interested me in the movie schedule I decided to take a shower, hoping it would extinguish my restlessness. I pressed the button to the control panel and the wall moved, revealing the bathroom and then the closet area. My glance diverted to my side of the closet and rested on the items that concealed the glider. Suddenly a thought struck me like an electric current. I bounded over to the closet and started removing the glider. Only one thought consumed me now: *I'm out of here!*

Because of the winds, I assembled the glider flat on the terrace. From experience, I knew it was best not to erect the control bar into flying position until I was ready to launch. When I had the glider set up, I went back into the bedroom and packed thermal underwear, three shirts and three pairs of jeans, a down jacket, and hiking boots. I placed everything in the backpack that came with the kit. I went down to the kitchen and sliced some turkey, got a block of cheese, a roll of salami, a loaf of bread, crackers, a container of vitamins, and filled both canteens with water.

I returned to the bedroom, packed the food items with the rest of my belongings and put on the weather-resistant suit. After that I arranged everything back in its usual place, studied the maps and stepped out onto the terrace, closing the glass doors behind me. I confirmed the course I planned to take, then secured the flashlight to my right forearm, the special navigational instrument, airspeed indicator, and compass to my other forearm above my watch, and then tucked the maps into my gloves.

Maneuvering the picnic table into a position against the railing that extended the outer perimeter of the terrace created a perfect launch pad. I made a circular walk around the glider to complete my preflight inspection, and then I erected the control bar into its flying position. While climbing onto the top of the picnic table I could feel that the glider was a little tail heavy so I held the nose slightly elevated and the wings level. I draped the Trimmer on the outside of the control bar, performed a hook in check, and eased the control frame out for lift-off, simultaneously taking three quick steps across the table, over the railing, and out into space. It was like an elevator going straight up, and the 196-story building was quickly distanced beneath me.

The glider handled the launch with ease; due to its tight rigging it behaved quite reasonably for the windy conditions. The thermals were turbulent and as soon as I stopped climbing I decided to go on course. It wasn't until then, with the Main Complex far beneath and behind me that my heart stopped its sledge-hammer pounding. From the instant I stepped into midair there was no turning back, even if I wanted to. At last, I was able to admit to myself with conviction that I was free; I was on my way to Peaceful Valley.

By checking the instruments, the compass, and the map I determined that I was heading in the right direction, southwest. The full moon afforded me a clear outline of the tops of the mountains I had to cross in order to reach my destination. If I maintained my height, currently at 5,300 feet, there wouldn't be any problem clearing the mountains.

I relied on the instruments to maintain my direction, keep me on course and up to speed. A *beep, beep* sound emanated from the navigational instrument. Checking it revealed that I needed to fly faster to maintain my speed, so I pulled in on the bar. A *deep, deep* meant not so fast, and a *burp, burp* meant slow down. I finally became synchronized with the instruments and was quite surprised to discover that flying at night proved to be no more difficult than flying during the day.

My watch read eleven o'clock. I had been flying for over four hours with plenty of time before dawn. I would have to land at first light to avoid the possibility of being seen. The State had now centralized the people into individual colonies or islands as they were referred to, which removed my fear of inadvertently coming upon campers or travelers.

The United Nations Environment Program was the force behind the Environmental Protection Agency that monitored emissions and made recommendations for controlling pollution. The strategic goal, under the guise of emissions control, was to completely eliminate the internal combustion engine in order to restrict people's ability to travel, thus keeping them confined to the island communities.

Erroneous propaganda campaigns by the EPA convinced the world that America's industry, utilities, and automobiles accounted for over three-fourths of all sulfur and carbon dioxide emissions and more than

50 percent of all greenhouse gas emissions. Supposedly to help curb pollution and impede global warming and acid rain, the State conformably established stringent environmental controls.

They also implemented a preposterous EPA acid rain-emissions trading program directed toward removing older model cars. Polluters were able to buy stock certificates from the government for a cost that was considerably less than the cost of installing expensive vapor-control equipment or removing sulfur dioxide from the air. These certificates could then be traded for another emission source that was less costly to reduce, such as a large number of used cars four years old or older that were claimed to emit an equivalent amount of pollution. Junking the cars removed them from the streets and eliminated their ability to spread toxin, while the major polluters were allowed to continue spewing their pollution as usual.

Although the attack on automobiles was worldwide, the focus was primarily on the United States. To further effectuate this goal, policies were implemented to make the cost of operating automobiles too expensive for all but a privileged few.

Progressive gasoline taxes, pay at the pump insurance costs, six-month smog checks with increasing emissions standards, and other such tacked-on charges reaped billions of dollars for the government on an annual basis. This also resulted in most vehicles over four years old failing the stringent emissions requirements, which immediately rendered them inoperative and candidates to be junked through the EPA's acid rain-emissions program. Likewise, this escalated the overall cost of operating a vehicle far beyond the reach of the average person. Knowing these facts helped dismiss my fears of possibly being seen by a random driver.

By 4:00 a.m. the mountains were far behind me. I was growing sleepy and starting to tire. My ability to fly this long was due to the practice sessions in False Reality and the good shape I was in from playing racquetball with Fred.

Approximately two hours of flying time remained and I found myself looking at my watch repeatedly. My mind was wandering aimlessly so I directed my focus on the people who had affected my life for the past year. I thought about Monique and what would happen when she reported my disappearance. The authorities would not be pleased, and I was sure she would be interrogated intensely. But Monique was a needed entity; the State wasn't about to deprive itself of her genius merely because I had escaped. She could only tell them that I was gone when she returned from her work assignment and that I might be headed for a place I called Peaceful Valley. With regret, I was forced to admit that Monique was content under the conditions of the totalitarian, New Age New World Order and she would never adapt to the type of environment in which the Freemans lived.

I didn't know if my escape would have any negative effect on John's position. He was my immediate supervisor and therefore responsible for my security, but he also maintained a high degree of notability within the Region.

Fred was the real victim. I had actually stolen his glider and there was no way of me avoiding that fact. And yet, knowing Fred as I did, he would rejoice over my escape. If the guard that performed the monthly search of his quarters admitted to concealing Fred's glider by informing on him, his confession would be his own ruin as well.

Fred was a seasoned warrior and would thumb his nose at whatever punishment the authorities threatened him with. If he was upset with me at all, it was only because I didn't take him with me, not because I had taken his glider. Undoubtedly he would be questioned extensively. Unless given a memory-scan, which was unlikely under the circumstances, it would never be known that Fred owned a glider and he would probably come out of this all right.

With Amanda banished to the labor camp, she didn't have any way of knowing that I had escaped. If someone like Hal Copeland were cruel enough to tell her, she would probably self-destruct on the spot.

I pitied them. They were caught up in a fabricated world contrived by the most satanic perpetrators ever to take a breath of air. And yet, they had been deceived and I hadn't. I made a knowledgeable choice to further the cause of the most insidious enemies ever known to humanity; and I did it strictly for personal advancement. Surpassing my pity for them was remorse for my disloyalty to humanity and myself.

The dawn's light began to brighten the sky behind me, and I knew that I was going in the right direction. To confirm my position, I checked the compass to make sure I was still on course.

It was time to start looking for a landing zone, preferably one that would double as a launch pad. I was having a little difficulty getting down; there were still lifts everywhere. At five forty-five I spotted a steep, grassy knoll about a mile beyond a group of trees. Since I hadn't seen any signs of a community for miles, I headed in that direction. Managing to find a sink, I was able to fly my downwind leg, base over the trees, and make a dive into my final descent. Just before I got to the top of the hill, I flared and made a perfect two-step landing.

I didn't bother to break down the glider but I did secure it firmly. The camouflage coloring would make it almost impossible to detect from the air, and I wouldn't have to reassemble it before launching. Totally exhausted, I removed my backpack, slipped underneath one of the wings of the glider and lay down. By now the sun had cleared the horizon, absorbing most of the chill with its ascension. It wasn't long before I was overcome with sleep.

I woke up eight hours later, very hungry. A few swallows of water washed down the turkey and cheese, bread, and vitamins. I pulled the binoculars from my pack and studied my surroundings for anything unordinary. Satisfied that all was well, I sat down in the grass to calculate the distance I had traveled and conclude how much farther I had to go.

I left the Main Complex at seven thirty the night before and landed around five forty-five the following morning; approximately ten hours and fifteen minutes. Averaging 45 miles per hour, I had traveled close to four hundred and fifty miles, covering slightly over half of the distance to my destination. I could easily go the remaining distance by morning if I flew all night. I doubted that the authorities would send out a search party before dawn, which would give me at least a nine-hour head start. Not knowing which way I went, it would be impossible to determine my location without using a satellite surveillance camera.

Part of my plan was physical exercise: stretches, knee bends and toe touches, jumping jacks, and push-ups. It was essential that I maintain good blood circulation. This would also help to keep my joints and muscles from becoming stiff.

Sleep would be my biggest enemy; fatigue would be next. I needed strength and stamina to sustain me during the long, grueling flight ahead. Being suspended in mid-air for another night would be exceptionally taxing both physically and mentally.

The winds were picking up and the sun was sliding down the side of the sky. It was time to go. I ate enough to satisfy my hunger, and then I attached the pack to my back, the flashlight and the instruments to my forearms, and climbed into the harness. I maneuvered the glider into the best position for takeoff, took three steps toward the cliff side of the knoll and the ground instantly distanced beneath me. I found good lifts everywhere, but they carried a slight southeast drift, so going up also meant going a little off course. When I felt the cold air that is usually prevalent at cloud-base, I steadied my course. Again, I was in full flight.

By midnight I was growing weary. I needed to do something to stimulate my mind. One of my favorite songs came to mind, so I sang it three times before singing another. One by one I sang song after song until I grew tired of singing and couldn't remember any songs. I began reciting poetry, and eventually resorted to any technique that would keep me alert and on course.

By 4:30 a.m., I was physically exhausted. My arms and legs started to stiffen. I was now maneuvering by sheer determination of will. I knew I would lose control of the glider if I continued much longer.

While straining through the darkness to see what lay beneath me, I spotted a cluster of lights. Caution signals went off immediately, snapping me out of my weary condition. The last thing I needed was to fly into an island community full of people.

With all I could muster, I forced my body to make the necessary flying adjustments. I was able to make a quarter turn, which took me slightly off course but allowed me to avoid the community. Using every ounce of my strength, I pressed on for another hour.

Sighting the town stimulated me mentally, but not physically. My body simply refused to cooperate; my limbs were completely numb. Then, from the corner of my eye, I saw the long-awaited gray of dawn. Seeing the dawn breaking over the edge of the horizon, pulling the daylight behind it, encouraged me.

A forest of trees covered the ground beneath me as far as I could see, with no landing zones in sight. I was forced to keep flying at the risk of a crash-landing. Dangling from a high limb unable to get down, or even worse, breaking a bone, were only a couple of misfortunes that could bring my journey and possibly my life to an end. I decided to go on until I spotted a clearing. A few miles farther, I noticed a small section of clear land. It would make a perfect landing zone if I could drop down over the tops of the trees. Under normal conditions it would be difficult to perform such a landing safely. In my present state, it was impossible to maneuver the glider properly. But I didn't have any choice in the matter since this was the only landing zone in sight.

With all the will I could summon, I forced my body to guide the glider toward the opening ahead. I based over the trees in order to make a hard dive into my final descent. The ground was rushing up to meet me entirely too fast. I flared hard, but it was too late. I hit the ground, sending both the glider and me tumbling. The sudden shock brought mobility back to my rigid body. I was shaken, but not hurt.

Picking up the twisted frame, I dragged the shattered remains of the glider to a covering of trees close by. I was totally exhausted and I collapsed beside a fallen tree. From fear of being seen, I burrowed myself beneath the camouflage material and fell into a deep sleep.

Hours later a rustling noise woke me. I opened my eyes just in time to see a skunk waddling off into the opposite direction. Since it was broad daylight, my first thought was that the skunk might be rabid. My second thought caused me to sniff the air, relieved to know that he hadn't released his sickening perfume. My body was stiff and a little sore from the tumble but that was the extent of my inconvenience.

It was noon, and I was hungry. There was still plenty of food and water. Although my taste buds preferred something tastier, my hunger demanded food, regardless of the taste.

I was sitting in the middle of no man's land, leaning against a fallen tree, eating salami and cheese and drinking water from a canteen to quench my thirst. My sole determination was to find a family I had met only once, almost two years before. What was more ironic was that they lived in a place they affectionately called Peaceful Valley, without a clue of its location indicated on an official map. The fact that I was familiar with the surrounding area was my only certainty of finding Peaceful Valley.

I checked my belongings to make sure everything was still intact, and then I changed into a fresh set of clothes. According to my estimate, I could reach Peaceful Valley by nightfall. Once I determined what direction to go, I put on the backpack and started walking due west through the trees until I reached a clearing. I stopped every other hour for a five-minute rest to help prevent exhaustion and give me time to assess my position.

I had been walking a couple of hours when I noticed a reflection from a moving object in the distance. I pulled out my binoculars to investigate. The flicker of light was the sun reflecting off the window of a passing car. According to my map, this was highway 59, which connected to Beaver Road, the only paved road in the vicinity of Peaceful Valley. I was far enough away to avoid being seen from a passing car and yet still able to see the highway for a guide to keep me on course.

As I walked, I regularly surveyed the highway through the binoculars. Finally, after three hours, I spotted a directional sign. The next turn off was Beaver Road, the only road that allowed access through the pass, which led down into Peaceful Valley.

It was 3 o'clock. It would be difficult finding the Freemans' house in the dark, so I wanted to reach Peaceful Valley before nightfall. Following the road at a distance brought me close to where I had buried my coins. I figured the coins could be useful, particularly if I was unable to find the Freemans.

I counted each step and calculated each turn. The boulder marking the spot was still there. I pulled a screwdriver from the toolkit and dug until I struck the metal box that I had buried over two years before. I put the coins into my backpack and returned to the road.

Before approaching the pass leading into the valley, I positioned myself upon a ridge and carefully appraised the town. I couldn't detect any signs of activity anywhere. Positive that I was entering a ghost town, I trotted down the dusty road leading into the town.

By the time I reached the Freemans' gas station it was dusk. I searched the premises without a clue. The gas station was nothing more than an empty shell. As I continued, I noticed that most of the structures made of wood had been burned to the ground. I began to feel like my surroundings looked: hopeless, desolate, and full of despair.

I continued cautiously through the empty streets toward the Freemans' house. I didn't know if they had left on their own initiative or were forced to flee. They could have been captured by the authorities or killed by looters, I didn't know. I only hoped their house would give me a clue that might answer my questions.

The dwellings that weren't burned to the ground were vandalized, and all of the windows were broken out. I decided to randomly examine a few of the houses that were still standing to see if I could determine whether the occupants were forced to leave, or left of their own accord.

I carefully investigated the interior of a few of the houses that were still intact. Because of the lack of debris I figured that the residents had removed all of their belongings before any of the looters had arrived. Had vandals taken them by surprise, some evidence of their personal belongings would still be there. I was certain these houses had been cleaned before they were vacated. Those who came to Peaceful Valley to pillage and plunder left empty-handed.

Many of the street signs had been spray-painted and covered with graffiti, or purposely turned the wrong direction to misdirect anyone passing through. It appeared like an act of revenge against the townsfolk for not making themselves and their belongings available for plunder.

The rapidly fading light and the inability to read the street signs added to the difficulty of finding the Freemans' property. I had only visited them once, and that was during daylight hours.

When I found the structure still standing and intact, I was overjoyed. I made a thorough search of the dwelling and found it to be spotless. Just as the other residents of Peaceful Valley, the Freemans had carefully removed their belongings from the premises. Learning that they left by their own free will renewed my hope of finding them alive. Suddenly Mr. Freeman's words echoed in my mind, *"If we have to, we'll move up higher into the mountains, above that place where you used to fly that kite of yours."*

It was too dark to continue, so I found a spot to sleep until morning. The night was growing cold, and I was thankful for the shelter. After getting a bite to eat, I bundled up as best I could and slept until dawn.

The next morning I ate the last of the salami and bread. Only a small piece of cheese and a small amount of turkey and water remained. I recalled that the Freemans had a pond in the back of their house. If it was still intact, I intended to bathe.

The water in the pond was cold, but I washed myself thoroughly and put on another of the clean changes of clothing I had brought with me. Regardless of my appearance, I felt better with a clean body under the clean clothes.

I had at least a two-hour walk before reaching the foot of the mountain where I believed the Freemans were now living. If possible, I wanted to reach the mountain and then climb it before nightfall.

I recalled that it took me about 30 minutes to get from the place I used to fly my glider to the Freemans' house in town that night they invited me for dinner. I was driving a car, and averaging 30 miles an hour. To determine the distance from the Freemans to the mountain, and the time it would take on foot, took a simple calculation. Greta and I used to walk five miles a day as a part of our daily exercise program. If we walked at a good pace we would easily cover five miles in an hour. By my watch it was 6:30 a.m. If I left now, I could reach the base of the mountain by five o'clock that evening.

I started on the last leg of my journey with renewed vigor. My spirits were high even though I was making my way through a maze of destruction. It seemed to symbolize the life I was leaving behind. I wanted to erase the thoughts of the Elite and all the devastation they had perpetrated upon the earth and the countless lives they had destroyed because of their lust for power. Every step took me further from the past and closer to the new life of freedom that I was seeking.

I didn't know much about religion. The little I did know confirmed that the Freemans' beliefs were more in agreement with what I believed. They described their God as a loving God who created the universe and everything in it. The so-called *Most Holy* was a self-proclaimed god. He forced allegiance on people, and demanded them to worship him. None of it fit my idea of God; that is, the God I always imagined God to be like.

I had met Mr. Freeman only once, but during that occasion he had thoroughly explained to me what he believed. From what I heard, I couldn't find anything that I didn't agree with. What stood out more than anything else was the fact that they were giving, loving people.

It was getting dark when I reached the foot of the mountain. To stop now meant that I wouldn't reach the Freemans until the following day. My food supply was down to a piece of cheese, and my water was almost gone. With every ounce of strength, I determined to keep going.

I climbed until I reached the spot from where I used to jump with my glider. Even in the rapidly fading light, the valley was a beautiful sight to behold. I stood there marveling over the glorious sight below; many hours were spent soaring these skies.

The impending night had now darkened my side of the mountain completely. I drew the flashlight from my backpack, secured it to my wrist and resumed my climb. Even though the most difficult part of the climb was behind me, it was extremely dangerous climbing at night. I carefully examined each footing before applying my full body weight. Very cautiously, I made my way up the side of the mountain. Unable to see little more than the small lighted area in front of me made the climb a slow, tedious job.

I felt that I should save the last of my water until I reached the top or found a stream where I could replenish my supply. My fingers and toes were growing numb due to the extreme cold that increased with the steady, blowing wind. With a fixed determination, I continued up the mountain.

It was 4:30 a.m. I had climbed through the night, taking only a few short rests. Finally my flashlight revealed flat ground and the trunk of a tree instead of the dry shrubbery that covered the mountainside. It was the beginning of a forest that ran along the outer edge of the mountain for a quarter mile in both directions. I made my way through the trees until I found a clearing. Too exhausted to go any farther, I stumbled to the ground and collapsed, falling fast asleep.

The sound of a dog barking woke me up. I was lying on my stomach, with my head resting upon my arm. When I opened my eyes the first things I saw were two black boots about a foot away. Following the boots upward, I looked directly into the eyes of Mr. Freeman. I couldn't think of anyone that I wanted to see more than him. He was standing over me holding the dog firmly by a leash.

"It's about time you woke up, son," he said in jest. "I thought maybe you'd planned to sleep here all day."

"How did you find me?" I asked, awkwardly climbing to my feet.

"John Jr. and his dog found you over an hour ago. He was sure it was you. I didn't want to alarm the townsfolk, so I personally came to check it out for myself. I just got here and was about to see if you were all right when the dog started barking and woke you up."

"I'm glad to see you, Mr. Freeman."

"Come on," he said, reaching down to give me a hand. "Sara's been keeping a plate of food warm for you in the oven. When you've had your fill of a good meal, then you can tell me how you got here, and where you've been hiding since I last saw you."

We walked about a hundred yards before turning onto a dirt road. The forest was now on our right and extended to the edge of the mountain. On our left was a stretch of bare land that extended about 50 yards before reaching cultivated farmland. From where we stood at the edge of the road, as far as I could see, lay acres of farmland.

As we walked, Mr. Freeman pointed out the pastures, the various orchards and the different kinds of crops they had harvested. He directed my attention to certain sections, explaining the planting procedure and the times of harvest.

"Being fall," he continued, "we've already harvested most of the crops. Altogether there's about a thousand acres of farmland up here. Behind that, there's a stretch of empty land that ends at the base of those snow-peaked mountains towering in the distance. It's good land, son. The Lord's given us more than enough to carry us through the winter."

We followed the road for half a mile until we reached a community of about a hundred individual properties. These people were farmers, tillers of the ground, keepers of livestock, and they were perfectly content producing their sustenance from the land.

The farther into town we went, the larger the gathering of people grew to greet us. A fresh smile appeared on Mr. Freeman's face with each group of people that approached us. Each time he introduced me, he exhibited a sentiment of kinship, as if I was a lost relative who had been miraculously found.

"This is Lance Roberts, the lad we've all been praying for these past two years," Mr. Freeman expressed to each new throng of people we encountered.

I'd done a lot of traveling and met a lot of people during my lifetime, but I hadn't smiled so much and shaken so many hands with such genuine sincerity as I did while walking down that dusty road with Mr. Freeman.

When we arrived at the cabin, Mr. Freeman led me to the water pump out back. Reaching into a box, he handed me a bar of homemade soap. "I'm glad to see you, son," he told me while pumping the water. "The only way you could have made it here is by the grace of God." Then he bowed his head and prayed, "I thank you, Lord, for giving Lance Roberts guidance and protection. You must really love him, Lord. Amen."

I followed Mr. Freeman into the cabin where the rest of the family stood in front of the large dining room table. Mrs. Freeman broke the silence by stepping forward with her arms open wide and greeting me with a warm hug, "Thank God, you're all right. When John Jr. told us he found you, we weren't sure if it was really you; although he insisted that it was. Then we weren't sure if you were alive or not, since he didn't stay long enough to find out; he was in such a hurry to get back to tell his dad. That's when big John said he'd better go see for himself. Yes. I thank God you're all right."

Her sincere display of graciousness overwhelmed me. "Thank you for your concern, Mrs. Freeman. I really appreciate it."

John Jr. was right behind her, offering his hand for me to shake. "Glad to see you, Mr. Roberts. I sure would like to hear all about where you've been, and the things you did while you've been gone. You gonna tell us what happened?"

I reached out and took his hand and shook it firmly. "I sure will, John Jr., every detail."

Mike and Mark came over to greet me next. "How old are you now, Mark?" I asked the youngest boy as he looked up at me.

"Almost eleven."

"You're almost eleven?" I responded with a look of surprise. "Let me see, that means that Jenny *is* eleven, Mike's fifteen, John Jr's eighteen, and Sara's twenty-two. You've all grown into lovely young ladies and handsome young men."

"How did you remember all of our names and ages?" Mark asked unbelievingly.

"Oh, a little something I learned a long time ago."

Mike reached out to shake my hand. "What did you do with that car you were driving when we first met you? I sure wanted to go for a ride in it."

"You didn't miss anything; it rides just like any other car. I don't have it anymore, Mike, and I don't need it anymore, either."

Jenny eased over from beside her mother and put out her hand for me to shake. "Hello, Mr. Roberts. Am I glad *you're back*! Now I don't have to keep hearing about how much a *certain person*," she stopped to glance back at Sara before she continued, "is *missing* you, and *worrying* about you."

"Jenny, please," Sara countered, stepping forward with a smile and an outstretched hand as though nothing had been said. "We're glad you're back, Mr. Roberts. And I'm also looking forward to hearing about your adventures."

"Please, all of you call me Lance," I said while shaking her hand.

"Well, let me get you something to eat. Would you give me a hand, Jenny," Sara asked. "Sit here, Lance. I'll get your plate." While eating two helpings of everything, I told the Freeman family the whole story. Mr. Freeman sat there listening expressionless. When I finished two hours later, he reached into his pocket, pulled out his handkerchief and wiped his moist brow. I wasn't sure if the moisture on his brow was due to the warm kitchen or the details of my story.

We both pushed away from the table and walked outside to sit on a bench resting against a large oak tree in the backyard. "I want to let you know that I brought $50,000 worth of gold coins with me. I don't know if they have any value here, but if you need them, they're yours if you'd like."

"I sure appreciate it, son. But I can't think of one thing I could do with a bunch of gold coins," he stated, and then added with a grin, "except maybe look at 'em, just to admire their beauty.

"Now Ed the jeweler, he may be interested in some gold for making wedding rings and other pieces of jewelry. If you don't mind parting with them, remind me later on and I'll take you by his shop."

"If you're not interested, I'll just hold on to them. I felt that it was only fair that I tell you, in case you needed them," I responded before changing the subject. "Okay, Mr. Freeman, now it's your turn to tell me what happened while I was gone," I challenged.

Mr. Freeman gave me his account of the Christians' reaction to the collapse of America and the introduction of global governance. With my knowledge of the Elite's overall plan, along with what Mr. Freeman told me, I could visualize the whole ordeal.

None of the major news sources accurately reported the events that ushered in global governance. According to Mr. Freeman, and to my surprise, for years Christian investigative reporters had attempted to disclose the activities of the Elite. As attacks against the constitutional rights and freedoms mounted, Christian and patriot authors, journalists, and radio talk show hosts started investigating these atrocities. These two distinct groups made strange bedfellows. Their only commonality was preserving the United States Constitution and the true, American way of life. Through every source available, they fearlessly disclosed the identities of the perpetrators and their treasonous acts.

History proved that America was founded on Judeo-Christian principles and that these principles were interwoven into the fabric of our United States Constitution. Initially, Christian journalists were unaware of the international conspiracy. They believed the diverse attacks against the foundational beliefs of this country were independent efforts made by unrelated sources. When the battle lines were finally drawn, it was obvious these issues were the precise focus of attack to eliminate the major roadblocks preventing global governance. By the time it was discovered that these varied attacks were part and parcel of a well-organized plot to overthrow the United States, as well as all sovereign governments of the world, the enemy was solidly entrenched in every major institution.

While these findings were well documented, secular publishing houses refused to publish their works. These invaluable truths were kept isolated within the Christian and nationalist camps, and they rarely reached the general public. If they did, the liberals loudly labeled the information as fanaticism, prejudicial, bigoted or intolerant.

Since I wasn't a Christian, my source of news was limited to the secular news media. This left me with only the partial, biased reports that the Elite-influenced news media portrayed. My advantage was the insight derived from reading *The Master Plan*.

There were seven heavily financed organizations that influenced legislators to rewrite constitutional law: the American Civil Liberties Union, the homosexual movement, the National Organization of Women, Planned Parenthood, the National Education Association, the National Endowment for the Arts, and the Environmental Protection Agency. On the surface these powerful organizations appeared to represent their individual cause. They were, however, all socialist programs sponsored and orchestrated by the Elite to destroy the fundamental principles and the sovereignty of America.

These organizations maintained a relentless attack on every tradition that was known to be good and right and just. With an overwhelming number of highly paid professional lobbyists, they campaigned for every detestable cause imaginable.

The abortion issue, the homosexual agenda, and the New Age religion—which had crept into the traditional churches to create a *new form of Christianity*—were most threatening to the true born again Christian. Abortion, which was actually infanticide, murdered babies— some 35-50 million in a 30-year period since its legalization in America alone. Homosexuality perverted the natural and logical progression of life and was considered an abomination to God. The New Age religion, with its mixture of all pagan religious beliefs, its worship of the environment—fish, insects, birds, animals, and trees—directly challenged the belief that mankind, not creatures, were created in the image of God. Affronting every level of decency, these organizations shamelessly spurned the Creator, sound morals, and family traditions.

Propagating infanticide was the fundamental purpose of Planned Parenthood. One segment of the U.S. government's financial-aid package, whether nationally or internationally, was a condition to implement genocide; Planned Parenthood's abortion program was one of those conditions.

Desensitization, deceptive propaganda, and pseudoscience were the ideals proselytized through the news media, television, movie theaters, magazines, and books.

Homosexuals and their supporters harassed, intimidated, and played on the emotions of the public, the business owners, and legislators to accommodate the homosexual agenda. To further support the idea that homosexuality was more than just an individual choice in lifestyles, a false study was widely publicized that claimed homosexuals were different than heterosexuals due to a difference in brain chemistry and an unique cell characteristic only to them. A law was finally passed making the sexual preference of homosexuals a Civil Right. Once their deviate, sexual lifestyle became civil law, they pressed forward with an ever-increasing thrust. Although they represented only a small percentage of the population, they were well organized, heavily financed, and firmly entrenched in the areas of government, education, business, and the media.

Those that opposed the homosexual agenda were labeled as intolerant, bigots, hatemongers, and often equated with Adolf Hitler of Nazi Germany. Many Christians and nationalists were tried under Civil Rights law, heavily fined and/or imprisoned for refusing to adopt the homosexual agenda in their churches, workplaces, and schools.

Despite the unanimous rejection by the majority, homosexuals attained the right to wed. Never before in the history of the world had humanity fallen so low as to sanction two people of the same sex in marriage.

While at first difficult to accept, Mr. Freeman presented convincing evidence that environmental controls were fostered by a Green-Peace Religion, which was spawned by Earth Worshipers. The medium used to impose global governance upon the people of the world was contrived threats of global environmental holocausts fabricated by pseudoscience.

Christians of all denominations banded together to form a coalition. They networked across the country, educating Christian organizations on how to defeat these assaults upon their freedoms. By supplying copies of documents such as the Earth Charter and the IUCN's recommendations proposed by the Commission on Global Governance, many were able to temporarily delay attempts to implement the environmental agenda in their community. They encouraged everyone to contact their Representatives and to support pertinent issues that would further their cause. They utilized their right to picket, boycott, and lobby by standing against those enterprises that refused to adhere to their pleas for morality and basic family principles.

Christian lawyers united. They searched the annals of jurisprudence to find a way to save the country. The only legal remedy was impeachment. Impeachment procedures were initiated against those members of the judicial branch, the legislative branch, and executive branch that transgressed their oath to uphold the Constitution of the United States. This well-organized, powerful, and influential group of Christians, often assisted by nationalists, made a bold effort to thwart the attempts of global governance. These efforts, however, only alienated Christians from others, incited further hatred, and increased the persecution against them. Exposing the Elite's conspiracies only forced the Elite to accelerate their takeover.

There was another international, religious-based movement that rose to the forefront. Their leaders held vast resources of oil. This powerful religious sect didn't tolerate other beliefs and sanctioned the extermination of those that did. Their claim to glory was death in holy battle, initially using brutal acts of terrorism. But as they grew in ranks, they also grew in power. This power brought international acceptance. They mounted ruthless and unmerciful attacks on anyone that refused to worship their god of war and violence. Their desire to annihilate the uncompromising Jew and Christian only supported the Elite's agenda.

None of this happened behind closed doors. People had read lies printed next to truths for so long that most of them didn't know the truth when they saw it.

The cost of living always exceeded the wages earned. Most people were too busy trying to provide for themselves and their families. Very few had the time nor the education needed to study the lengthy and complex material pertaining to candidates and the political issues they endorsed. All of these were created conditions, designed to keep the people in a state of frustration and despair.

Government debt mounted beyond thirty trillion dollars, Corporate debt followed closely, and consumer debt exceeded the trillion-dollar mark. Thousands of businesses vacated the United States in pursuit of cheap labor—often slave labor—available in the third-world countries. And if that weren't enough the result from the Y2K took its toll, virtually paralyzing the economy and leaving most people destitute.

With no viable alternative, the people struck out in riotous profusion. They first attacked the public officials and then the rich. Once property and possessions were consumed, the raging mob turned inward. The basic instinctual cry, *everyone for themselves*, and, *survival of the fittest,* vibrated across the country. Violence in unheard-of proportions and of every form swept the cities.

Petty disputes erupted into wars. The whole world was in despair. People were starving; black market was the way of life; gold and silver were the only means of exchange for food, clothing, and shelter, since common currency was obsolete.

Under Executive Orders, UN troops consisting of armed forces from around the world were deployed to restore law and order. These foreign troops, however, had no allegiance to the governments, no relationship with the peoples, no investment in the countries in which they were stationed. Using a higher degree of precision, these troops duplicated the violent acts of the raging mobs that they were sent to eradicate. Finally, after months of military abuse, the masses begged for relief from the cruelty and depravation administered by the UN troops.

It was to this end that the Elite had worked over the centuries to attain. Realizing the means in which they succeeded was terrifying. This group of Elitists now governed the thinking and actions of billions of people, regulated the international financial system, and controlled the political arena in every country. The misery and loss of human lives, the devastation to animal and plant life, along with the destruction of property were mere unfortunate sacrifices.

A universal cry for deliverance resounded from the earth.

With the stage now set, a truly majestic orator emerged. He was born royalty. Through his veins flowed the bloodlines of emperors, kings, boyars, grandees, and monarchs of every great empire. His ancestry could be traced from King Nimrod down through the mighty Persia and Babylonian dynasties to the present-day kings and queens.

Being indirectly related to all of Europe's gentry, an incredible force ran through the veins of this prince. Fused within his lineage of greatness were strong ancestral ties to cults, occults, generations of satanists, and particularly the Illuminati coven. From amongst the predecessors of this prince the self-professed illumined or enlightened ones derived.

The most prominent Illuminati bloodline was the Merovingian dynasty, considered to be the Holy bloodline. Through a process of selected marriages the concealed connections of the most important satanic occult bloodlines were interwoven to strengthen the occult lineage and increase its magnitude.

In order to achieve total dominance the Jews, Christians, and Muslims had to be satisfied. This prince claimed—although indirectly—to be a descendant of Israel's King David. He also asserted to be of the lineage of Jesus—the legend being, Jesus didn't actually die on the cross but was surreptitiously removed from the tomb and later wed Mary the Magdalene who bore him children, of which this prince is a descendent. His ancestry could also be traced, according to further claims, to Mohammed the prophet and founder of Islam. As an offspring from the lineage of King David, Jesus, and Mohammed he considered himself to be deity, while appeasing the demands of Judaism, Christianity, and Islam.

This prince was groomed from birth to rule the world. Being nobility as well as an eminent member of the Elite's inner circle he grew in power and authority. And yet, it was through intrigue and covert manipulation that he became the reckoning force. As a master of deceit he caused deceit to reign, and by it he grew very powerful. One means of increasing his strength was by affixing himself to governing bodies of other countries, particularly third-world countries, and nurturing them until they grew prominent under his dominion.

Confirmation of his vested supremacy quickly spread throughout the world. Once the prince established his lordship his entire personality changed. Pride, conceit, and disdain consumed him. His allegiance was unto himself. No longer content with ruling the world, he wanted to rule the universe.

Through the Security Council of the UN, the prince sent forth a decree informing all nations that their sufferance on population had ended. Quotas for reducing the population on a yearly basis would be enforced by selective or total embargo of credit, items of trade including food and medicine, or by military force when required. The Major Nations of the Security Council would now enforce complete legal, military, and economic jurisdiction in all regions of the world. All natural resources were to be used and preserved for the good of the Major Nations of the Security Council. All races and peoples were not equal. Those races proven superior by superior achievements were to rule the lesser nations, caring for them only on sufferance that they cooperate with the Security Council. All decision making, including banking, trade, currency rates, and economic development plans, would be made by the stewardship of the Major Nations. All of the above constitute the New World Order, in which all nations, regions and races will cooperate with the Major Nations of the Security Council.

The prince had fostered the prophet to international prominence. The prophet, also a master of intrigue and deceit, likewise practiced black magic. He ordered the people to setup an image in the likeness of the prince and deceived all the inhabitants of the earth into worshipping the prince and his image.

Everything pointed to this prince as being the savior of the world. Between him and the false prophet, they deceived everyone, small and great, rich and poor, free and slave, causing all to receive a mark on their right hand or forehead as a sign of total submission; all except born again Christians who refused to denounce their love for Jesus Christ. Without this mark no one could buy or sell.

Those who worshiped this false messiah were given sufficient credit to purchase a month's supply of food, clothing, and shelter. Those who initially rejected this false messiah and his totalitarian regime were forced into seclusion, hunger, and eventual submission. Born again Christians that refused to worship this man and denounce Jesus Christ as their Lord and Savior forfeited their property, risked starvation, imprisonment, and death by fire or decapitation.

In an attempt to expunge the name of God from the earth, this prince attempted to change the times and reset the dates by eliminating BC and AD. He mounted a vicious attack against born again Christians and Jews. While these two groups appeared to be his target, it was apparent that his hostility was being vented toward God. For he believed that he was a god and thus cursed the true God of heaven and the earth, Jesus Christ, and everything that was good, right, and just.

The day I told the Mr. Freeman about *The Master Plan* he gathered the elders and devised plans to leave the valley. Men were sent to ferret out a suitable way to transport their families and livestock up the mountain. Once they found the safest and easiest route, the elders convened to find a method of transporting their belongings. They divided into groups and began to instruct the people in various tasks according to their qualifications and capabilities. Upon hearing the first reports of anarchy in the major cities, the entire community of Peaceful Valley made their move up the mountain.

They used mechanical pulleys to hoist the heavy equipment, the livestock, their belongings, the elderly and anyone unable to climb the mountain under their own power. Step by step, piece by piece, animal by animal, the community of Peaceful Valley relocated to a thousand-acre plateau entrenched halfway up the mountain.

The new location was ideal. The mountain formed a semicircle around the tableland, which was 1,500 feet above sea level, and provided a protective wall that practically encircled the mesa. The only direct access onto the plateau, other than scaling the almost vertical surrounding cliffs, was through the forest that extended inward for a distance of about a mile. This was the same forest that I came through the night before I collapsed on the road. The only other means of detection was from aircraft or high-powered surveillance satellites.

This land was exceptionally fertile; there was a natural, continuous runoff of fresh water from the mountains; the air was thinner than the valley but clear and clean. This produced excellent crops, hearty livestock, and a healthier life for everyone. Within a year the people from Peaceful Valley were a thriving community again.

When Mr. Freeman finished describing the events that took place, he offered the same proposition he had made when we first met. "The same requirement still stands, son. In order to live here, you have to be a born-again Christian who loves the Lord with all your heart, and with all your mind, and with all your strength.

"After a month, if you accept the Lord into your heart, we'll help build you a place to live and supply you with whatever you need to get started. When you're able to provide for yourself, then you'll be an established member of the community."

"I have two questions," I asked after he finished. "What if I confess to being a Christian just so I can stay?"

He grinned, chuckling to himself, before stating with conviction, "Why that would be impossible, son. Jesus makes it real clear that *'You will know them by their fruit.'* The fruit of the Holy Spirit is love, joy, peace, longsuffering, kindness, goodness, faithfulness, gentleness, and self-control. There's no way you or anybody else can fake these characteristics. He's got to be living inside you for you to act like Him—actually it's Him working His plan through you. But, in any case, you'll either come all the way into the Lord and this body of Christians or you won't be able to stand this place or us either; you'd be glad to leave.

"What's your second question, son?"

"What if I decide not to become a Christian?" I asked, looking him directly in the eye.

He paused, and then he lowered his head in serious thought. Once he found the exact words and the obstinacy to say it forthright, he raised his head and returned my stare. "Then you'd have to leave, Mr. Roberts! And may God be with you if that's the choice you make."

Fall had made its mark upon the earth. Days were growing shorter and nights were growing longer. Mornings and evenings brought a progressive chill, preparing all for the coming cold. Leaves were turning a variety of bright reds, yellows, and golden browns. Trees, as if aware of the needed strength to endure the cold temperatures, dropped their multi-colored leaves like excess baggage. Everything was in harmony with the seasonal change. Not only the weather, but also the plants and the living creatures began to alter their appearance and behavior patterns in preparation for the winter ahead.

Word traveled fast throughout this mountain community. It wasn't long before everyone knew I was the one who forewarned Mr. Freeman of the distressing times that were about to come; they also knew about my one-month contract. People told me that they had been praying for me the whole time I was gone, and because of the decision I would soon have to make, they would continue to pray more fervently.

The entire community worked. Unless they were too young or too old, everyone performed two functions and I was no exception to that rule. Each person had a regular job which provided a means for exchanging either services or goods with the rest of the community. Each person also volunteered a certain amount of hours each week to fulfill his or her service to the community.

Those who were able gave ten percent of their time or goods to the community as tithes. Tithes were considered God's portion that was being returned as gratitude for all He had given them. This assured unlimited provisions in the community storehouse for the ill or injured.

During my first community meeting I was asked what I could do to help. I described my past experience in engineering, designing, and drawing commercial and residential structures. In order to fulfill my obligation for community service, it was agreed that my talents would be utilized best in the town's planning and building department.

Later that day Mr. Freeman asked me what I wanted to do in trade for my room and board. I remembered the labor camp and offered to set up an irrigation system to water the fields. "That would be a great help, son. If you can figure a better way to direct the water off those mountains for irrigating the crops, it'd be a blessing to everybody in the community."

This became my job. I surveyed the land and examined the sources of the water's runoff. I also estimated the distance the water traveled down the mountain, the approximate rate of travel, and the amount of pressure it would generate. Once I discovered an ideal location for a dam, I started building it. My plan was to construct a system of aqueducts that would distribute the water evenly to all the farms. If my calculations were correct, which I wouldn't be able to accurately determine until the coming rains, the community would have a fresh, natural-flowing water source year round.

Imposing upon someone's generosity had never been my style in the past, but volunteering my services to benefit an entire community had never been my style either. However, this place was different from any place I had lived before. The system that this small community of believers had developed was far more rewarding than anything I had experienced in my past. Even though I wasn't being compensated with money, my compensation was sufficient and my services were a benefit to the entire community.

Every weekday when the women finished their chores they gathered the children into the Community Center and taught them reading, writing, and arithmetic. Included in these daily lessons were studies from the Bible. They believed that a child taught from God's Word and trained in Biblical ways by their parents would never depart from what they were taught.

For every ten families an elder served as an overseer. Every six months the elders would rotate, overseeing another group of families. This gave each of the elders a personal relationship with the whole community and allowed them to discuss any problems with each other for counseling purposes. Three evenings a week each of the elders would alternate teaching a Bible study.

Since I was completely ignorant about the Bible and its teachings, the elders recommended that I attend the Beginners Bible Class. Everybody in the class was younger than I, but it was necessary that I learn the fundamental teachings of the Christian beliefs in order to make a knowledgeable decision about accepting the Lord when my probationary period ended.

Ever since my first meeting with the Freeman family I held a high regard for the invisible God they worshipped. My belief system usually combined senses with reason. I used the process of elimination, first with my senses, and then by reason. Normally, if I couldn't see it, hear it, smell it, taste it, touch it, or feel it, I would dismiss it as not being real. And yet I was also aware that that concept contained an obvious flaw, since it restricted reality to the experiential realm of sense. So if I based my conclusion solely on my senses, the logical conclusion would be that the metaphysical God who couldn't be perceived through my senses couldn't be real.

Knowing that the human experiential sense-realm was limited and often exaggerated, I then usually reverted to the realm of reason. That is, what is conceived as being true based upon logic and rational thinking must exist in reality. Although I couldn't relate to God in the sense realm, I witnessed Him in the daily lives of these people. Therefore, through a logical and rational thought process, coupled with my visual senses and personal experience with the people of this community, I concluded that the God they worshipped had to be real. From that point on, I desired to know God's master plan with the same insoluble curiosity that I desired to know the Elite's master plan.

While working on the dam I often reflected on what I was learning in the Bible classes. The elders taught that the Holy Bible was the true Word of God revealed by God to His prophets, the patriarchs, and the disciples of Jesus Christ. To dispel any doubts that the Bible contained errors, contradictions, or omissions, the elders clarified that if God can create something from nothing, He can get His Word across to His people without error. They taught that the Bible contained the account of creation, the deterioration of life and the destruction of earth, and a new heaven and earth where Christians will live with God in bliss forever.

I learned that the Bible was divided into two testaments or covenants. The Old Testament was written before the birth of Jesus Christ, and the New Testament was written after His death and ascension into heaven. The teachers likened the Bible unto a puzzle. When the scriptures are correctly fitted together God's truths would unfold. The teachers also emphasized that when two scriptures didn't fit—the same as when two pieces in a puzzle don't fit—then you shouldn't try to force them; that would only create false doctrines, erroneous teachings and provide a platform for skeptics. In due time God would reveal His truths to you as they are needed in your life.

According to the Bible, mankind was created different from any other earthly creature. Humans were created spiritual beings and were endowed with intelligence, understanding, emotions, and a will. They are the only earthly creatures capable of making a logical, rational, intelligent decision.

God created Adam and Eve and placed them in His garden to take care of it. Upon doing this, He gave them one commandment and told them that the consequence for disobeying that commandment would bring death. Disregarding God's warning, Adam and Eve sinned by disobeying God. The results of their sin brought spiritual death, a separation from God, and severed their communication with God on a spiritual level.

Instantly, the human race was in a fallen, spiritually dead state. The opposite of the spiritual is the sensual. Thus, being enslaved to the senses became the eternal sin that dominated the existence of mankind. Therefore God had to expel His beloved children from His spiritual, heavenly kingdom. Because humanity was now spiritually dead, the only way God could communicate with mankind was through their physical senses.

Irrespective of the sin and death that prevailed for hundreds of years after the fall of mankind, God continued to seek out anyone willing to do His will, and grant mercy to those who sought Him. However, due to the chasm that separated humanity from God, it was virtually impossible for man, by his own will, to break the hold of sin and death that held him in bondage.

Driven by a deep love for His children, God reserved a provision for their salvation. Jesus Christ was the propitiation for the sins of mankind. Christ enabled humanity to re-enter God's spiritual kingdom and renew fellowship with the Father. Jesus Christ was the door to salvation for all who received Him as the Lord of their lives.

I found these studies informative, interesting, and heart warming. Their concept of a God in heaven with no death or pain or suffering was extremely inviting. I couldn't deny my daily witness of the way these people lived, or the existence of some unseen force working powerfully in their lives. To merely say that it works for them but it wouldn't work for me would be preposterous. I was reasonably certain that it would work for anyone who applied these teachings, including me.

Taking everything into account, the thoughts still plagued me as to why an all-knowing God would allow humanity to fall into such a state of devastation. *Why would a holy and loving God tolerate the wickedness that engulfed the earth He created out of love? If the Creator of everything was so almighty, why in heaven's name didn't He give the world another alternative?* These were only some of the many questions that caused me to doubt.

Due to the respect I held for the elders I didn't air my objections before the whole class. The following evening I approached Mr. Freeman alone. "If God is so holy and loving, why is the world so wicked? Why does He tolerate a group of people like the Elite, and why does He allow them to carry out their treacherous plans on His earth? If He really knew the outcome in advance, why did He create these evil people? And why—due to so much wickedness running rampant in the world—are we forced to live on this mountain instead of wherever we want to live?"

"Take it easy, son," he consoled me in a soothing voice. "Let's take this thing one step at a time. All your questions will be answered. And if they're not, then I'll personally sit down with you, and I'll go through the Bible and show you the answers to everything you want to know."

I resigned to be patient a little longer. If Mr. Freeman could truly answer my questions, he would also have the solution to the dilemma facing the whole world.

I was living in a one-room cottage behind the Freemans. Every morning at 5:00 a.m. the alarm would wake me. When dressed for work, I joined the family in the dining room beyond the kitchen. We gathered there each morning to sing hymns and pray before we ate breakfast and started the day.

I normally left for the fields around seven each morning. At noon I would return for lunch. After eating I went back to work until four that evening. I volunteered to spend two evenings out of the week in the planning department to fulfill my community service.

On Saturday evenings everyone gathered together in the Community Center, which was a huge barn-like structure that was used as a storehouse, church, and meeting house. The women prepared a special dish for what they called the Saturday Night Fellowship, which was actually a social gathering for the community to draw closer together.

Sunday was our day of rest. Everyone living on the mountain came together in the Community Center for services on Sunday morning and Sunday evenings. They would sing and worship the Lord, pray for one another, and then one or more of the elders would bring a message from the Bible.

One afternoon while working on the dam, I ran into complications. Unable to make it back to the house for lunch, I decided to keep working until I fixed the problem. About an hour later I looked up to see Sara coming across the field with a picnic basket over her arm. As she came closer I could see the gentle breeze blowing her long, brown hair and pressing her cotton dress firmly against her body. For the first time, I realized that Sara was a woman, and a beautiful woman at that. My facial expression obviously revealed my thoughts because she lowered her eyes self-consciously before setting the basket on the ground between us.

"Hello, Sara," I greeted, hoping to relieve her apparent discomfort.

"Hello, Lance," she replied with flushed cheeks and a quick glance before returning her gaze to the basket. "I noticed you hadn't come home for lunch, so I asked father if I could bring it to you. Here's a couple of roast beef sandwiches, a slice of pie, and some lemonade."

She really is beautiful, I thought to myself, unable to shake from my mind the sight of her coming across the field. "I sure appreciate it," I told her. "I was having some problems and I didn't want to leave before fixing them."

Picking up the basket, I pointed to a large stump a short distance from where I was working, "Let's have a seat over there."

We walked over to the stump and sat down together. As I picked up one of the sandwiches to take a bite, she promptly asked for a blessing on the food. When she finished, she asked me, "Lance, do you know why father says you have to become a Christian to live here?"

After pondering her question for a moment, I answered. "At first I thought he was reacting out of fear that outsiders would take over their beautiful valley. Since then, I've learned that you people, especially your father, don't react out of fear. Before you act there's usually a well-thought-out reason behind what you say and do.

"I must admit, there's a definite difference between the people here and those I've seen anywhere else. You're one big family here. Everybody is a part of the whole, a community family so to speak. You're not only responsible to and for one another, you're committed to one another, which is something I've never witnessed before. To be honest, in this day and age, I would never have believed it was possible.

"I know I still haven't answered your question why it's necessary for me to become a Christian in order to live here. So you tell me, Sara, why?"

"It's really simple," she replied after I finished. "The Bible tells us, if two people aren't in agreement they can't walk together."

Offended by her obvious narrow-mindedness, I asked, "Are you saying, if we disagree on something we can't live together as neighbors?"

"No, I'm not talking about a minor disagreement. I'm talking about two completely different ways of thinking, speaking, and acting. What I'm saying is this, God's system is one way and the world's system is the exact opposite. The two worlds are going in different directions and they won't ever agree. Jesus tells us, either you're with me or against me; you're either gathering or scattering."

I interrupted her again, "You're telling me that life is either black or white and there's no in-between. And that's not acceptable in the real world, Sara."

Unmoved by my objection, she continued. "Okay, let's look at it this way; if the truth is twisted in any way, it's not the truth, it's a lie. If right is changed in any way, it's wrong. Truth can't be conditioned to fit the circumstances; the ends don't justify the means; truth is absolute. Either it's black or white, right or wrong; there's no in-between.

"Let me give you another example. One of the spiritual laws that God teaches in the Bible is to give and it will be given back. And yet, the world system teaches to take whatever you can get because nobody's going to give you anything. These are two different ideals that represent two different worlds. Two people with such different views can't live together in agreement.

"Lance, when a person truly asks Jesus Christ into his heart, God instantly creates a new spirit within him; at that instant he's born again. As he learns more about Christ, he learns to trust in Him. That person begins to give Christ control over his life and Christ becomes his Lord. Until a person is willing to make Jesus Christ the Lord of his life, whatever he thinks, says, or does is working against Him. Whether that person is conscious of it or not, that person is not furthering God's kingdom, but hindering it."

I didn't understand everything she said, nor did I agree with everything I understood. But if she was right, it was best not to oppose her. I had made more than my share of blunders for the day already.

As I finished the last bite of pie, Sara gathered her things and hooked the basket over her arm. When she finished, she faced me, and while staring me straight in the eyes she asked, "Who's your Lord, Lance?"

Before I could answer, she had turned and started across the field on her way back to the cabin. I felt bad. Sara was nice enough to prepare my lunch and bring it out to me and I returned her kindness with harshness. "Sara," I hollered across the field. "Thanks for bringing my lunch."

She turned, just long enough to reply, "You're welcome, Lance," before continuing on her way.

During one of the Bible classes that week, I learned that God is the master designer who worked out everything to conform to the purpose of His will before speaking it into existence. The Biblical explanation of creation was similar to the way I formulated the plans to design the Main Complex. My experience with False Reality gave me an excellent mental picture of how God designed the world, inspected it, and then brought it into existence.

God's design was the universe. He went to the drawing board to design the world and everything in it. He engineered the formulas to produce atoms and molecules, the sun and moon, air and water, and everything that exists. God formed each grain of sand, counted and weighed them, and placed them where He wanted them to be. He calculated the wind patterns and steered its erratic course for the length of earth's existence. God uniquely conceived each blade of grass and each leaf. He even gave the flowers their multi-varieties and glorious colors. He established the depths of the valleys, the heights of the hills and mountains. He gave the oceans their boundaries and formed the channels for rivers, lakes, and streams. God determined the precise temperature to freeze water and its point of boiling.

Whether the flight pattern of a butterfly or the birth of a child, an animal, an insect, or the salvation of a person on his or her deathbed, all events were known by God before He created the world.

God's entire creation was contrived as one continuous life-sustaining, self-existing unit. Water freely offers its substance; the sun freely offers its radiant light, heat, and other life-supporting elements. The plants produce oxygen and provide food supplements. God's creation harmoniously maintains a life-producing cycle that works in conjunction with each other.

As the Creator freely gives life to all, His creation was designed to freely give of itself, with no expectation of receiving anything in return. Constant giving is eternal life; this is the true *Master Plan* that was brought forth out of love, only to be accomplished by love.

As all good designers, God took every possibility into account. Foreseeing each choice that every creature could make in any given situation, He manipulated each millisecond of existence to conform to His perfect will.

On the sixth day of creation God completed His labor of love. After a thorough assessment of what had been made, He determined that everything was very good. And then God spoke His creation into existence with powerful, creative words of truth. The instant God spoke the Word, the substance and form of all created things, both visible and invisible, started materializing in the exact order He had ordained them. As a sequence of events appears on a movie screen, God's creation continuously unveiled itself second by second, day by day, year by year. What we see today was prearranged from the beginning of time.

On the seventh day of creation God rested from all His work.

This was more than my mind could fathom. Human beings are constantly faced with situations that require decisions. According to the elders' teachings, God foresaw each situation and foreknew the alternatives that confronted each living person for eternity. Without violating mankind's ability to choose, God manipulated each situation to fulfill His purpose in their lives, simultaneously furthering His eternal plan for the universe.

Throughout the day I continued to ponder these beliefs that the elders considered basic Biblical principles and fundamental Biblical truths.

The next day while working on the dam, Sara brought her basket just before my usual quitting time for lunch. This time she brought a small pocket Bible.

Curious, I asked. "How were you able to keep your Bibles when they issued the decree that prohibited them?"

"A long time ago, when I was still a young girl, the Lord told father to bury a large number of Bibles in various places. So he brought the issue before the elders. After explaining, it was agreed that the world's philosophies were eventually going to conflict with the Word of God. They all contributed Bibles and helped to bury them in marked locations throughout the valley. Before we left the valley we dug them up and reburied them here on the mountain, just in case they find us and take the ones we have."

"You said that the Lord told your father to bury the Bibles. Exactly how did the Lord tell him?"

"There's an Old Testament scripture written in Amos 8:11-12, that says: *"Behold, the days come, saith the Lord God, that I will send a famine in the land, not a famine of bread, nor a thirst for water, but of hearing the words of the Lord: And they shall wander from sea to sea, and from the north even to the east, they shall run to and fro to seek the word of the Lord, and shall not find it."* It was through these verses that the Lord spoke to father's heart. Believing that its dogmatism would offend and convict the hearts of a godless society, father also realized that the Word of God would be outlawed. That's why he consulted with the other elders to get as many Bibles as possible buried."

"I just wanted to know if you believed that God speaks to us in an audible voice as I'm speaking to you now."

"God speaks to us in many ways. He talks to us through others, with a gentle tug upon our heartstrings, or through scriptures that suddenly invade our thoughts, the same way it did with father. God has talked to me in an audible voice in my mind, and I've also heard a resounding voice round about me. God loves His children very much. He'll do whatever it takes to get our attention, even if it takes a miracle, like He did with Moses when He spoke to him from the burning bush."

"Well," I replied with a smile, "I'm sure He'd have my undivided attention if He spoke to me from a burning bush."

We laughed and then Sara began to read from the book of Romans, chapter thirteen, verses eight through ten, while I ate my lunch. *"Owe no man any thing, but to love one another: for he that loveth another hath fulfilled the law. For this, Thou shalt not commit adultery, Thou shalt not kill, Thou shalt not steal, Thou shalt not bear false witness, Thou shalt not covet; and if there be any other commandment, it is briefly comprehended in this saying, namely, Thou shalt love thy neighbor as thyself. Love worketh no ill to his neighbor: therefore love is the fulfilling of the law."*

When she finished reading these verses, she asked, "This is the way *true Christians* live; can you live this way, Lance?"

Her questions were starting to upset me. All of my life I had been proficient in witticism and communication. No one could paralyze my thinking ability with questions the way Sara did. Despite her limited education and lack of experience in worldly affairs, she continued to confound me with her wisdom.

"Probably not," I responded, "But then I've never tried."

She continued: "The Bible tells us that God's thoughts and ways are foolishness to the world and what the world considers wisdom is foolishness to God. According to the ways of the world, meekness, kindness, gentleness, and humility are signs of weakness; and those who love their enemies are foolish. And yet, Jesus tells us to love our enemies and pray for those who persecute us; and we're commanded to love our neighbor, as we love ourselves.

"Pride, boasting, and arrogance are foolishness to God. And yet the world encourages people to exalt themselves, focus on their qualities, and flaunt them before others as if they created themselves. The talents, attributes, or intelligence we possess are all gifts from God. It's the selfish human nature that refuses to acknowledge there's a God. If they did, they'd have to admit that they were nothing without Him, and that they needed His help, which means they would have to submit to Him and change their ways."

"It reads good on paper, Sara," I replied authoritatively. "But you'd be destitute, hungry, and in awfully bad health if you tried living like that in the world that I came from. It just doesn't work."

"That's why we're told to come out from among them and be separate. It's impossible to take part in the world's system and not be abused by those living in that system. It takes close fellowship with God and His people to live the way God wants us to live. It also takes the support and prayers of a body of believers for anyone to live God's way, which is the way He planned it."

"Does that mean cut yourself off from the rest of the world and become hermits?" I asked.

"No. While Jesus was still on earth He prayed and asked the Father not to take us out of the world, but to protect us from the evil one while we're in the world. He also warns us that as long as we're in the world we're going to meet with all kinds of trials and tribulations, but not to worry, because He's defeated the ruler of this world."

Sara placed the basket on her arm, and started across the field toward the cabin. After walking a short distance she turned around to face me, "I'm baking a special dessert for dinner, Lance. I hope you'll like it,"

I stood there feeling like an imbecile. This wasn't going the way I wanted it to go at all. According to what Sara had just said, the principles I believed in were based on erroneous information.

Before she was out of range, I finally managed to conjure another, "Thanks, Sara."

When she was gone I thought about Haile. His understanding of the existence of mankind was as faulty as mine was. Sure, he believed that life was the only thing that counted, but it wasn't an eternal, spiritual life. In this respect, Haile's beliefs were as erroneous as mine were. In the end, he senselessly traded his life for selfish revenge.

Every new bit of knowledge challenged my old opinions. I could see why Mr. Freeman was amused when I made the suggestion of pretending to be a Christian. In a close community such as this, people's thoughts and behavior would ultimately become apparent to everyone. There wasn't any way around it, if I planned to become a part of this community, I had to become a Christian. Just as Mr. Freeman asserted, I couldn't fake it.

One by one, I heard answers to questions I had pondered most of my life. Did the Bible really have the corner on truth? I was skeptical whether I should believe the Bible or continue believing the theories of the leading authorities of the day. The secular psychiatrist, psychologist, therapist, and sociologist set the order for most of the thinking and behavior that was prevalent in the world. Whenever these leading authorities claimed to ascertain that an established method of thinking or behavior was harmful to their secular agenda, the people unquestioningly implemented those theories.

But weren't these emissaries for the Elite? Practically everything publicized by secular sources contained a deceptive agenda to further enslave the people psychologically as well as bodily.

Through these Bible studies, I was confronted daily with information that forced me to reassess my entire course of thinking. It wasn't easy to accept that my decision-making process was darkened by untruths and all of my past conclusions and judgments were based on erroneous information. No, I needed a better understanding of God's Word before I could make an intelligent decision.

Even though I had heard talk of Satan since my early childhood, during most of my life I never believed that a literal devil existed. So I was somewhat skeptical when one of the elders began to teach on the subject of Lucifer, the devil.

While studying *The Master Plan,* I learned that the original Elitists considered themselves to be the cream of the intelligentsia—the select of the elect—and the only people with the mental capacity, the insight and understanding to govern the world and bring it peace. They called themselves the *Illuminati,* and their avowed purpose and goal was the establishment of a *Novus Ordo Seclorum* or New World Order. The ultimate aims of this secret sect were sevenfold: abolition of all ordered government; abolition of private property; abolition of inheritance; abolition of patriotism; abolition of all religion; abolition of the family, particularly in the areas of morality, marriage, and the proper education of children; the creation of a New Age New World Order or Global Governance.

The Illuminati, by their own admission, were Satanists who worshiped Lucifer, the illuminator or light bearer. As well, each member of the inner circle, as occultists and disciples of Lucifer, were themselves rays or points of light, of which the head was referred to as having a thousand points of light.

Angels and humans were created with the ability to make logical choices between right and wrong. Although Adam chose to go against God, he wasn't the first one to do so.

Lucifer, the bearer of light, was the first of God's creations to turn against Him. God created Lucifer as an angel of great power and brilliance. He ordained him to be a guardian cherub and anointed him for this high position. God had endowed Lucifer with a high level of intelligence; he was full of wisdom, possessed exceptional beauty, and was a model of perfection. He was blameless in his ways from the day God created him, until wickedness was found in his heart.

It was through his God-given wisdom, understanding, and position of authority that he was able to gain prestige amongst the other angels. By his great skill he bartered for favors with other angels and increased his standing amongst them. He began to assume power and gain the allegiance of many. Through his widespread, dishonest trading, he became filled with violence and wickedness. It was on account of his beauty that his heart became proud; it was because of his splendor that he corrupted his wisdom, desecrated his sanctuaries, and sinned.

Instead of Lucifer glorifying his Creator, he glorified himself. He said in his heart, *I will* ascend to heaven; *I will* raise my throne above the stars of God; *I will* sit enthroned on the mount of assembly, on the utmost heights of the sacred mountain. *I will* ascend above the tops of the clouds; *I will* make myself like the Most High.

Lucifer, the light bearer, became the bearer of darkness, lies, and deception. He was renamed Satan, which means the accuser. Because of his wickedness he was also referred to as the devil. Satan became God's adversary, and an adversary to anyone that opposed him.

The first words God proclaimed was, "Let there be light." This light was truth, which produced substance, order, and purpose. Darkness is uncertainty and confusion, which is a product of lies and deception. The devil took God's truth and reversed it, creating the lie. Lies aren't real because they're not based wholly on reality, while truth is real because it is based solely on reality.

Sanity is being in touch with reality and truth. Insanity draws from something that's nonexistent and untrue. The state of insanity is being incapable of comprehending reality and truth. Without God's truth, Satan descended into a deeper state of insanity.

Satan's wickedness consumed him, until there wasn't any light of truth in him. The devil believed that his lies were truth and God's truths were lies. Since a lie isn't real, and it doesn't contain substance, the only thing it can produce is pandemonium and death. Through Satan's lies, death made its entrance into God's perfect creation.

Although God had given Satan a wealth of knowledge and wisdom he was still unable to foretell future events; an intelligent guess is still a guess. Since God created all things to follow an exact sequence of events, He knows everything in advance.

The devil went about God's kingdom exalting himself while accusing, abasing, and slandering God. Satan gave favorable treatment to the angels that followed him, while he accused, taunted, and tempted those angels that remained faithful to God.

God allowed the devil and his followers to taunt, tempt, and test even the most faithful of His servants. He allowed this in order to confirm those who truly believed in Him.

Through these tests, the faithful angels came forth refined and purified. They learned to trust in and depend upon God for their protection and safekeeping. As they drew closer to their Creator and learned of His loving, selfless ways, they acquired an utter disdain for the devil and all the wickedness he represented.

Two-thirds of all the angels chose to follow and serve Almighty God; one-third chose to follow the devil. Once the line was clearly drawn, God expelled the devil and all his cohorts and cast them down to the earth. Those that proved themselves worthy of God's kingdom remained.

God banished the devil from heaven. He cast him down to the earth to continue the same refining process on humanity. It's now man's turn to overcome the temptations, persecutions, and tribulations brought about by the devil and his demons.

The elders explained that temptations reveal the evil desires within us, while persecution proves faithfulness, and trials work patience. Just as fire burns away dross and removes the impurities, so God uses Satan to purify His people.

I was starting to see the picture more clearly. Maybe God *did* know what He was doing after all. If I took into account the entire existence of humanity, my few years didn't amount to a millisecond in the span of man's existence. If the basis for what I did or didn't believe were lies, then I probably made a lot of incorrect judgments and reached a lot of inaccurate conclusions.

I spent the better portion of my time in the field trying to sort out what I was going to do about my predicament. Time was running out, I was going to have to make a decision, and I wasn't ready. If I were asked to leave the mountain, where would I go? How would I survive? Living off the land and eluding the authorities would constitute a way of living that I wasn't prepared for. I was facing the biggest decision in my life; the choice that I made would be final.

The elders taught that Jesus Christ is the Word of God; He is before all things and in Him all things exist. He was with God from the beginning as the Master Builder working at God's side. Everything was created through Him, by Him, and for Him. God, the Father and designer of all things, gave His Son dominion over His creation as an inheritance.

Due to the state of the fallen human race, Jesus agreed to leave His Father in heaven and come down to earth as a human being. Although He was equal with God, He emptied Himself and became a man to serve all of mankind. In spite of the fact that He was tempted like us in every way, He withstood the influences of the sinful nature. He denied Himself, laid down His life, and lived strictly to do His Father's will. He humbled himself and was obedient to the point of death on the cross. By these acts, Jesus defeated sin and delivered mankind from the punishment of eternal death. Therefore God was able to raise Christ from the dead and exalt Him above every name on earth and in heaven.

The first Adam was created a living spirit, so Jesus Christ, the second Adam, was born a living spirit. Adam's sin of disobedience and spiritual death resulted in all humanity being born spiritually dead. In this respect, Jesus was different from all the descendants of Adam, being born of the Holy Spirit through the virgin birth He was born spiritually alive. But prior to Adam's sin of disobedience, Jesus and Adam were alike as far as their spiritual condition was concerned.

Since Adam was a man, redemption had to be accomplished through a man. A sinless man was the only payment acceptable for redeeming humanity and the earth from the sentence of death. The sinless life that Jesus led met all the requirements of the Old Testament laws that called for death as a result of sin. Since Jesus walked in love and desired to please His Father in every way, His life and eventual death also met the necessary requirements of God's spiritual laws. Because disobedience is sin and death is the result of sin, Jesus couldn't experience death because He had never sinned. In which case, the law of death couldn't hold him in the grave.

By virtue of Christ's life of obedience and His death and resurrection, spiritual rebirth was made available to all humanity. At the moment a person is born again, the living spirit of Christ is instantaneously created within him. He has then received the spirit of Christ, the spirit of sonship. The born-again believer is now embodied with a spiritual power to overcome sin, a spiritual capability of loving selflessly, and a spiritual mind equipped to understand the spiritual truths of God.

The opportunity to sin is always present with the born-again believer the same as it was with Adam and Jesus. But as the born-again believer gradually surrenders his life to Christ, God empowers him to prevail where Adam failed.

Jesus Christ, the living Son of God, paved the way so that anyone who desires to partake of God's love and eternal life can become a child of the living God. After pioneering the way, He sent back the Helper, God's Holy Spirit, which takes residence within the heart of each born-again believer. The Holy Spirit is the helper and teacher who guides the believer into all truth and a closer fellowship with the Father and the Son.

I was beginning to see that God had planned Christianity to be a combined effort that included the believer, the Father, the Son, and the Holy Spirit, all working in conjunction with each other and all believers as a whole; they literally become one.

That evening after supper, Sara placed on the table a large carrot cake with cream cheese icing. It was my favorite dessert. She handed a slice to each of the family and then placed a slice before me, "I heard you liked carrot cake, so I baked one for you."

Again, my only reply was, "Thank you, Sara."

Later that night we had a town meeting. There was an announcement given by one of the elders: "This Saturday is our annual barbecue. We need to have a record of the volunteers and their contributions. You can see sister Bethel, sister Anna, sister Judy, or myself after the meeting. We need to hear from you as soon as possible. Thank you."

No sooner than he had finished his appeal, Sara raised her hand and addressed the elder. "Elder Brooks, on behalf of Lance and myself, we'd like to contribute a side of beef."

"That'll be *most* appreciated, sister Sara," elder Brooks replied, nodding his head with a smile. "Sister Bethel, would you please put Sara and Lance's names down for a side of beef."

After the meeting we had a Bible study. The Bible teacher expounded on what was called the rapture of the church. Included within the promises of the New Covenant agreement were promises that Jesus Christ would return for His faithful followers. These followers are also referred to as Christ's church and the bride of Christ. As part of their reward, they are joint heirs with Christ and will reign with Him for a thousand years.

Jesus promises that He will return as King of Kings and Lord of Lords and He will gather His bride from the four ends of the earth. According to the Bible, when Christ comes for His church, He will appear in the clouds with His angels and it will be like lightning that comes from the east and flashes to the west. In an instant, in the twinkling of an eye, when the last trumpet sounds, the bride of Christ will be changed from mortality to immortality. Those who have already died in Christ will be gathered to Him, and then He will send forth his mighty angels to gather the remaining members of His church who are still alive, and they too will meet Him in the air. Then, with the wrath of the Almighty God, Christ will destroy the wicked with the two-edged sword that proceeds from His mouth, which is God's Word of Truth. The devil will then be bound in a bottomless pit, unable to tempt the people for a thousand years.

Christ's bride—those who have made themselves ready through their righteous deeds of faith—will be arrayed in all her splendor. This is the body of believers who have overcome the world by the shed blood of Jesus Christ, the word of their testimony, and didn't love their lives so much that they were afraid to die for Him. These are the ones who are invited to the wedding supper of the sacrificial Lamb of God. Therefore Christ will serve them at the banquet table and they will reign with Him for a thousand years here on earth. After that, they will be with Him in His Father's glorious heavenly kingdom forever. As far as I could tell, this was the Christian's only real hope.

Making an agreement to sacrifice the rest of my life for a future hope that may or may not exist was a serious concession to make. The promise of being a child and an heir of God and co-heir with Christ was a notable consideration, but in order to share in His glory I also had to share in His sufferings. The Biblical statement that the present sufferings aren't worth comparing with the eventual glory of living with Him eternally left a lot for my imagination. Even though there was a condition that God would reveal His supernatural kingdom to His children through the Holy Spirit, I had to first become a child of God in order for His Spirit to give me that revelation.

Considering everything I was being taught, the scales still remained heavily unbalanced. This tangible world that I lived in outweighed the spiritual, unseen world by a hundred to one. It was imperative that I count the cost before making such a decision.

The next day, when Sara brought my lunch, she went directly to the stump. She spread out a small cloth on the ground before her, unpacked a lunch for two, and said, "I haven't eaten yet. I thought we might eat together."

I walked over and sat down beside her. She looked at me and said, "You know, Lance, the Bible tells us that 'God created man in His own image, in the image of God created he him, male and female created he them.' Apparently God created the man as a complete individual, with all of the attributes of both sexes. God saw that it wasn't good for the man to be alone, so He brought all of the animals before him and asked him to give them names. God did this so that the man would see that he was the only one without a mate.

"God put Adam to sleep and from within him He selected the necessary components to create a woman. Since the woman was originally a part of the man, she was made from him to be a helper and an expression of his completeness. The Bible tells us, when a man finds a wife he is to leave his father and mother, be united to his wife and the two of them become one flesh and one spirit. They're no longer two people going individual ways, but they're two people that have become one.

"I guess that's kind of hard to understand at first, just like it's hard to understand that the Father, the Son, and the Holy Spirit are separate beings, and yet one and the same. Their thoughts, their words, and their deeds are in total agreement with one another. One of them wouldn't think, say, or do anything that the other wouldn't think, say, or do; that's what makes them one. That's what made Jesus one with the Father. Jesus didn't do or say anything that the Father wouldn't do or say. And, that's also what makes us one with Christ; we want to please Him in everything we think, say, and do. But getting back to the man and woman, they gradually learn to deny themselves for the benefit of the other. Through this selfless love they're being conformed to the image of Christ, and eventually they become one with each other and one in Him.

"As you know, it wasn't long before they disobeyed. We're told that the woman was deceived. The Bible also tells us that the man *knew* what he was doing. In fact, Adam is called a traitor because he understood what God told him, and yet he chose to go against God.

"In the beginning they only knew God's way. Now they knew good *and* evil, and were faced with the choice of doing it their own way or doing it God's way. It took death and separation from God to learn that He's all-knowing, He's all-loving, and He only wants the best for His children; man's way will always end in heartache and death. That's why the Father had to send His Son to redeem those who are willing to deny themselves because they believe His ways are good and right and perfect."

When she finished my heart was yearning. It was as though a bright light had come on. I finally realized what this whole thing was about; it's a love story. The Biblical account of the history of humanity from its inception is a heart-throbbing love story between God and His children.

Like Eve, I had been deceived. I thought I was going the right way, when all of my life I was really going the wrong way. My upbringing, my education, my choice of employment, how I dressed, the car I drove, where I lived, the people I chose as companions, all of my past decisions were made from erroneous information. My education was a product of the world system, which taught me how to succeed in the world *without* God! I sat there with my arms folded across my knees staring at the ground and deeply pondering what I had just heard.

Sara stood up and gathered her belongings into the basket. Stooping down in front of me she said, "Don't be so hard on yourself, Lance. Everyone has to come to the same place of decision where you are now. Some people come sooner than others; some don't come until judgment day. But everyone's eventually faced with the question that you're faced with now: what are you going to do with the One called Jesus Christ?"

That was the last thing I wanted to hear. I couldn't even say "thanks" to a statement like that.

Later that evening Elder Brooks' cow was in labor. Mr. Freeman asked me if I wanted to go along and give him a hand. I felt that it might be a useful lesson for later, so I went along.

This was my first time witnessing a cow giving birth. It was a long delivery because the calf was incorrectly positioned inside its mother and Mr. Freeman had to reposition the calf for delivery. When the calf finally came, it fell to the ground with such force I thought it had broken its neck. But after examining it thoroughly, we learned that it was fine.

It was late when I returned to my cottage. Although I was tired, I couldn't sleep. In the quiet solitude of the night, I examined my life. I was confused and hurting inside. Maybe it was the emotional experience of seeing the newborn calf fighting for its life, or maybe it was the mind-boggling truths I was being taught in the Bible classes. Or maybe it was Sara... My feelings for her were growing daily. All I knew for certain was that a feeling of heaviness was mounting inside me and I didn't have the vaguest idea how to stop it.

The next morning, while working on the dam, Sara constantly invaded my thoughts. I appreciated her concern, since I knew she was trying to help. But how was I going to impress someone who believed that I didn't even know right from wrong. Just because I didn't know the Bible didn't mean I was incapable of making a right decision. And her million dollar questions and profound Biblical statements were trying my patience.

Sara Freeman didn't have a monopoly on what was right. In fact, she was young and inexperienced. She didn't know anything about my past successes. I felt that most of the choices I made were pretty good.

For over two weeks now, Sara had been faithfully bringing my lunch around noon. I didn't bother taking the long walks back to the house any more, so my anticipation of her coming only heightened my anxiety to tell her what was on my mind. My anticipation of seeing Sara grew with each passing minute.

Shortly after noon, I saw her coming across the field. The dress she wore fit snugly around her small waist and hung loosely below her knees. Although it was simple, on Sara it was lovely. Had she been prepared by one of the top modeling agencies in the world, she couldn't have been more appealing.

I felt that Sara cared for me and the only way I knew to impress her was relating some of my past accomplishments. This would help give me the upper hand in our relationship and show her that I was as capable of handling my affairs as anyone, including those living on this mountain.

Sara made her way over the recently cultivated soil and approached me, "Hi, Lance," she greeted with a smile that caused her eyes to sparkle like diamonds.

"Hello, Sara," I began, confidently reaching out to take her hand and draw her closer to me. For the first time in my dealings with her I felt in control of our relationship. "There're a few things I'd like to say. But first, let's have a seat."

Since this wasn't my typical response, she began to scrutinize me, as if trying to read my thoughts. Suddenly her expression changed into puzzlement. Perplexed, she cautiously sat down beside me. I was too impressed with myself to consider what she was thinking or how she felt.

"I've been all over the world," I said, starting the speech I had planned all morning. "I've seen some incredible sights and done some exciting things, some of which I'd like to share with you. I've also met some very important people, Sara, but I haven't met anyone quite like you. You're intelligent and you're beautiful; one of the most beautiful women I've ever met…"

Every word seemed to boost me higher. And yet, the more I said, the more she withdrew. Finally, she wouldn't look at me; she just hung her head. Apparently unable to bear it any longer, she stood up. With an expression that revealed her feelings, she shook her head in disappointment.

Under the circumstances it was impossible for me to continue, so I stopped in mid-sentence. With a look that was now more pity than disappointment, she asked: "What are you saying, Lance…? No, not what are you *saying*, what are you *doing*, is the question I should be asking."

I felt I had violated the trust of a cherished friend; it was like I had broken into her home to steal her prized possessions, only to learn that she was watching me all the time.

Without another word, Sara turned away and started back across the field. With her head lowered to release the falling tears, she headed for the house.

I saw my folly immediately. My selfish, immature behavior was evident to Sara from the start. Had I been more sensitive, I wouldn't be standing here alone, regretting what I had done.

I finally found my voice and cried out: "Sara?" She turned with an expression that spoke louder than the words that followed: "What do you want from me *now*, Lance?"

I shouted with honest sincerity, "Sara, I'm sorry."

While shaking her head in disappointment, she replied, "You really don't understand, do you, Lance?"

Before I could respond she asked me to bring her picnic basket when I came in from work, and then she turned and walked away.

I tried to convince myself that my motives were sincere and above-board. But after honestly examining my intentions, I was forced to admit that the entire ordeal was to satisfy my selfish desires. Had I once considered Sara, I wouldn't be feeling so wretched now. When was I going to learn...? Was I ever going to learn...?!

Normally when I finished working in the fields I returned to the house to shower and eat. Three evenings during the week I attended the Bible class. The other two evenings I usually spent in the town's planning and building department or helping Mr. Freeman around the farm doing small jobs. I didn't have an appetite this evening, so I only stopped at the cottage long enough to drop off the picnic basket. I saw John Jr. in the yard and told him to tell the rest of the family that I was going to the Bible class and not to expect me for dinner. From there I went to the Community Center to read the Bible and wait for the teacher. It wasn't long before he arrived and the lesson began.

We studied from the book of Job. It was a lesson that revealed the devil's satanic character. On two separate occasions all of the angels came before God. Each time God asked Satan had he considered His servant Job, who was an upright man that feared God. In this first account, Satan replied, "Doth Job fear God for nought? Hast not thou made a hedge about him, and about his house, and about all that he hath on every side? Thou hast blessed the work of his hands, and his substance is increased in the land. But put forth thine hand now, and touch all that he hath, and he will curse thee to thy face." God gave the devil permission to destroy all that Job had, but he was forbidden to lay a finger upon Job.

After the loss of everything he owned, including the lives of his sons and daughters and servants, Job still dropped to his knees and worshiped God. His very words were: "Naked came I out of my mother's womb, and naked shall I return thither; the Lord gave, and the Lord hath taken away; blessed be the name of the Lord."

On the second account, God again asked the devil about His servant Job. Satan replied, "Skin for skin, yea, all that a man hath will he give for his life. But put forth thine hand now, and touch his bone and his flesh, and he will curse thee to thy face." The devil was clearly expressing his belief that a man will do anything to save his life. This time God placed Job in the devil's hands but forbid him to take his life.

But Job proved the devil wrong, again. Although the devil afflicted Job with painful sores from the soles of his feet to the top of his head, when his wife told him to curse God and die, without hesitation he replied, "What? shall we receive good at the hand of God, and shall we not receive evil?"

These direct quotes from the devil reveal his thoughts and beliefs. The devil actually believes that there must be a reciprocation of some kind since no one would freely give without expecting something in return. According to Satan, there was always a personal motive and no one would worship God just because He's God.

This lesson illustrated the dark depravity that obsessed the devil. It also revealed that the human character had been conformed to these same depraved characteristics. Attitudes such as survival of the fittest, dog-eat-dog, and self-preservation were all the results of the devil's nature being manifested through the human nature since the fall of Adam and Eve.

These teachings weren't mere principles that I could accept or reject whenever I felt like it. Nor were they simply good things to do. These God-ordained fundamentals of selfless giving were the foundation of existence; they were the way to eternal life. There were only two choices in life; God's selflessness that leads to eternal life or the devil's selfishness that leads to eternal death. It was black or white, gathering or scattering, helping or hindering.

This self-satisfying nature of the devil, which now indwelled the human nature, was actually self-destructive. The insoluble lust of the five senses couldn't be quenched. This addictive nature demanded satisfaction until there wasn't anything left.

The world's present condition hadn't transpired simply because these power-hungry Elitists wanted to rule the world; this was the consequence of spiritual death and separation from God.

This was why Mr. Freeman insisted that I become a Christian before I could be permitted to live among them. Had Mr. Freeman allowed me to stay here without being born again, he would've been responsible for bringing the devil's nature, the world's system, and all of their destructive ways to this whole mountain community.

So what was I fighting? What was I hanging onto with such stubborn refusal? Was it my integrity, or my individualism? I felt imprisoned by my past, my self-centered emotions, and my sensual desires that seemed to have a nature of their own. What I rationally deduced to be right warred against my instincts that demanded constant satisfaction at any cost. This battle between my rational thoughts and my sensorial desires was exactly why I had hurt Sara.

Even though the elders taught that Christ offered freedom from the fleshly bondage that held humanity prisoner, I wasn't sure whether it was true freedom or a greater restriction of do's and don'ts.

All things considered, I still didn't want to give up my rights. I enjoyed being my own boss. If I laid down my old life, I would be giving up *my right* to live the way *I* wanted to live; I couldn't do it *my way*. I just wasn't ready to relinquish the lordship over *my* thoughts, *my* wants and *my* desires to someone else, not even to God. I was at a crucial crossroads, and I still needed more information before I made my decision.

When I returned from the Bible study, I was tired. I knew that everyone had already eaten, which was fine with me since I wouldn't have to face Sara and the rest of the family. A shower helped to refresh me, but it didn't satisfy my hunger. Just as I finished dressing, I heard a knock on the door. "Come in," I shouted in response to the knock.

"I noticed you missed dinner tonight," Mr. Freeman stated as he stepped through the door. "Is there anything wrong?" he asked with concern.

"I'm not feeling too well, Mr. Freeman," I countered, hoping I wouldn't have to give him an explanation.

"Well, you need food; it's like fuel to the body. Sara's got a warm plate on the table for you now. We're having a family meeting and we'd like for you to be there."

I didn't know if Sara had told her family about what had happened today or not. If so, I was prepared to take my punishment, even if it meant leaving the mountain.

Everyone was sitting at their normal places around the table except Sara, Jenny, and Mrs. Freeman; they were still cleaning the dishes from the evening meal. I greeted everyone and sat down at my usual place.

Mr. Freeman began talking as if he was unaware of what had taken place between Sara and I. "You know, son," he said, while turning in my direction, "tomorrow's the barbecue. It's a community affair and everybody has a part in these gatherings.

"There'll be games for the kids, with plenty of food and prizes. Sara told me that you two are contributing a side of beef. John Jr., Frank, and I are in charge of the other half of the cow. Mama and Jenny are baking some pies and cakes. The boys and me already butchered the heifer, set up the pits, and started the coals burning for tomorrow so that part's been taken care of. We'll have to be up early to get this show on the road. I'll wake you at dawn, okay?"

"Actually, I would like to be excused from attending the barbecue, if you don't mind?"

"Well, we can use your help," he replied after a moment's hesitation. "And it sounds to me like the barbecue is just what you need. It'll help you take your mind off your problems and put them on helping the rest of us.

"We sing a song that says it all in a few lines. 'Turn your eyes upon Jesus. Look full in His wonderful face. And the things of earth will grow strangely dim, in the sight of his glory and grace.' Whether you're able to put your eyes on Jesus at this point, I don't know. What I do know is this, problems are only as big as we make them out to be. Personally, I give all of my problems to the Lord, since He's the best problem solver I know. He tells us to cast our cares upon Him, 'cause He cares for us; and I know He does, 'cause He gave His life for us."

After we finished eating, I excused myself from the table and started toward the back door. Sara fell in step beside me, "Let's go for a walk, along the levy by the creek bed."

I reluctantly answered, "All right."

"We'll take the long way," she added, "down the main road through the center of town, until we reach the levy."

"Father," she said as we approached the door. "Lance and I are going to take a walk along the levy, okay?"

"Okay, Sara. It's getting dark a bit earlier now. Maybe you ought to take one of those small lanterns with you, just in case. There's not going to be a moon tonight and you won't be able to see your hand in front of your face. You better grab your sweaters on your way out, too."

"There's still a couple of hours before dark. We should be back before then, but just in case, we'll bring a lantern," she added.

We got our sweaters, picked up a lantern from the shed, and started down the road. It was the same road Mr. Freeman and I came into town on when he first found me. As we passed each of the cabins, Sara gave a portrayal of each family member and how their unique talents blessed the rest of the community.

Children played in their yards and along the roadside. People sat on their porches in rockers, smiling and waving as we passed.

I noticed a flock of chickens playing hunt and peck from one place to another. A large pair of geese honked with outstretched necks, warning us to keep our distance. A couple of dogs chased a cat up a tree, then she sat on a branch looking down teasingly at the barking dogs. The biggest pig I've ever seen rested against the side of a barn feeding her piglets. It was a pleasant, peaceful, late afternoon, the kind that made you glad to be alive.

There wasn't any rush-hour traffic or mounting pressure from impatient drivers that normally took place this time of day in the major cities throughout the world. No one was too busy to speak. There weren't any signs of anxiety or stress attacks. Everyone seemed to possess a peace that showed they were content in the state they were in.

The smell of country filled the air and the tranquil atmosphere was contagious. I felt total contentment walking with Sara along this country road, enjoying the wonders and natural beauties associated with life.

Once we passed the cabins, the road began to narrow. We were leaving the town and approaching the open country. On our left was the forest, which began to broaden as the tree line curved inland with the road.

We were approaching the spot where John Jr. found me sleeping after I had made my way through the forest to the side of the road. On the cliff side of the forest, for a distance of a few hundred feet, was the only section accessible to the plateau from the valley below. This was also the place where the townsfolk hoisted their belongings when they moved up from the valley. The remaining terrain that surrounded the mountain was steep and covered with jagged rocks that made it impossible to climb unless you were a professional mountain climber with the proper equipment.

The road began to narrow considerably as we approached the bridge that crossed over the creek. "During the winter the creek usually overflows," Sara informed me. "That's why it's going to be a blessing when you finish the dam. That way the water can be saved and then channeled to irrigate the farmland during the summer months." These were the first words spoken since we left the town.

The levy ran alongside the creek in a gradual uphill climb all the way to the base of the mountains a mile away. On the downside of the bridge, it ran to the edge of the mountain, sending the water plummeting over the mountainside during the seasonal rains.

The scenery was so lovely, I could have walked for hours oblivious of time or distance. When we reached the base of the mountain there was a bench that someone had carved out of a tree stump with just enough room for two people to sit comfortably.

From our elevated position, we could see the entire plateau. Since we left the bridge, neither of us had said a word. Again, it was Sara who broke the silence. "Earlier today I had a long talk with father about you. We discussed your arrest, your imprisonment, and how you managed to escape and make it back here alive. You're probably the only person *ever* to escape from one of those places without getting caught or killed. I know for certain you're the only person who's found this place—hidden so high in the mountains and all. You're also the only one who's been given a choice to live with us.

"When I thought about all the things you went through since that morning you left, I realized that none of it happened by chance. Think about it: your arrest, and the foul-up on the memory-scan. You even became the head draftsman so that you'd be able to get the maps you needed. Then there's the man with a glider, who just so happened to live right under you. There're too many coincidences for them to be all by chance. Even if you believe in luck or some other foolishness as that, you'd still have to stretch your imagination pretty far to believe that *you* could be so lucky.

"Well, that's when I saw it as clear as day. Lance, you're here because God wants you here. I don't know *why,* but He has a purpose for you here."

"I haven't given that much thought," I replied cautiously, not wanting to respond too hastily. "I know that I'm facing the biggest decision of my life, and I don't quite know how to handle it."

"That's exactly what I'm saying. Your whole life depends on you becoming a Christian."

"It's not that simple, Sara. First I have to believe that there *is* a God, and then I have to believe that He'll accept me as His child."

"That's what faith is. First, you have to believe that God exists. Then, you have to believe that He'll respond to you if you seek Him with all of your heart. What makes Him God is that He has the power to do everything that He claims He'll do. I worship Him because I know that He loves me and He's always got my best interest at heart."

"That's not an easy thing to do," I replied, realizing this was precisely my dilemma. "I've never believed in anyone or anything but myself. My gods are knowledge, status, success, possessions, and the ability to use them to get more of the same. My world has never gone any higher or any further than what I could attain.

"When I discovered *The Master Plan,* it wasn't long before I realized that I had been brainwashed, just like everybody else in the world. My first reaction was rebellion. I was pretty upset when I learned that I had spent my life helping a group of people whose whole purpose was to enslave me. It wasn't that I knew a better way—in fact, I function quite well in the kind of society they were putting together. I rebelled because I couldn't stand the thought of someone controlling my life and telling me what I could and couldn't do. Now, I'm starting to see that God's way is the only way."

"*Today* is the day of salvation, Lance," she countered. "Tomorrow's not guaranteed to any of us. And don't think I'm trying to scare you into heaven, because I don't believe anybody really comes to the Lord like that. You come because you see how wonderful and loving and caring Christ is, and how wretched and ugly and selfish you are. You actually fall in love with Him and want to be like Him. When I said tomorrow's not guaranteed, I said it because it's true. God's knocking on your heart today! He might not keep knocking forever."

"You're asking me to give up my *life*, Sara. You're asking me to cast aside my thoughts, my feelings, and my desires. You're asking me to take a lifetime of learning, all the desires I've cultivated over the years, all my beliefs and my personal feelings—which is me—and bury them as if they don't exist anymore. You want me to exchange Lance Roberts for a Biblical version of Jesus Christ.

"Look, I've been given an ultimatum. Either I accept Jesus Christ into my life or I leave this mountain and a lot of people I've grown to care about. Accepting the teachings of Jesus Christ means that I'm admitting that my whole life's been a failure. I won't do that, because I don't believe that's so."

"Well... How *do* you sum up your life, Lance? Do you claim success *now?*"

"I didn't live a carefree, lazy, pleasure-seeking life, Sara. I worked hard and sacrificed a lot to accomplish what I had. I'm not a liar, a thief, or a murderer. And I didn't hang out in bars or use drugs, or run with loose women. I just wasn't ever taught Biblical principles, that's all. Compared to most people, I'm a pretty good person!"

"The things you just mentioned would've stopped you from reaching your goal, that's why you didn't do them. You're comparing yourself with other people, not Christ. You're also boasting about the good deeds that you did, when most good deeds are done for self-satisfaction. Lance, your motive is self-seeking unless you're doing it for the good of others, without expecting anything in return. The Bible says, 'All men have sinned and come short of the glory of God.' The problem is, we're all born with a selfish, sinful nature. Until the selfish nature is changed, everything we do is self-motivated."

Sara had a way of cutting through the frill and getting right to the point. "The question is," I stated honestly, "will God accept me? There are a lot of things in my life that I still need to get rid of before I can come to Him. Just last night I read that God can't tolerate sin. Well, if I judged myself according to His standards, I'm one of the biggest sinners there are!"

"That's a mistake a lot of people make. They think *they* have to clean up their lives before they come to God. *You* can't do it, Lance! You have to come as you are. You can't change the sinful nature you're born with. If *you* had the power to change, Jesus' life, death, and resurrection was for nothing. No, *He's* the one who does the changing in us, and He does it from the inside out. He puts *His* nature inside you, *then* you can do it His way."

"There has to be *something* that I have to do, Sara. It can't be that simple."

"The only thing you have to do is love Him with all your heart. If you do that, *God* will make you like His Son."

"What about all the things I still want to do that go against what He commands?"

"Before Jesus went to the cross, He knew that He would have to carry all the sins of the world. During His whole life He always had fellowship with the Father. As you said, God couldn't tolerate sin. Jesus knew that He would have to take on the sins of the whole world. He knew He had to be separated from His Father. Three times Jesus asked the Father if there was any other way to carry out the salvation plan. After asking the third time, without an answer, Jesus knew that there was no other way. His response was: 'Not *my* will, but *thy* will be done.'

"He placed His life into the hands of the One who judges all things justly. Jesus wanted to please the Father no matter what the cost. If you have that same desire to please Him, no matter what the cost, He promises to see you through to the end, Lance."

"Why do Christians worship Jesus as though He were God?" I asked.

"It's *all* about Jesus, Lance. The Bible teaches us that God loves us so much that He gave His only Son as a living sacrifice for the whole world. And don't forget that Jesus had a choice in the matter, too. He didn't have to come to earth and die for you and me. It was His love for us that made Him leave heaven and come down to this sinful earth as a man. He sacrificed His life so that we could have eternal life.

"For three days and three nights Jesus was alone in the grave believing that God would raise Him from the dead. And God honored that faith by raising Him from the dead. Even in death, Christ was tested and proved that He trusted in the Father. That's why God was pleased to give His Son all power and authority over His creation.

"Those of us who accept God's love gift of eternal life make Jesus our Lord. If we continue to obey God to the end, the same as Jesus did, death won't be able to hold us in the grave either. God will raise us from the grave the same as He raised up Jesus.

"The Bible says that all creation is under the judgment of death because of man's sin and its curse on the earth. The Bible also tells us that the creation cries out, as if in birth pains, until we're conformed to His likeness. The last enemy to be defeated is death. When there's no sin, the death-enemy is defeated.

"In these last days people have a choice to worship the Antichrist or Jesus Christ. Those who reject Jesus will be thrown into the lake of eternal hellfire with the devil and his demons. Once Jesus restores everything, He'll turn it back over to the Father and we'll be with them forever. That's God's desire for everyone, including you, Lance."

"Okay, I understand why it's all about Jesus. But you just said that we're living in the last days. What do you mean by *last days*?"

"We don't know the day nor the hour that Jesus will return and bring an end to this existence as we know it today, but the Bible describes certain signs that will take place so that we'll be prepared when He comes."

"Sara, people have predicted the end of the world since Jesus walked the earth. So tell me about some of these *so-called* signs that prove that Christ is coming soon?"

"The Bible tells us in Second Thessalonians, chapter two, verse three that two things must happen before Jesus returns to get His bride. The first thing is the apostasy of the church or the falling away of believers. The second thing is that the Antichrist will be revealed; he'll exalt himself above God and he'll sit in the temple in Jerusalem, proclaiming to be God and everyone will worship him. Everyone, that is, except the ones that know Jesus as their Lord and Savior.

"The Bible says that no one will be able to buy or sell unless they take the mark of the beast. Remember when everyone was offered the mark if they worshipped the false prophet? There were a lot of people we thought were Christians who took the mark. They turned against true believers and had them imprisoned, persecuted, and even put to death. We knew then that this was the great falling away of the church. And when we heard that the prince sat in the new temple in Jerusalem, claiming to be God and cursing the true God of heaven, we knew that he was the Antichrist."

Puzzled, I asked, "Why would God allow this Antichrist to persecute His church?"

"Jesus warned us that the whole world would hate us because of Him. During the last ten years they've killed millions of Christians just because they refused to denounce Christ. These believers are showing everyone—including the devil and his demons—that they won't worship anybody but the Lord Jesus Christ!"

"It almost sounds like their looking forward to being martyred," I stated.

"Jesus is *the* sacrifice for sin, and nobody else can do that. These saints aren't taking their own lives; if they did, it would be self-righteousness. But they wouldn't kill in order to protect themselves either. That would be going against the commandment to love your neighbor as you love yourself and pray for those who spitefully abuse you. If we've truly died to this world and everything it has to offer, then there's nothing to lose and everything to gain by dying for Christ. The issue of dying for Christ has to be settled in our hearts long before we're confronted with actual death.

"Just as God permitted Satan to test Job, God's given Satan the authority to test the whole world through the Antichrist. Everyone who's not committed to Christ will worship the Antichrist and take the mark.

"Our faithfulness to Jesus Christ is proven by how we stand firm while we're going through the tests. Simply disagreeing with the world system doesn't mean you're living for Jesus Christ. The Bible says that God allows the unbelievers to reach the fullness of their depravity; He allows the devil to give them a strong delusion so that they actually believe the lies of the Antichrist. Because they love the lie and hate the truth, and love wickedness and hate righteousness, God turns them over to their own depraved thinking."

"While I was in the labor camp we were forced to attend the services on Sundays—they were pretty eerie, to say the least. But the false prophet, as you call him, often boasted how he and the prince were bringing about a state of Utopia throughout the world."

"The Antichrist and his army are forcing countries to sign peace agreements, but it's a false peace. People still hate each other; they're just being forced to suppress their hatred. Without the peace that comes through knowing Jesus Christ, there can't be peace on earth. The Bible says, 'For when they shall say, Peace and safety; then sudden destruction cometh upon them, as travail upon a woman with child.' Even now there are mass killings like never before. In fact, Jesus says, if He weren't to return when He does, everyone will be killed.

"God is shaking the heavens and the earth, angels and humans alike. Everything that can be shaken will be shaken loose. Only those who are established in Jesus Christ and the Word of God will be able to stand through these terrible things that are happening."

"When Jesus comes back for His church, how will we know for certain that it's Him and not a counterfeit?"

"'For as the lightning cometh out of the east, and shineth even unto the west; so shall also the coming of the Son of Man be.' He will appear in the clouds with His angels. Those who've already died in Christ will be raised first. Then He will send His angels to gather His elect, those of us who are still alive on earth when He comes. In the twinkling of an eye, at the last trumpet call, we'll be changed into His likeness and caught up to meet Him in the air. In an instant, our mortal bodies will be changed into immortality.

"Dressed in pure white garments of righteousness and riding white horses, we'll join Him as He comes down to make war against the Antichrist and all the enemies of God. This will be God's wrath poured out upon the earth with all vengeance. So heavy will the weight of wickedness be upon the earth that the oceans will roar and toss about without restraint; the sun will refuse to shine, the moon will turn blood red, the stars will fall from the sky and the heavenly bodies will be shaken.

"With the breath of His mouth, which is the Word of God, Jesus will defeat the Antichrist, who will then be cast into eternal darkness, which is the lake of hellfire that burns forever.

"At that time, a mighty angel will come down from heaven with a chain to bind the devil; he'll throw him into a bottomless pit and seal it up for a thousand years. The rest of the dead won't come to life until the second resurrection, which takes place after the thousand years is over. Jesus tells us that all of His followers will be seated at a huge banquet table and He'll serve us personally. What a glorious day that will be. Hallelujah!"

I could see the picture clearly, and I wondered why she stopped. "What happens next?" I asked.

"Although I know it's in the Bible, I don't thoroughly understand everything that will take place during the millennium, or thousand years. But those who've been faithful to Christ will live and reign with Him for a thousand years right here on earth. During that time, all the weapons will be beaten into plowshares, the lamb will lie down with the lion and there'll be peace over the whole earth. It'll be real peace, because the devil will be locked up and Jesus will reign as King. God's creation will live in safety, and we won't have to worry about war.

"When the thousand years are over, Satan will be let out of his prison. He'll go out to tempt, test, and refine the people again. He'll stir up a large multitude against Christ and His followers. This multitude will probably be the young who died before they were old enough to be proven; they may even be those born during the millennium and haven't yet had their faith in God tested, I'm not certain. But they'll march to Jerusalem, the holy city, to make war against Christ and His saints.

"This time God acts quickly. With hailstones, fire, and brimstone He zaps the devil and everyone who follows him and they're immediately thrown into the lake of eternal hellfire.

"Then comes the Day of Judgment. Everyone who ever lived will be brought before the Great White Throne of Judgment. Everybody will see the Father and the Son sitting upon their thrones in glorious splendor. They'll see the heavenly hosts and thousands times ten thousands of angels delighted to be in the presence of the Father and the Son. The books will be opened and also the book of life. They'll be judged according to what they had done, as recorded in the books. It'll be like waking from a bad dream with their whole life behind them. They won't be able to change one wicked thought, one harsh word, or one cruel deed. They'll re-experience the times that people told them about Christ and they ridiculed them and shunned Christ. They'll realize that it was God who gave them life; that each breath of air they breathed was His; that each drop of water they drank was His, that He freely gave His wondrous creation for their pleasure, and not once did they thank Him for it. They'll see the spear marks in Jesus' side and the nail prints in His hands and feet; they'll see Him as the sacrificial lamb who died for them. Then they'll drop to their knees and worship the Lamb of God who was slain for the sins of the whole world; they'll confess that He is King of Kings and Lord of Lords.

"Those whose names are not written in the Lamb's book of life will be thrown into the lake of fire with the devil and his demons and tormented forever and ever. Those whose names *are* written in the Lamb's book of life and served Jesus Christ with all of their hearts while here on earth won't experience the second death.

"Then God will bring forth the new heaven and the new earth. The old order of things will pass away. There won't be any more weeping, or pain, or heartache. He'll wipe away our tears and cleanse our minds from all the old thoughts of this Godforsaken world. Everyone who enters the new heaven and the new earth will be there because they have been proven faithful to God and worthy of His eternal kingdom. It'll be worth it all. Amen."

"It sounds almost like a fairy tale," I told her. "But I know that it's true. I've done a lot of serious thinking about my life during these past few weeks, Sara."

"Like what, Lance?" she asked.

"The things I've learned in the Bible classes have seriously affected me. I've been forced to consider whether or not I'm capable of living the Christian life, and if not, what my life will be like if I had to leave the mountain."

"Well, what's your decision?" she asked anxiously.

"Sara, I know that I'm a sinner, and I really do want Christ to change me. I just don't know how to go about it." I answered impulsively.

"Oh, Lance," Sara replied. "It's so simple. Just tell Jesus everything you feel inside. He's waiting at the door of your heart. All you have to do is ask Him; He'll come and live inside you forever."

The burden that was accumulating over the past few weeks was now unbearable. Unable to endure it any longer, I begged God for forgiveness.

Instantly, as soon as the words left my mouth, a miraculous, unspeakable joy overcame me. I was free! The turmoil was gone, the burden was lifted, and I wasn't confused any more. With God in control it seemed senseless to entertain worry or fear. All I wanted to do was rejoice and thank the Lord for saving me.

When I expressed this to Sara, she fell upon my neck with joy. "Praise the Lord, Lance, you've been born again. Do you know what that means?"

"All I know is that I don't have any more worries and fears. Sara, I was at the bottom of the pit. My whole life was one big mess and there wasn't anywhere for me to turn. Now I feel a thousand pounds lighter. The blindfold is off, and I can see beyond *me* and all of my problems."

"Praise you, Lord Jesus," was her immediate response. "Let's pray, Lance?"

While kneeling on the ground beside the bench, Sara led me through the sinner's prayer.

I now realized that God had created me for a specific purpose that fit within His overall plan. I wanted to know His purpose for my life, and how I fit into that plan. Perhaps, through my desire to please Him, I could give back to Him some of the joy that He just gave me.

When we finished praying, we noticed the sun was approaching the crest of the mountain. We silently watched its huge fiery surface drop from view. A curtain of darkness, spotted with glittering stars, followed the last ray of light. We marveled, realizing that this was just one more of God's magnificent creations created for our pleasure. In the midst of this serenity, we thanked God for His wonderful creation.

"Do you think your family will be worried about us being gone so long?" I asked Sara, thinking about Mr. and Mrs. Freeman's concern for their daughter. "Maybe we ought to start back."

"My family trusts me, Lance, and they know that I'm in the Lord's hands. It gets pretty dark out here with no moon. The lantern will probably keep the animals away, but I don't think it's wise to take that long walk along the levy on a moonless night."

We talked through the night. I saw everything differently now. I knew that Sara cared for me, but I also knew that her major concern was for my soul and where I would spend eternity. God needed someone faithful like Sara to bring me His salvation plan. Mr. Freeman or the elders' teachings of the gospel couldn't do it alone; God knew it would also take Sara. I felt an eternal bonding with her that caused me to desire her in a different way than I had ever desired a woman before.

Without another thought, I asked, "Sara, would you *please* marry me?"

As soon as I proposed, she bolted to an upright position. From the flickering light of the lantern I could barely make out the look on her face as she beamed with joy. "Lance, now that you're a child of God, I'd be honored to share the rest of my life with you."

"Does that mean, *yes*?" I asked, wanting to be certain that she was giving her consent.

"Yes, that means *yes*!"

"Thank you, Lord!" I shouted. Overwhelmed with joy, I pulled her toward me and kissed her. I suddenly wanted everyone on the mountain to share in my excitement.

"It's starting to get light, Sara," noticing the dawn breaking over the tops of the mountains. "Let's hurry back to the cabin so that we can tell your parents the good news. Do you think they'll be upset?"

"No, Lance. They wanted you to come to the Lord as badly as I did. The Bible tells us that even the angels in heaven rejoice whenever a person becomes a part of the family of God. The whole mountain will rejoice at your salvation."

"I was talking about us getting married, Sara. But I can see where they'll be excited about my salvation, too."

The levy and thick terrain now lay behind us. About a mile from town I suddenly heard a clacking noise in the air high above us. It was unmistakably an Army helicopter. When I told Sara, she stopped, listening and searching the sky attentively.

We spotted them at the same time. There were two helicopters following each other in single file, apparently on a mission together. They were traveling to the left of us, in a northerly direction away from town. The crafts continued to grow smaller until they finally disappeared out of our sight. The town lay far to the right of the direction they were traveling, so we were relieved they hadn't noticed it.

For no apparent reason, I continued to glance in the direction the two helicopters had disappeared. After a few minutes I spotted a small, black dot beginning to materialize in the distant sky. It was too far away to hear, but I believed it was one of the helicopters. I was now certain that the dot was growing larger, so I kept my sights locked on its position.

Seeing only one aircraft puzzled me. Was this another helicopter or one of the two that disappeared earlier? I decided not to alarm Sara until I was certain.

With every step, the dot grew larger. Now I was positive that it was an aircraft of some kind, but I couldn't yet determine whether it was a helicopter or a small airplane. Then I saw the second craft coming out of its turn, as if finally agreeing with the suspicions of the first. They were a good distance apart, but they were both now heading in our direction.

"Sara, I believe our friends are coming back," I calmly mentioned, pointing in the general direction of the two helicopters.

Again, she searched the sky. "I see them," she said, "and this time it looks like they've spotted the town."

"I think we should hurry back to warn them," I said, not knowing what else we could do.

As we picked up our pace, Sara began to talk to me. "Long before we left the valley, God warned us about the violence that would sweep through the country. God would speak to father or one of the elders and reveal what was ahead. When you came, you just verified what we already knew was coming. God's never failed to show us the direction He wanted us to go. As far as I know, nobody's said anything about us leaving the mountain, and that's puzzling me."

She took a moment to gather her thoughts and then she said something that shocked me. "Lance, I know that God is in control of *everything*. There's nothing in all His creation that He's not aware of before it takes place. He's the Creator of all things, and He's in control of *everything*. If those pilots spotted the town, God has allowed it for His glory and our good."

"That doesn't make any sense, Sara. Why would God want us to be tortured, or killed, or imprisoned in a concentration camp for the rest of our lives?"

"I can't answer that, Lance. All I know for certain is, '*Everything* works for the good of those who love God and are called according to His purpose.' Do you love Him, Lance?" she asked, not really as a question to me, but as a reminder of the commitment I made to God.

"You know I do," I answered, somewhat offended.

Sara continued. "There's a story in the Bible about a man named Joseph. His older brothers were jealous of him so they sold him into slavery. He was only 17 years old at the time, but God was with him and caused him to become ruler over the household of the captain who bought him. Some time later the captain's wife made advances toward Joseph. When he refused, she told her husband that he tried to rape her, and Joseph was sent to prison. But he trusted God and remained faithful, so God gave him favor with the prison warden and he was placed in charge of the whole prison. Joseph learned how to rule wisely, and proved that he was ready for the job God created him for. The way that God had Joseph released from prison placed him in a position of authority over the whole kingdom; he was the king's only advisor. God had prepared Joseph all of his life for that position.

"During the whole time Joseph was in prison he never complained once. He was a witness to those around him, and everyone knew that he was different because God was with him. Through Joseph, God was able to preserve the Israelite people until the time they left Egypt four hundred years later.

"God had to have a man in a position of authority over this ungodly nation. Joseph was tried and tested and proved to be that man. On the other hand, Joseph didn't know what the future would bring; he only knew that his trust was anchored in the Almighty God and that was enough for him.

"God knows what's best, Lance, and He has *everything* under control. We can't see past our noses, but God sees forever!"

"All right, that answers my question about imprisonment, but what about death? How is God glorified when His children are killed by ungodly, wicked men?" I asked with a hint of sarcasm.

"Most of the prophets died horrible deaths. All of the apostles of Christ were nailed to a cross, burned at the stake, beheaded, or martyred in some way except John. He was banished to the Island of Patmos to spend the rest of his life alone because he wouldn't stop preaching the gospel of Jesus Christ. He was the only one that died a natural death.

"When Jesus' disciples asked him to describe how it would be at the end, He warned them about the things that would take place. These are also warnings for us. Here's what He tells us, 'But before all this, they will lay hands on you and persecute you. They will deliver you to synagogues and prisons, and you will be brought before kings and governors, and all on account of my name. *This will result in you being witnesses to them.* But make up your mind not to worry beforehand how you will defend yourselves. For I will give you words and wisdom that none of your adversaries will be able to resist or contradict. You will be betrayed even by parents, brothers, relatives, and friends, and they will put some of you to death. All men will hate you because of me. But not a hair of your head will perish. By standing firm you will gain life.' Eternal life, Lance!

"This isn't God's world; He's preparing another world for us, and at the same time, He's preparing us for it. We're only passing through on our way to heaven. Jesus' words are forever encouraging us; 'I will be with you always, even until the end of the age.' *If* we trust Him and remain faithful *to the end*!

"The Word says, 'And they overcame him by the blood of the Lamb, and by the word of their testimony; and *they loved not their lives unto the death.*' There's no greater honor than to die for the One that saved you and gave you eternal life. It's only reasonable to make your body a living sacrifice to Christ. After all, He died for us first. But if we won't *live* for Him, we won't *die* for Him either."

"This isn't that easy to accept," I assured her, without any sarcasm this time. "But I understand."

As we approached the town we could see the helicopters hovering overhead. We expected them to fire on the town any second, but they didn't. The two helicopters circled masterfully above, taking everything into account before they sped away.

"Evidently they're returning to their home base," I commented, while trying to keep them in view as long as possible. "It looks like they're heading toward Camp 1100. If they are, they'll be back, and there won't be just two of them when they return."

Most of the people were asking each other questions or making general comments about what had just happened. "It looks like the whole town is here, Sara," I commented.

"That's because everybody is getting ready for the fellowship barbecue. Most of the women have been up since dawn preparing their special dishes and baking their favorite cakes, pies, cookies, and other delights. And every elder seems to have his own special sauce, or special method for barbecuing a side of beef, a pig, lamb or goat. With all the games and activities that'll be going on, it's almost like Christmas to the kids.

"This is the time of year we lay our cares aside, thank the Lord for His mercies and blessings, and fellowship with each other. In fact, one of the rules is that everybody has to speak to every person in the community at least once before the day is ended."

When Sara saw Mr. Freeman, she grabbed me by the hand. "There's father, let's go meet him" she said as we rushed toward him.

"Father? Father, over here," she shouted over the crowd, waving to get his attention. When he saw us, Sara released my hand and rushed to meet her father. Without hesitating, Mr. Freeman opened his arms and hugged his daughter tightly.

"Let's go to the house; we have so much to tell you," she told him while beaming all over with excitement.

Mr. Freeman put his arm around her, and then he turned to me and held out his hand, "Come on son, breakfast is waiting for you; I'm sure you're both hungry."

I was hungry, and yet, because of all the excitement, eating was the last thing on my mind.

Most of the elders were gathered around the kitchen table drinking coffee and discussing the inevitable consequences of the two helicopters finding our location. When Mrs. Freeman spotted us, she made room at the table, insisting that we eat.

"I'll be back in a flash with your breakfast," she told us. Turning to Jenny, she asked for her help as they went into the kitchen together.

"Sweetheart," Mr. Freeman said, looking across the table at Sara, "what did you want to tell me?"

The room grew silent as Sara began to speak. "Last night, in the most touching way I've ever witnessed, Lance gave his heart to Christ."

Instantly the room was filled with shouts of joy. "Praise the Lord!" "Hallelujah!" "Glory to God!"

"Well, well, well...it's *brother* Lance, now!" One of my Bible teachers roared with laughter.

"But that's not all," Sara continued. "He also asked me to become his wife."

Mr. Freeman jumped to his feet, scurried around the table and lifted me from the chair with a hearty bear hug: "You're really my son, now."

I tried to hold back the tears that were welling up within my eyes, but I couldn't. "Thank you, sir."

One by one, the elders filed by. Some shook my hand while others grasped my shoulders as they each stepped forward to express their congratulations.

"What's all the fuss about," Mrs. Freeman asked, carrying two plates overflowing with eggs, bacon, fried potatoes, and hot cakes.

"Last night Lance asked the Lord into his heart. Now, Sara and him are going to be married. That's what all the fuss is about, mamma," Mr. Freeman answered, choking as he spoke.

"Praise the Lord! Hallelujah! Thank you Jesus!" she shouted, almost dropping both plates before setting them on the table. Cupping Sara's face in her hands, she sobbed while kissing her profusely on the cheeks.

As quickly as she had started, she stopped and turned to me. "God bless you, Lance. *God* did this. No one else could've done this but God! They can be married today. What do you say, papa?"

"Why sure. I can do it myself. Since today's the big barbecue we'll just tell everybody before it starts that we'll have the marriage ceremony later in the evening."

I was pleased with the way things were going, but I couldn't get my mind off those two helicopters.

"Mr. Freeman, I don't want to put a damper on things, but I think those helicopters are a pretty serious matter. When Sara and I first saw them they were leaving the area. Evidently one of the pilots saw something that caused him to investigate further. The other one seemed reluctant to come back at first, but he came. After they saw what they wanted to see, they left in the direction of Camp 1100, the place from where I escaped. In case they return, I want everyone to know, if it's me they're after, I'll go with them peacefully and the rest of you don't have to worry."

"That's mighty big of you, son. I'm sure everybody here appreciates that. Don't we brothers?" he asked, looking at the men seated around the table.

All the elders answered in unison with an affirmative, "Yes."

"I don't mean to slight your act of heroism, son, but they want all of us—every last one of us! Just last night we discussed this in a meeting. The Lord's already revealed to us what's about to happen.

"Brother Fred, would you please pass me my Bible. It's right there on the table, by your elbow. Yes, sir. Thank you very much.

"This may sound strange to most people, even to some Christians, but God gives this Antichrist power over the saints for a reason. The Bible, in Revelation, chapter thirteen, verse eight, says it a lot better than I can. 'And all that dwell upon the earth shall worship him, whose names are not written in the book of life of the Lamb slain from the foundation of the earth. If any man have an ear, let him hear. He that leadeth into captivity shall go into captivity; he that killeth with the sword must be killed with the sword. Here is the patience and the faith of the saints.'

"Just like the devil, the Antichrist is a tool God uses to refine His people and punish the wicked. Spending the rest of our lives in a slave labor camp isn't something I'm looking forward to. It takes patient endurance and a deep love for God to stand in front of a firing squad, or place your neck across the chopping block, or submit to being burned alive because you refuse to denounce Jesus Christ as your Lord.

"Daniel tells us in chapter eleven, verses thirty-three through thirty-seven: 'And they that understand among the people shall instruct many; yet they shall fall by the sword, and by flame, by captivity, and by spoil, many days. Now when they shall fall, they shall be holpen with a little help: but many shall cleave to them with flatteries. And some of them of understanding shall fall, to try them, and to purge, and to make them white, even to the time of the end: because it is yet for a time appointed. And the king shall do according to his will; and he shalt exalt himself, and magnify himself above every god, and shall speak marvelous things against the God of gods and shall prosper till the indignation be accomplished: for that that is determined shall be done. Neither shall he regard the God of his fathers, nor the desire of women, nor regard any god: for he shall magnify himself above all.'

"Purification and refinement come through persecution. For some reason, the only way God can keep our eyes steadfast on Him is through persecution. But don't fret, He won't put more on us than we can bear; His Word says so. Jesus is our strengthener, and He'll be with us to the end.

"Standing firm under persecution also shows the devil and his demons that God's got some faithful servants down here. It doesn't matter if the devil destroys everything we have; it doesn't even matter if he strikes our bodies with sickness or death, we've made up our minds to glorify Christ Jesus no matter what he does, or what happens.

"Lance," Mr. Freeman said, "you need to be ready in your heart to face what's about to take place. Some of us might be burned to death, some of us might lose our heads, and some might go to prison. It doesn't matter how we get to heaven, as long as we get there and God is glorified on the way. After all, we're all going to get new bodies anyway," he related with a smile.

"I know you just came to the Lord, Lance, so my question is not an easy one. But are you ready to take a stand for Jesus Christ, no matter what the cost?"

"Mr. Freeman, there's no other place I would rather be than right here. I would prefer to die today and be with Jesus Christ than live forever under this present world system. This morning on our way home Sara explained most of the things you're discussing. Regardless of what may happen, I've already resolved it in my heart to follow Jesus to the end."

"Praise God! Well, do you have any questions then, son?"

"Yes, there is one. I understood that Jesus was coming back to rescue those Christians who've been obedient to Him. However, judging from the Scriptures you just read, it sounds like Jesus is *not* coming back to rescue His body. So, is Jesus coming back for His Church, and if so, when?"

"Those are two good questions, son. The word rapture isn't in the Bible, but that's the word Christians have used for years when they talk about Christ coming back for His people. There're three different beliefs about the rapture. Some say Christ is coming back for His church before the Tribulation, some say He's coming in the middle of the Tribulation, and some say He's coming at the end of the Tribulation. In the 1900's a teaching started that Jesus Christ was coming back to get His church *before* the Tribulation. One of the Scriptures that's often used is: 'For God hath not appointed us to wrath, but to obtain salvation by our Lord Jesus Christ.' And that's true, God's wrath is directed against unbelievers, not believers. When we rightly divide the Word of truth, we see that there's a big difference between tribulation and God's wrath.

"Before we go any further, we need to make an important point: there's only *one* body of Christ. Starting from the first born-again believer to the last born-again believer, all of them make up the body of Christ. Since we know for sure that He's coming, I guess the real question is, would He come before the last member of His body is born again. God knows them all by name, since He wrote their names in the Lamb's book of life before the foundation of the earth. And if He comes before the Tribulation, He would be coming to get only part of His body; He would be leaving behind thousands upon thousands of born-again believers, who the Bible says will be persecuted during the Tribulation period.

"So, when the Bible says Christ is coming for His *body*, that has to mean the *whole* body, including the last person whose name is written in the book of life. As the Bible clearly shows, there'll be Christians alive before the Tribulation, there'll be Christians alive in the middle of the Tribulation, and there'll be Christians alive at the end of the Tribulation.

"So let's first look at some verses to see what the Bible says about the body of Christ during the Tribulation. Afterward, we'll see what it says about Jesus coming back to get His body.

"In the book of Revelation, Jesus sends letters to seven churches. Christ has nothing but praise for two of those seven churches, the church of Smyrna and the church of Philadelphia. To the church of Philadelphia, Jesus promises: 'I also will keep thee from the hour of temptation which shall come upon all the world, to try them that dwell upon the earth.' But to the church of Smyrna, He says, 'Fear none of those things which thou shalt suffer: behold, the devil shall cast some of you into prison, that ye may be tried; and ye shall have tribulation ten days; be thou faithful unto death, and I will give thee a crown of life.' There's a part of the church that'll be spared the Tribulation and a part that'll be imprisoned and suffer persecution during the Tribulation.

"In Revelation, chapter six, verses nine through eleven, we see Christians in the beginning of the Tribulation. 'And when he had opened the fifth seal, I saw under the altar the souls of them that were slain for the word of God, and for the testimony which they held: And they cried with a loud voice saying, How long, O Lord, holy and true, dost thou not judge and avenge our blood on them that dwell on the earth? And white robes where given unto every one of them; and it was said unto them, that they should rest yet for a little season, until their fellow servants also and their brethren, that should be killed as they were, should be fulfilled.'

"In Revelation, chapter fourteen, verses twelve and thirteen, we Christians in the middle of the Tribulation: 'Here is the patience of the saints: here are they that keep the commandments of God, and the faith of Jesus.' Notice it says, 'faithful to Jesus', which makes them a part of His body.

"'And I heard a voice from heaven saying unto me, Write, Blessed are the dead which die in the Lord from henceforth.' Here it says, those who die in the Lord from now on are *blessed.*

"Revelation, chapter seven, verses nine and thirteen through fourteen, describes a great multitude of Christians that go through the Tribulation. 'After this I beheld, and lo, a great multitude, which no man could number, of all nations, and kindreds, and people, and tongues, stood before the throne, and before the Lamb, clothed with white robes, and palms in their hands.' Since they're from every nation, tribe, people and language, we know they are not just Jews.

"'And one of the elders answered, saying unto me, What are these which are arrayed in white robes? And whence came they?

"'And I said unto him, Sir, thou knowest. And he said to me, These are they which came out of great tribulation; and have washed their robes, and made them white in the blood of the Lamb.'

"After reading the Scriptures, there's no doubt that there'll be Christians going through the Tribulation. To find out when Christ is coming for His bride, let's take a look at First Thessalonians, chapter four, verses fifteen through seventeen. 'For this we say unto you by the word of the Lord, that we which are alive and remain unto the coming of the Lord shall not prevent them which are asleep.' Some of the members of Christ's body have already died, but there are still Christians living when Christ comes back. 'For the Lord himself shall descend from heaven with a shout, with the voice of the archangel, and with the trump of God: and the dead in Christ shall rise first.' This is what Christians call the rapture.

"So let's look at the verses that tell us what *trumpet call* this is. In First Corinthians, chapter fifteen, verses fifty-one through fifty-two, we read: *'Behold, I show you a mystery; We shall not all sleep, but we shall all be changed, in a moment, in the twinkling of an eye, at the last trump: for the trumpet shall sound, and the dead shall be raised incorruptible, and we shall be changed.'*

"Now that we know the rapture takes place at the *last trumpet*, the question is, when is the *last trumpet*? Revelation, chapter eight, verse six, tells us that there are seven angels and seven trumpets. In Revelation, chapter eleven, verse fifteen, the last trumpet sounds, and 'The kingdoms of this world are become the kingdoms of our Lord, and of his Christ; and he shall reign for ever and ever.' In Revelation, chapter fourteen, verses fourteen through sixteen, is the perfect picture of the rapture. 'And I looked, and behold a white cloud, and upon the cloud one sat like unto the Son of man, having on his head a golden crown, and in his hand a sharp sickle. And another angel came out of the temple, crying with a loud voice to him that sat on the cloud, Thrust in thy sickle, and reap: for the time is come for thee to reap; for the harvest of the earth is ripe. And he that sat on the cloud thrust in his sickle on the earth; and the earth was reaped.

"In Matthew, chapter twenty-four and verse thirty-one, Jesus says: 'And he shall send his angels with a great sound of a trumpet, and they shall gather together his elect from the four winds, from one end of heaven to the other.' This has to be the *last trumpet call*, since afterwards, the world starts falling apart, plus it's the exact same picture we saw earlier in First Thessalonians.

"At the *last trumpet call*, those members of the body of Christ who have died will rise first, *'Then we which are alive and remain shall be caught up together with them in the clouds, to meet the Lord in the air: and so shall we ever be with the Lord.'*

"In Matthew, chapter twenty-four, verses twenty-one through twenty-seven, Jesus says it this way, *'For then shall be great tribulation, such as was not from the beginning of the world to this time, no, nor ever shall be. And except those days should be shorted, there should no flesh be saved: but for the elect's sake those days shall be shortened. Then if any man shall say unto you, Lo, here is Christ, or there; believe it not. For there shall arise false Christs, and false prophets, and shall show great signs and wonders; insomuch that, if it were possible, they shall deceive the very elect. Behold, I have told you before.*

"'Wherefore, if they shall say unto you, Behold, he is in the desert; go not forth: behold, he is in the secret chambers; believe it not. For as the lightning cometh out of the east, and shineth even unto the west; so shall also the coming of the Son of man be.' Then he continues in verse twenty-nine through verse thirty-one. *'Immediately after the tribulation of those days shall the sun be darkened, and the moon shall not give her light, and the stars shall fall from heaven, and the powers of the heavens shall be shaken: And then shall appear the signs of the Son of man in heaven: and then shall all the tribes of the earth mourn, and they shall see the Son of man coming in the clouds of heaven with power and great glory. And he shall send his angels with a great sound of a trumpet, and they shall gather together his elect from the four winds, from one end of heaven to the other.'*

"Saint Luke says it like this in chapter twenty-one, verses twenty-five through twenty-eight. *'And there shall be signs in the sun, and in the moon, and in the stars; and upon the earth distress of nations, with perplexity; the sea and the waves roaring. Men's hearts failing them from fear, and for looking after those things which are coming on the earth: for the powers of heaven shall be shaken. And then shall they see the Son of man coming in a cloud with power and great glory. And when these things begin to come to pass, then look up, and lift up your heads; for your redemption draweth nigh.'*

Christ also says in Matthew, chapter twenty-four, verses forty and forty-one, *'Then shall two be in the field, the one shall be taken, and the other left. Two women shall be grinding at the mill; the one shall be taken, and the other left.'*

"Well, Lance, God doesn't tell us the day or the hour, but He makes sure that when Jesus comes back, we won't be caught unaware."

"The way you fit the verses together doesn't leave much room for doubt, Mr. Freeman. The Bible is really a fantastic Book. In order to thoroughly understand it, it takes a lot of study."

"Yes, it takes a lot of study, *and* the help from the Holy Spirit. Leading you into all truth is one of the Holy Spirit's job descriptions. You seemed to catch on mighty fast, son. I'm proud of you!"

"Well, I've had some good teachers, including your daughter. I've also seen a personal demonstration of Christ's love through all of you here. I thank God for all of you."

One of the elders asked us to take the brother's hand beside us. We formed a circle, and he began to pray. "Father-God, you created us for this very hour, and we need the power of your Holy Spirit more than ever before. So we ask you to touch each and every member of this body; strengthen us with the same mighty strength you gave your

Son when He went to the cross. And give us *your* words to speak to our adversaries, that we may glorify you before men.

"And we thank *you*, Lord Jesus, that you find us worthy of giving our lives for you, just as you gave your life for us; we think it's an honor and a privilege. We pray this humble prayer in the name of our glorious Lord and Savior, Christ Jesus. Amen."

After the prayer, Mr. Freeman addressed the group. "Okay, everybody get ready for the three biggest events to hit the mountain since we moved up here. There's a barbecue, and a wedding to attend, and we just may be hosting some outside guests."

Sara held my hand during the Bible reading and Mr. Freeman's explanation of the Scriptures. Afterward, Sara walked with me to my cottage. Stopping at the entrance, I reached down and pulled her to me. "I may not show it, but I'm pretty excited, Sara. This is the biggest day in my life. I was born again, I'm getting married, and I may see Jesus face to face all on the same day."

"Do you think they're coming back today, Lance?"

"I don't know when they're coming, but I know it'll be soon. I'm sure they're thinking we'll try to escape."

"Well, until they get here, I'm not going to give it another thought," Sara exclaimed boldly. "The Holy Spirit will give us exactly what we need, exactly when we need it."

"Good thinking," I responded with a smile. "I love you, Sara. I'm glad God gave you to me, even if it is at the end."

"I love you, too, Lance. And I'm glad God gave me to you, too. Even if it is at the end."

I kissed Sara for the second time. Her eyes sparkled as she studied my face. "It's just ten o'clock, we're both tired, so why don't you rest for a couple of hours. Nothing really starts happening until noon, anyway. I'll ask father to wake you up around twelve o'clock."

"That's a good idea," I replied before kissing her the third time.

I walked into my cottage and lay across the cot. The past 24 hours were heavy on my mind. "Well, Lord," I said, "there's nothing left for me on this earth, anyway. I pray that you give me peace in what's about to happen. Thank you, Lord. Amen." Within minutes I was sound asleep.

Mr. Freeman woke me at noon. "Son. Son...," I heard his voice slowly penetrating my consciousness. "Yes, sir," I answered, as I sat up on the side of the cot.

"When do you think they'll be coming for us, Lance?"

I went over to the water basin. "Sara asked me the same question," I replied, splashing water on my face. "I really don't know, Mr. Freeman. But I'm sure it'll be soon. The pilots acted like they weren't prepared for what they found, which is understandable. Apparently they radioed to their base for further orders and were told to return to the home base to make a detailed report of their discovery."

"How can they find out who we are without talking to us?"

"Actually, they can't. They can only make an educated guess through the process of elimination. By keying in our exact location, the satellite will send back area photographs and the most current data. They'll search the computer for the legal titles and descriptions of the nearest recorded property, Peaceful Valley will probably surface. Then they'll run a check to see what became of the residents. Eventually they'll discover that Peaceful Valley wasn't under the jurisdiction of the State as an authorized city. They'll also learn that it wasn't ravaged and there weren't any captives or executions. Then they'll probably conclude that the community they discovered today was the same one that disappeared. That's when they'll come back to inquire. And I don't think they'll be back just to ask a few questions; they'll be prepared for war."

"That's just about the way I figure it. How long do you think that'll take, son?"

"I believe they'll be back before the day's over, or right at daybreak."

"Okay," he sighed in resignation. "God hasn't told us to do anything. Until we hear from God, we'll keep doing what we're doing. God couldn't have given me a better son-in-law. Maybe we better marry you two before we start the festivities. Is that all right with you, son?"

"Yes, it is. I'm as ready as ever, *dad*," I answered with a smile.

We left the cottage together. The family was dressed for the barbecue and waiting for us at the dining room table. Mr. Freeman walked up behind his wife and placed both hands on her shoulders. "Is everybody ready for the barbecue?" he asked, totally disregarding what had transpired earlier that day.

Jenny and the boys jumped to their feet. "Yeah, dad," they answered in unison. "We're ready!"

"All right. That's what I wanted to hear. Let's go have some fun."

The whole town was assembled at the Community Center. To accommodate everyone, chairs were arranged so that the entire group could enjoy the events comfortably. The various foods on display filled the wooden building with pleasant aromas that set my taste buds yearning to sample everything I saw.

According to Sara, this was the biggest event of the year. Everyone, especially the children, looked forward to this festive event.

To my astonishment, I was in a state of perfect peace with God and humanity. I wasn't the only one; the whole town portrayed a peace that surpassed all understanding. Considering the inevitable fate awaiting us, the atmosphere was incredibly placid. I recalled the words of Jesus: "Peace I give unto you, but not as the world gives." This was truly the peace of God that I was experiencing within and witnessing in the people around me.

Since the boys had reserved chairs for the family, Sara and I were able to sit together. While we waited for the festivities to begin, Sara and I talked, "You know, Lance, for some reason known only to God,

He chose words, *the gospel*, to save mankind. Coming to know Jesus and His undying love is what draws us to Him. In order to realize this, somebody has to tell you about Him.

"It's the gospel, the Words of Life planted inside our hearts, that delivers us from our sinful condition. When the gospel begins to blossom within us and the fruit of the Spirit becomes ripe, we're compelled to share it with others. It's a joint effort; it's God working through us.

"God has chosen people to manifest Christ's love and spread the gospel and the power of salvation throughout the world. We're ambassadors for Jesus Christ and the kingdom of God. Sharing the love of Christ with others is the only way to reach unbelievers and develop a relationship with believers. Christians are one enormous body that God lives in and works through to touch every human being on the face of the earth with His message of love and eternal life.

"At the same time, we're learning to overcome the world and walk in love right here in this wicked world system. That's why it's so important to have fellowship with other Christians. Jesus is forming His glorious bride, without spot or blemish or wrinkle, while at the same time preparing us to be citizens of heaven.

"When Jesus came, He gave one commandment, although it's really two in one. 'and thou shalt love the Lord thy God with all thy heart, and with all thy soul, and with all thy strength.' And the second one is just like it, 'Thou shalt love thy neighbor as thyself.' Jesus calls it a new commandment, but what makes it new is by adding, '*as I have loved you.*' And then He explains: 'Greater love hath no man than this, that a man lay down his life for his friends.' He demonstrated this new kind of love by laying down His life for us. When we walk in love we fulfill the Old Testament law just like Jesus did, since walking in the Spirit is walking in love.

"It takes fellowship with other Christians in order for us to learn how to lay down our lives for one another. First John, chapter one, verse seven, says: 'But if we walk in the light, as he is in the light, we have fellowship one with another, and the blood of Jesus Christ his Son cleanseth us from all sin.'

"It's a threefold instruction. First, we must walk with Him in His light or truth—that's what it means to have fellowship with Him— then we will walk in fellowship with our brothers and sisters in Christ— by laying down our lives for each other. While we're doing this the blood of Jesus Christ is cleansing us and purifying us from all sin."

"This body on the mountain has learned to walk in His light and have fellowship with one another. The fact that God's allowing us to suffer for Christ—as most of His disciples did—means that we've found favor in His sight; the lives of the saints are very precious in God's sight.

"Lance, I know God loves you very much—the miraculous way you got here proves that. And I just want you to know that I feel very fortunate for God allowing me to be your wife."

"Actually," I replied, "I was the one feeling pretty grateful. Of all the people in the world, Christ chose you to bring me to Him. He trusted you with my eternal soul, knowing that you wouldn't blow it. My concern is that I haven't had a chance to learn how to walk in this love. And from the looks of things, I'm not going to have much of a chance to learn."

"Jesus told the thief next to Him on the cross, 'Today you will be with me in paradise.' You're just as clean now as you'll ever be. Even so, God can grow a person up as fast as they let Him. You, just like the rest of us here on the mountain, are going to drink from His cup."

"What do you mean, drink from His cup?" I asked.

"One day John and James asked to sit next to Jesus in His kingdom. Jesus told them that they didn't know what they were asking. 'Are ye able to drink of the cup I shall drink of, and to be baptized with the baptism that I am baptized with?' He asked. They answered, 'We are able.' Then He said to them, 'Ye shall drink indeed of my cup, and be baptized with the baptism that I am baptized with: but to sit on my right hand, and on my left, is not mine to give, but it shall be given to them for whom it is prepared of my Father.'

"Just as Jesus said, they all drank the same cup of suffering and were baptized with the same baptism in their death. As I told you before, all of the disciples but John died as martyrs."

"So this cup represents a life of *suffering* for righteousness' sake and the baptism represents a type of *dying* for righteousness' sake?"

"That's right. Paul says in Philippians, chapter three, verses ten and eleven, 'That I may know him, and the power of his resurrection, and the fellowship of his sufferings, being made conformable unto his death; If by any means I might attain unto the resurrection of the dead.' Paul wanted so much to be like Jesus. But he also knew that sharing in the cup of Christ's suffering and the cup of Christ's baptism insured that he would be like Him when he was resurrected from the dead.

"In Ephesians, chapter one, verses eighteen through twenty-one Paul gives us another clue to this resurrection power. 'The eyes of your understanding being enlightened; that ye may know what is the hope of his calling, and what the riches of the glory of his inheritance in the saints, and what is the exceeding greatness of his to us-ward who believe, according to the working of his mighty power, which he wrought in Christ, when he raised him from the dead, and set him at his own right hand in the heavenly places, Far above all principality, and power, and might, dominion, and every name that is named, not only in this world, but also in that which is to come.'

"Can you imagine, Lance? It wasn't the creation of the universe or designing the glorious wonders we witness every day here on earth; it wasn't creating the magnificently intricate details of the human anatomy or bringing about something from nothing. No. The *incomparably* great power of God was exerted in Christ when He raised Him from the dead. This took God working along with the faith of Christ. That's why Paul said I want to know Christ and share in His sufferings so that I can be like Him and somehow attain the resurrection from the dead.

"In Colossians, chapter one, verse twenty-four, Paul talks about the fellowship of suffering for the members of Christ's body. 'Who now rejoice in my sufferings for you, and fill up that which is behind of the afflictions of Christ in my flesh for his body's sake, which is the church.' This shows that there's still a certain amount of suffering that we must go through in order to fill up what is lacking in Christ's afflictions concerning His body, the church.

"Exactly how much suffering is still lacking, I don't know, but God does. He's in control, and He knows what He's doing. Our job is to place our lives in His hands and trust Him no matter what."

"Well, Sara, some of what you said went over my head and I will probably never understand it. But this I know, I trust Christ for the very air I breathe. If our physical death hastens our being together with Him in His glorious kingdom, so be it. Whether we're actually able to stand when faced with death is yet to be seen. But if that's His will for us, then my prayer is that He strengthens us.

"Praise God for you, Lance. We all need that kind of faith. I know God will see us through to the end."

Elder Brooks stepped to the microphone and called us to order. When everyone was assembled, he led us in a prayer of thanksgiving for all the blessings that God had bestowed upon them over the years.

When elder Brooks finished, he summoned Mr. Freeman to the small platform to address the body. "Brothers and sisters," Mr. Freeman began, "I have three pieces of good news I'd like to share with you today. The first piece of news is that brother Lance Roberts—yes, I said *brother* Lance Roberts—accepted the Lord Jesus Christ into his heart last night."

At once the entire body stood to their feet and began to thank the Lord. Then they began to clap. A loud thunder of clapping echoed throughout the Community Center. It continued until I thought they would never stop. Tears began to fill my eyes. I tried to hold them back but they ran down my cheeks like rain. Gradually, one by one, hands were raised high into the air as they began to sway back and forth. Shouts of "Glory be to God in the highest" rang throughout the Community Center.

I wept uncontrollably.

"The second bit of good news I'd like to share is that brother Lance Roberts has asked my little Sara to be his wife."

The previous incident started again. I had barely recovered from the first wave of applause when the clapping thundered throughout the large enclosure. As before, Mr. Freeman waited for the last "Glory be to God in the highest" to fade from the room before he proceeded.

I continued to weep uncontrollably.

"Before I share the last piece of good news with you, I'd like to honor Lance and his bride-to-be as they come together in holy matrimony."

Mrs. Freeman leaned over and whispered, "Please take my wedding rings, Lance; just for the sake of the ceremony. You can have brother Smith make you a set of wedding bands and return these later." She kissed me on the cheek and hugged my neck.

"Thank you, Mrs. Freeman, I appreciate this," I replied, returning the hug.

Sara beamed with pleasure as Mr. Freeman called us to the front of the hall. "It's a privilege to bring two of God's children into His throne room and ask Him to bless their union in marriage—especially when one is your daughter and the other is someone you love like a son.

"Today two children of God are going to take their marriage vows. They're making vows to each other and to God. It's better not to make a vow at all than to make it and then break it. To break the marriage vows means that your heart has become hardened and unforgiving.

"When two people are ordained of the Lord in marriage they become one in spirit and in flesh. They're entering into a covenant agreement. Part of this agreement is to love, honor, and obey, whether in sickness or health, whether rich or poor, till death they won't part. That doesn't leave much ground for a divorce.

"The Bible tells us that the wife is to respect her husband and submit to him, as the church submits to Christ. For as Christ is the head of the church, His body, the husband is the head of his wife, who has become a part of his body. It also says that the husband is to love his wife and lay down his life for her the same way Christ loves the church and laid down His life for us. He's required to cleanse her through the Word of God so she'll become radiant, without spot, blemish, or wrinkle of any kind. This is the way a husband is to love and care for his wife.

"It's a message of selfless giving that starts with the husband and wife, works its way through the children, and then throughout the whole body of Christ. The wife puts aside her will and respectfully submits to her husband; the husband puts aside his will in order to love, cherish, and care for his wife. Each member of the body of Christ puts aside their will for the betterment of the other and the glory of God. 'Greater love has no man than this, that a man lay down his life for his friends.' This is God's way, and the root of the tree of life."

Mr. Freeman turned to me and asked, "Do you agree with this, Lance?"

"Yes, I do," I answered.

"Sara," he continued, "Are you in agreement with this?"

"Yes, I am," she answered.

"Well, Lance Roberts, do you take Sara Freeman to be your wife, till death you will not part?"

I turned to Sara, and with all my heart I replied, "I do."

"Sara Freeman, do you take Lance Roberts to be your husband, till death you will not part?"

"Yes, I do," Sara responded.

"Lance, please place the rings on Sara's finger. As this ring forms a continuous circle, so let them represent your love for each other, a never-ending circle of love.

"I now pronounce you man and wife. Brothers and sisters, I present to you Mr. and Mrs. Lance Roberts. You can kiss the bride now, son; she's your wife."

While cheers and whistles and shouts of congratulations echoed throughout the hall, I tenderly kissed my bride.

One by one the mountain community came forward to congratulate Sara and me. Some of the men offered to help build a cabin and others offered to help build a barn; some promised to make furniture and others offered livestock. The women offered dishes, silverware, glasses, curtains, sheets, quilts and other household furnishings. It seemed that all of our needs were going to be met through these wedding gifts.

After the last person filed past Sara and me, Mr. Freeman made his way back to the platform.

"Please, everybody return to your seats," he announced. When everyone was seated and silence fell over the hall, Mr. Freeman began. "I mentioned that there were three pieces of good news I wanted to share with you. Well, it looks as if God's found this little body of believers worthy of suffering persecution for His name's sake. There's no greater honor than to suffer for the sake of Christ and His righteousness. Even if it means going to prison, or the loss of our property, or torture and death. Yes, some of us may have to suffer death."

Mr. Freeman reached over and picked up the Bible sitting on a table behind him and began to read. "'What shall we then say in response to these things? If God be for us, who can be against us? He that spared not his own Son, but delivered him up for us all, how shall he not with him also freely give us all things? Who shall lay anything to the charge of God's elect? It is God that justifieth. Who is he that condemneth? It is Christ that died, yea rather, that is risen again, who is even at the right hand of God, who also maketh intercession for us. Who shall separate us from the love of Christ? shall tribulation, or distress, or persecution, or famine, or nakedness, or peril, or sword? As it is written, For thy sake we are killed all day long; we are accounted as sheep for the slaughter. Nay, in all things we are more than conquerors through him that loved us. For I am persuaded, that neither death, nor life, nor angels, nor principalities, nor powers, nor things present, nor things to come, Nor height nor depth, nor any other creature, shall be able to separate us from the love of God, which is in Christ Jesus our Lord.'"

Before Mr. Freeman finished, we could hear the loud clacking sounds made by the propellers of the helicopters circling above. He stopped to listen. "They'll be coming for us any minute now.

"Heavenly Father," he began to pray, "we thank you and praise you for choosing us to be witnesses for you and your Son, Jesus Christ. We pray that you strengthen us with your mighty power through your Holy Spirit, that we may be at peace with what's about to happen. Give us your words to speak, Lord, have your way in us, and don't hold this to their account, we pray. Amen."

As Mr. Freeman prayed the last word, there was a thundering crash and the huge wooden doors burst open. We heard a loud, threatening voice, accompanied by the sounds of thick-soled boots that were worn by the heavily armed, military men as they ran into the Center, positioning themselves in a circle around us."Everyone remain where you are, or you'll be shot!" echoed the voice of the Lieutenant Colonel who led the men dressed in United Nations camouflage fatigues. The Lieutenant went straight for the platform where Mr. Freeman was standing.

"Are you the spokesman for these people?" he asked Mr. Freeman.

Mr. Freeman turned to face us. "Would anyone object to me being their spokesman?" he asked, appealing to the body of believers seated before him. After a unanimous nod of approval, Mr. Freeman looked at the Lieutenant and answered, "Yes, sir. I'm their spokesman."

"Very well," the Lieutenant retorted.

He ordered everyone to be seated, and he then turned back to Mr. Freeman. "The State, under the authority of the World Government Constitution, has not authorized nor permitted any of you to live here. Therefore, you are in violation of ordinance 2138, Section 32, which includes among other infractions, conspiracy to misappropriate State property! This violation carries up to ten years imprisonment and up to a $250,000 fine."

"Sir, for almost two years we've lived here by the sovereignty of

God and the United States Constitution. Many of our grandfathers homesteaded this land almost a hundred years ago. Since it's our land, we didn't know we needed an authorization or permission to live here. If you'd care to see our Title Deeds, we can have them brought directly," Mr. Freeman responded politely.

"The United States Constitution doesn't exist, so you have no sovereignty! Only the World Government Constitution exists, which clearly mandates that the entire earth, along with every creature living upon it and all items attached thereto, is the property of the State. That automatically nullifies any deed of title that you may hold!

"And regarding your mention of God, are you referring to the Most Holy Prince?" the Lieutenant asked craftily.

With an unusual calmness, Mr. Freeman boldly retorted, "No, sir. I'm talking about the one and *only* God, the Creator of heaven and earth and everything in it. He sent His Son Jesus Christ to die for the whole world that we might be saved from our sins. He died for you, too, Lieutenant, and all these fine looking young men you brought with you."

"Are you implying that the Most Holy Prince is *not* God?"

"Sir, I don't even know this person you call the Most Holy Prince, but I can attest that he's not God. I know for certain that he's not, because I know the Almighty God personally, and so do all these people..."

"Enough!" the Lieutenant interrupted. "Enough of these treasonous remarks denouncing the Most Holy Prince whom the entire earth has elected to worship and serve."

The Lieutenant, full of self-assurance turned to face the rest of us, "Anyone that wants to spare his or her life stand to your feet, clasp your hands behind your head, and form a line against the wall behind me!"

I looked at the faces around me. Their expressions conveyed compassion for the lost souls that held them captive because of their faithfulness to the living God and Jesus Christ His Son.

No one made the slightest indication of going forward.

As if in disbelief, the Lieutenant searched the faces before him, jerking his head mechanically from one side to the other. Apparently thinking he had found weakness, he ordered: "You! You in the yellow dress, come here and form a line against the wall behind me!"

The voice was delicate, almost childlike in response. "Oh no, sir. I'd rather stay here. I might not ever see Jesus if I did that."

As the Lieutenant continued searching the faces, the atmosphere grew unbearably intense and an extreme heaviness fell upon the Community Center. Suddenly my mind was flooded with all sorts of pernicious thoughts. What I had come to believe about God, His glorious

Son and their wonderful kingdom was being challenged. Grotesque lies that assaulted the authenticity of the gospel suddenly invaded my thoughts. The foundation of my faith was being shaken to the core. In order to combat these horrible lies that intruded my mind at will, I thought desperately to remember Scripture verses.

As soon as I started to recover, I was struck with waves of fear and began to doubt whether salvation truly existed. This fear was crippling my ability to reason intelligently; the depths of my faith and love for Christ was starting to crumble. I helplessly searched the faces of those around me for someone able to give me the encouragement I needed to stand. But instead, I could plainly see that everyone was entrenched in battle, and they were all fighting for their spiritual lives.

In my distress, I called upon the name of the Lord; I cried out to God with all of my heart and asked Him for help.

He heard me; my desperate cry reached His ear. The Lord is my shield, there's only refuge in Him. He's my strength; He gives me the victory. It's God's hand that sustains me. Jesus is my rock, the Rock of my salvation.

I began to thank the Lord for Sara, the Freeman family, and all the residents living on the mountain. I asked the Lord to strengthen them as He had strengthened me.

The demonic forces, blinded by a hatred for Christ, were forced to acknowledge defeat. With the help of the Lord, and His body now standing firm against their lying accusations, I felt the battle start to diminish. Apparently driven by frustration, the demons turned their voices toward the men that held us captive. They shouted demands for vengeance into the receptive ears of the Lieutenant and his soldiers. You could almost read their thoughts by the expressions on their faces. Finally, the same frustration, anger, and hatred that drove these demonic forces to attack us were unleashed upon the Lieutenant and his men.

Without another word the Lieutenant stormed across the room toward the exit. Before reaching the door he turned, "Burn them all and kill anyone that tries to escape!" he commanded his troops.

One by one the soldiers backed out of the Community Center with their rifles aimed toward us. When the last soldier exited the building, the wooden door was shut and bolted.

No one spoke a word. We smelled the kerosene, the smoke, and heard the crackling sound of burning wood. The flames began to spread throughout the wooden structure; the smoke and heat were unbearable.

Mr. Freeman pulled the microphone to him and quoted Revelation, chapter twelve, verse eleven, in a very loud voice. "'They overcame him by the blood of the Lamb, and by the word of their testimony; and they loved not their lives unto the death."

Mr. Freeman began to sing. The hymn was one of my favorites. Sara and I stood to our feet. I put one arm around her and pulled her close. With my free hand I grasped the hand of Mrs. Freeman who was standing on my other side. While singing the chorus together, one by one the whole mountain community rose to meet their Lord: "O, how I love Jesus. O, how I love Jesus. O, how I love Jesus, because He first loved me."

****

EPILOGUE

In the Book of Revelation, chapters two and three, the churches to which Jesus Christ ascribes praise—without any form of rebuke—are the church of Smyrna and the church of Philadelphia. Beside many promises, Christ encouraged the church of Philadelphia with these words: *"Because thou hast kept the word of my patience, I also will keep thee from the hour of temptation, which shall come upon all the world, to try them that dwell upon the earth."* The church of Smyrna, however, was gi.   a far different recountal for being faithful: *"Fear none of those things which thou shalt suffer: behold, the devil shall cast some of you into prison, that ye may be tried; and ye shall have tribulation ten days: be thou faithful unto death, and I will give thee a crown of life."* The only reward for their faithfulness unto death was eternal life. [For] *"...as it is written, 'Eye hath not seen, nor ear heard, neither have entered into the heart of man, the things which God hath prepared for them that love him.' But God hath revealed them unto us by his Spirit,"* 1Corinthians 2:9-10.

In *The Master Plan*, I purposely portray the most extreme scenario, not to displace hope but affirm it; "In hope of eternal life, which God, that cannot lie, promised before the world began." There is no hope on earth! My paramount aim is to exhort the body of Christ to prepare for the Lord's coming, that we should be "Looking for that blessed hope, and the glorious appearing of the great God and our Saviour Jesus Christ."

None of us are certain whether we've been called to the church of Philadelphia or the church of Smyrna, and it shouldn't matter, *"For where your treasure is, there will your heart be also,"* Matthew 6:21. As Christians, we're merely sojourners on this earth, passing through, looking forward to our heavenly home. *"These all died in faith, not having received the promises, but having seen them afar off, and were persuaded of them, and embraced them, and confessed that they were strangers and pilgrims on the earth. For they that say such things declare plainly that they seek a country. And truly, if they had been mindful of that country from whence they came out, they might have had opportunity to have returned. But now they desire a better country, that is, an heavenly: wherefore God is not ashamed to be called their God: for He hath prepared for them a city,"* Hebrews 11:13-16.

"Cast not away therefore your confidence, which hath great recompense of reward. For ye have need of patience, that, after ye might receive the promise. For yet a little while, and He will come, and will not tarry. Now the just shall live by faith: but if any man draw back, my soul shall have no pleasure in him. But we are not of them who draw back unto perdition; but of them that believe to the saving of the soul." (Hebrews 10:31-39)

I pray that God, the Father of our Lord and Savior, Jesus Christ, establish and keep you, and all that you think, say, and do, be for His glory.

Amen.

ABOUT THE AUTHOR

Many of my early adult years were spent in prison. I actually considered myself a Robin Hood-type of character that stole from the rich and gave to the poor—mainly myself! In 1979, after serving close to five years of a ten-year sentence in Federal prison, I began to have a strong urge to read the Bible. As I read, I began to see that there was a God, that He was good, and just, and loving. In fact, He loved me so much that He gave His only begotten Son so that I could have eternal life. I then learned that I was not a Robin Hood-type, but actually selfish, unjust, and wicked.

During that time another inmate loaned me a copy of *The Fourth Reich of the Rich*, by Des Griffin. Through reading this book, I learned that there was a powerful group of elitists—being driven by the devil himself—whose sole aim was to enslave me, along with all humanity, under a New [One] World Order. This newfound knowledge, which corresponded with what I was reading in the Book of Revelation, helped me to realized that my past lifestyle was furthering the efforts of these elitists.

The more I studied the Bible, the more I found myself falling in love with Jesus Christ, even to the extent that I was willing to denounce *my* way of life for *His Way;* I was willing to lay down my life, pick up my cross, and follow Jesus Christ.

Approximately two years after I started studying the Bible, one night while alone in my cell, I accepted Jesus Christ as my Lord and Saviour and was born again. My life was instantly and miraculously changed. I was no longer the same person and everyone in the prison knew it, from the guards to my fellow prisoners, many of whom I had known most of my life.

Sixteen years and what seemed like a lifetime later, I found myself teaching the adult Sunday school class for the third year in the church that my wife and I attend. For two years I was given the privilege of leading a Bible study twice a week in a local High School. Because of my past experiences, I have spoken in Churches, Full Gospel Businessmen's meetings, and other Christian functions. To prevent what I say from being misinterpreted as bragging about an exciting life of crime, I prefer to proclaim the gospel of Jesus Christ, alone. Therefore, I only briefly mention my personal testimony, lest *I* get in the way of Christ and the cross.

I previously owned and operated Al Duncan's Secretarial Service, a service that offered the public everything from general correspondence to Living Trusts. I am currently a Real Estate agent and find it a challenge as well as an excellent opportunity to represent my Lord and Saviour. Through *The Master Plan* the Lord has given me the opportunity to share with you what He has shown me. I pray with all of my heart that Christ will graciously open your eyes to the plan and purpose He has for you, as a member of His body and the Church, in these last days. May God truly bless and keep you, that you may be able to stand, loving His appearing.

Come Lord Jesus.